# ON THE BANKS OF THE ROYAL BLUE MERSEY

CHRISTOPHER BEESLEY

# ON THE BANKS OF THE ROYAL BLUE MERSEY

## Inside Everton's First Season at the Dock

FOREWORD BY DAN MEIS

pitch

First published by Pitch Publishing, 2026
1

Pitch Publishing
9 Donnington Park, 85 Birdham Road
Chichester, West Sussex, PO20 7AJ
www.pitchpublishing.co.uk
info@pitchpublishing.co.uk



Set in Warnock Pro 11/16pt

Typeset by Pitch Publishing

Cover design by Olner Design

Printed in Great Britain by TJ Books, Padstow, Cornwall

The authorised representative in the EEA is Easy Access System Europe OÜ, Mustamäe tee 50, 10621 Tallinn, Estonia gpsr.requests@easproject.com

A CIP catalogue record for this book is available from the British Library

ISBN 978-1-83680-425-3

Papers used by Pitch Publishing are from well-managed forests and other responsible sources

MIX
Paper | Supporting responsible forestry
FSC® C013056

# Contents

This book, a far more personal account than my previous one, is lovingly dedicated to my mother and father, Aileen and Raymond; plus to the memory of my grandparents Emily (1918–2000), Irvine (1919–1992), Nellie (1921–2005) and Norman (1922–2018).

Each of them, in their own individual manner, have been exemplary when it came to showing me the right way and any goodness I now possess, as the man I am today, comes from them.

# Foreword by Dan Meis

AS AN architect, I am not often asked to contribute a foreword to the writing of a book about a building which I have designed.

In this case, it is one of so many unique aspects of this project that have been career-defining for me in so very many ways.

My journey with what became Hill Dickinson Stadium had an inauspicious start while sitting at a seafood bar in Heathrow Terminal 2.

What started as a simple sketch on a cocktail napkin grew some ten years later into the project that will for ever define who I am as an architect, and why I so love what I do.

More than that, I became part of a family that I will cherish long after I have retired as an architect.

As someone who has designed stadiums and arenas all over the world, I have had the opportunity to work with a number of historic clubs and passionate supporters. I learned quickly that Everton supporters were another level. They are the fan equivalent of Nigel Tufnel's amplifier in *This is Spinal Tap*.

Everton supporters go to 11.

Taking this on board, and the fact that I would be the architect to lead this club away from Goodison Park, a tired but beloved historic ground, and one of English football's greatest experiences, I realised quickly that this building had to be much more than just a shiny new stadium with more toilets, escalators and wider concourses.

This building would have to capture the magic and romance of Goodison Park. Most importantly, it had to provide that same 'bear pit' atmosphere that struck fear in the hearts of opposing teams. Not an easy feat.

Once I realised that the site for the stadium was to be Bramley-Moore Dock, I was faced with an additional challenge.

Besides the technical complexity of building on a historic, water-filled dock, it quickly became clear that the development of the stadium would cost the city of Liverpool its status as a UNESCO World Heritage site.

I hope that history will prove that this was an incredibly short-sighted decision on the part of the World Heritage Committee.

Prior to the stadium build, the dock was essentially derelict after generations of neglect. We worked very hard to design a building that, while contemporary, drew carefully on the history and heritage of the docks and surrounding context.

For all of the attention paid to creating an intimidating home-pitch advantage and a new home for one of England's most storied football clubs, I am most proud of the fact that Hill Dickinson Stadium feels to me like it is part of the historic fabric of the Liverpool docklands.

I have been very fortunate in my career to design several important stadiums and arenas in exciting cities all over the world. I am quite confident in saying that there has never been, nor will there ever be, a project quite like this for me.

This city, this club, and its amazing supporters have left a mark. As Alan Ball said, 'Once Everton has touched you nothing will be the same.'

I am very grateful to Christopher Beesley for choosing to document this project.

While it is true that it started on a cocktail napkin, it became the product of a collaboration of literally thousands of talented architects, planners, engineers and builders.

I would be remiss to omit special mention of the incredible work of Laing O'Rourke in delivering the building without compromise.

Lastly, my personal and eternal gratitude to the late Bill Kenwright. Being the chairman of a historic club can be a rollercoaster ride given the passions of thousands of supporters who fully expect a win every weekend.

I can say this with certainty, that while he endured at times a rocky relationship with the fans, no one loved this club more than Bill Kenwright and no one was more responsible for Bramley-Moore Dock becoming Hill Dickinson Stadium.

It couldn't have happened without the unwavering and significant financial support of owner Farhad Moshiri as well, but it was Bill Kenwright's incredible passion and vision that we see realised there today.

I am for ever grateful.

**Dan Meis, FAIA, RIBA**

# Acknowledgements

IT SEEMS as though books are like buses for me: it is often said everyone has got one book in them, but this is now two in as many years from myself.

The difference is that my first book, *Spirit of the Blues: Everton's Most Memorable Matches & Goodison Park's Greatest Games*, covered a time span of some 133 years, a period longer than any human lifetime.

This second publication covers a single football season, but one that is truly momentous in Everton's history and the lives of their legions of passionate supporters.

The record-breaking trophy drought goes on for the Blues, but after a long and painful decline from being one of the football superpowers in this country throughout an era when those 'across the park' (that's no longer the case but they are of course still the neighbours and biggest rivals) continued to dominate, Evertonians can now look to the future with renewed optimism in the hope that it at least has a chance of living up to their club's illustrious past.

I would like to thank Pitch Publishing for not only showing their faith in me by backing my writing projects, but for also suggesting that I get Paul Trevillion back on board to provide the cover illustrations in order to give a 'synergy' between my previous work and this title.

I do not say this with any bias because he is a dear friend of mine, but I consider Trevillion, as he signs his work, to be the greatest sporting artist in the world. He has not been dubbed the 'Master of Movement' lightly; the way in which he captures athletes in motion is unparalleled.

But while the two books might look similar, their content is actually very different. *Spirit of the Blues* was the story of Everton's time at Goodison Park told through reports on its most notable fixtures by those who were present to witness the action across 14 separate decades, while this is very much a personal account of my own experiences, covering Everton home and away over the landmark 2025/26 season.

Rather than relying on research and attempting to bring the past to life, these are my own observations from wherever I was over that period, whether that be Hill Dickinson Stadium, reporting on Premier League away days or varied points across pre-season from Accrington to Atlanta.

I was fortunate enough to meet many interesting people along the way – especially during the Blues' time in the USA, expats and American fans alike, as the team prepared for the campaign – and some of them get a mention among these pages.

At this point, I feel it is only right to give a nod to my regular travelling companion when Everton are on the road, Joe Thomas (more on that later).

As the two Everton reporters for the *Liverpool Echo,* it is imperative that we work as a team, and I hope that both Joe (who officially holds the title of correspondent) and our readers share my view that our respective journalistic attributes dovetail extremely well.

Given the amount of coverage *Echo* readers have become accustomed to with a live blog on matchdays before and during games, a verdict match report, player ratings, analysis, interviews with a player and both teams' managers plus additional video content, it is very much a two-person operation for Premier League fixtures.

Due to our respective considerable workloads, we are often the last journalists out of the press room before staff close the stadium, turn off the lights and go home themselves.

I am aware that many people would consider ours to be 'dream' jobs. But whereas we are fortunate to be in a profession that is a vocation for us, while social media and the digital age has enabled fans to share their voices and opinions whether good, bad or everything in between, and an increasing number of people like to 'play' at being football journalists, Joe is an outstandingly talented individual.

More importantly, he is a good person, which is a major boost for me considering that we have had to spend many hours in each other's company in cars and trains going up and down the country over the past four years.

The pair of us are also lucky to have gone from one great boss to another, with Joe Rimmer, who I worked under when this journey began, being succeeded by Paul Wheelock as head of sport, so I'd also like to thank him and all my other colleagues at the *Echo*, including fellow *Royal Blue* podcast regulars Gavin Buckland, Ian Croll, Connor O'Neill and Tony Scott for their continued support.

Last, but certainly not least, there is the person that means everything to me, my wife Chloe. In our 21 years together so far, we have experienced a lot – still no Everton trophy win – yet wherever I am, I know that I am truly blessed to share my life with her because she is my world.

In some ways, this story has come full circle. My journalistic career has spanned an era of unprecedented change: when I started in my first professional post at the *Ellesmere Port Pioneer* in 2000, we did not even have internet in the office.

But even earlier than that, as I will mention later in the book, while a student I had my first experience of interviewing David

Moyes, who at the time was in his first managerial position at Preston North End.

Fast forward to August 2025, and the by-then 62-year-old Glaswegian gaffer – back in charge of Everton for a second stint – was ribbing me when he asked what the assembled press pack had seen of Atlanta during the team's visit for the Premier League Summer Series and I told him I had been to World of Coca-Cola.

What I did not mention to Mr Moyes was that before then, my job and visit to the city had enabled me to do something very significant.

Like thousands of families across Merseyside, ours is a mixed household. My wife Chloe, along with most of her immediate kin, is a Liverpool fan. She might not recognise Dominik Szoboszlai, never mind being able to spell his name (for full disclosure, I had to look it up), as John Barnes and Patrik Berger remain her historic pin-ups, but her passion burns bright.

That stems mostly from her dad, Stephen Oldfield, a lifelong Reds supporter who was a season ticket holder at Anfield.

The full obituary to my late father-in-law, himself a former *Liverpool Echo* journalist, that I penned after his death on 28 April 2025, less than 24 hours after Arne Slot's side clinched the title, can be viewed online on the newspaper's website and I would implore you all to give it a read because he left a unique legacy which is a story that deserves to be told.

Chloe's parents, who had swapped Liverpool for life in the Bahamas at the time, got married in the city of Atlanta in 1969. But other than the date and the fact that a certain Judge Pressley presided over the ceremony, details were scarce and her mum couldn't remember exactly where it was.

A bit of journalistic digging from myself through Google revealed that the judge had often operated out of the Fulton County Courthouse, just a mile and a half south of my hotel in downtown Atlanta.

Having filed all my day's copy to the desk back in Liverpool, I took a walk there – passing through a few sketchy neighbourhoods en route – and arrived at approximately 4.30pm on a Friday as staff were no doubt winding down for the weekend.

Explaining my situation, I was ushered upstairs to a record office and sure enough, it was the right place. Not only was I able to take photographs of the building for the family back in the UK, having stood on the same steps and walked through the same door as Chloe's parents on the day that they had wed almost 56 years earlier, I also obtained detailed copies of the marriage licence for my wife, her mother and two sisters to go with the singular decorative one already at her parents' house.

My journalistic journey had taken me to this special spot at a poignant time. It was a once-in-a-lifetime moment to kick off a landmark season.

**Christopher Beesley**

# Prologue

EVERTON FC was Goodison Park and Goodison Park was Everton FC. That is all we had ever known. For myself and thousands of other football fans – whether Blue or Red – across Merseyside, and indeed the whole football world, for longer than anyone could remember.

Goodison Park was special.

Everyone thinks the ground where *their* team plays is special, and in their eyes, rightly so. But even if you take out personal bias, and football lives and breathes on such prejudices, even the most blinkered, dyed-in-the wool Kopite could not deny Goodison Park its unique position within the game.

The first purpose-built football ground in England, the first Football League ground to stage an FA Cup Final, the first to be visited by a reigning monarch, the first to have double-decker stands on all four sides, the first to have undersoil heating, the first to have a triple-decker stand, the venue for the most top-flight matches plus five World Cup games, including the status of being the only English club ground to stage a World Cup semi-final.

However, despite being the pre-eminent club ground in the country for most of her existence, 'The Grand Old Lady' had become tired-looking towards the end of her natural life.

Everton had been seriously looking at finding a replacement for Goodison Park for a generation since the mid-1990s and it is surely no coincidence that this period corresponds with the longest trophy drought in the club's history, the ground reaching a point where so many of its rivals had overtaken it and it was no longer financially viable.

As much as she was loved and the long goodbye produced an understandable outpouring of emotion from Evertonians, it was high time for this venerable football institution and its many loyal supporters to begin a new start and look forward to a brighter future at last – on the banks of the royal blue Mersey, as the terrace chant from the 1960s went. It had finally come to fruition – and in spectacular fashion.

Some, including David Moyes, had hankered for Goodison Park to be redeveloped, but unlike Everton's previous home at Anfield, where Liverpool had been allowed to buy up a series of streets in the surrounding area to increase their footprint and capacity, Goodison's landlocked status on three sides ensured that remained a pipe dream.

In the end, it was a case of the best things come to those who wait for the Blues.

Who knows where they might have ended up with Peter Johnson's ambitious yet vague plans for a bowl-shaped stadium in the 1990s that would have been the biggest club ground in the country at the time – in an unspecified location.

When Everton failed to secure a move to another riverside location at King's Dock in the 2000s, many felt that was an opportunity of a lifetime wasted, but then there were the fears that they could have been out of sight and out of mind if they had moved inland beyond the city of Liverpool's boundaries for the ill-fated Tesco project in Kirkby.

The Blues now boast the best stadium in the country again and it sits in an unparalleled location, taking its place as a 'Fourth Grace', also alongside the two cathedrals, as part of Liverpool's world-famous maritime skyline.

David Moyes is a manager who chooses the words in his programme notes carefully. Ahead of the inaugural first-team fixture in front of fans at Everton's new home against Roma, he remarked, 'We are starting from a blank page. We have built the stadium, and we are starting to rebuild the team.'

A fortnight later against Brighton & Hove Albion when the Blues played their first competitive fixture on the Mersey waterfront, he told supporters, 'There will be lots of new experiences today. You'll all be getting used to new seats, new matchday rituals and new facilities. What I know won't change is the way you've supported the team over all the years at Goodison Park. The move here wouldn't be worthwhile if we didn't bring the soul of Goodison Park with us to Hill Dickinson Stadium.

'We know we have to earn your support and we understand that watching a winning team is really important to generating that atmosphere. We hope to make this a stadium which is difficult for our visitors to play in, a phrase which so many said about Goodison.'

1

# Nothing less than the Evertonians deserve

THE PROJECT to build Everton's new home and what became Hill Dickinson Stadium was nine years in the making.

One man who was there from the start until after the Blues received the keys to the site from contractors Laing O'Rourke was Richard Kenyon, who served the club for over 11 years in a variety of senior leadership positions.

Working as Everton's chief commercial and communications officer for his final three and a half years, he had become chief executive of Nottinghamshire County Cricket Club by the time of publication, but as a lifelong Evertonian himself he remains immensely proud of what he and his former colleagues achieved by the banks of the Mersey. Speaking in an exclusive interview for the book, Kenyon spoke about the internal process in terms of choosing Bramley-Moore Dock and whether other sites were ever seriously considered as viable options.

He said, 'As Evertonians will know, the club had been researching potential sites for a new stadium for several decades. When we moved on from the opportunity at Walton Hall Park, the Bramley-Moore Dock site came into focus. Ultimately, through the work of consultants, this was shown to be the only suitable site available in the city.

'We knew from our research with fans and members of the public that people were keen for the club to stay in the city and in the north end of it, so despite some very obvious challenges – it being water – and potential complications around planning, we were keen to go all-in on the waterfront site.'

A month after visiting the dock, owner Farhad Moshiri declared that the club had 'taken soundings from fans' and added, 'In our mind, we know where we want to go. We are committed.'

In terms of risk and reward, while everyone could see the clear benefits of the waterfront site, there were still major hurdles to overcome in terms of practicalities.

Kenyon said, 'Logistically there were challenges – draining and then filling the dock and getting materials in and out of the site – but the teams were always confident these could be overcome.

'We also knew we would have to go to great lengths with our engagement processes. While we were hopeful and confident that Evertonians would be supportive of our plans for the site, there were many other stakeholders we needed to generate support from.

'At times, I know some Evertonians were frustrated by the lengths we went to in our engagement and consultation processes, but we had to get this right. From pubs to parliament, people needed to understand the importance of this scheme – not just to Evertonians but to the people of the city.

'I'm really proud of the team I led at Everton for the results they achieved – and there were many external agencies who supported us through what became an exemplar engagement and consultation process.'

The stadium build had to overcome some significant external obstacles during its construction process: the global coronavirus pandemic which caused professional football to be played behind closed doors for the first time; the threat of a breakaway European 'super league' and then Russia's invasion of Ukraine which impacted on sponsorship deals for the club.

Kenyon insists that Everton chiefs remained unwavering throughout though, 'It was a fairly tumultuous time and there were several external factors that presented challenges; there were times when it did feel like everything was working against us.

'Internally, however, we always remained focused and worked hard to find a way through the issues we faced.

'Once construction was started, we knew there was no option other than seeing it through. Across all parts of the club, we had to be creative and remain absolutely focused.

'I think it's fair to say that we were determined to deliver this project for Evertonians and the people of the city and couldn't let doubt creep into our work, no matter what was happening outside of our direct control.'

There were also other factors that proved additional hurdles and Kenyon added, 'Initially we had some concerns about getting a successful outcome through the planning process and we did lots of work behind the scenes to prepare for our engagement and consultation programmes.

'We always felt confident that we had a design that the fans would like and that this would convert into high demand for tickets.

'As is widely known, the club faced some financial challenges during the construction process, but the design and build process was never compromised.'

Looking now at the completed stadium in use, there are several aspects that Kenyon finds particularly pleasing: 'The stadium site and design was always going to make for a magnificent new home for the club, but until you see it being used and feel the atmosphere you are never quite sure how it's going to work out and compare to other venues.

'However, what has been created has been incredible. The intimacy and atmosphere have always made it feel like Everton's home to me, which is no mean feat given how much we all loved Goodison.

'The premium areas are fantastic of course, but to me, that home end and its concourse looking back to the city are my favourite features. I also love hearing feedback from others across the game who comment on what a great stadium it is, whether they be visiting fans, rival managers or others.

'In years to come, I'm sure we'll also be proud of how our new home has also played that catalytic role in regenerating that part of the city. I know north Liverpool and its communities well from my time as chief executive at Everton in the Community so that's really important to me too, as I know it is with all Evertonians.'

While Everton are now playing in front of the biggest regular crowds in their history, the capacity issue has been a hot topic with many supporters given that Manchester United have had a capacity of over 70,000 for a long time plus Liverpool, Manchester City, Arsenal, Tottenham Hotspur and West Ham United can all welcome over 60,000.

Architect Dan Meis has always passionately defended going smaller and Kenyon explains the thought process behind the size issue, 'There was a lot of debate about this at the time and while I can understand the argument for a greater capacity, one of the key principles we always worked to – and fans said they wanted – was an intense atmosphere, steep stands close to the pitch and for it to feel intimate and intimidating like Goodison and it being full all the time certainly helps with those last points.

'I think having a stadium that's always packed and is known for its intensity is better than being slightly bigger, and it could only ever have been slightly bigger – if at all – on that site, so that's another trade-off to consider.

'Would the fans who wanted a bigger stadium have been happy with a different site where a larger stadium could have been more comfortably accommodated – probably not?

'It should also be remembered that when we started this project, we had only just started selling Goodison out for every game.

'When I joined the club in 2013/14 we were usually only selling out a handful of games per season. So, while we always knew we were one of the biggest clubs in the country in terms of fanbase with amazing, loyal supporters, at that time the reality was that we did have empty seats in a stadium with a capacity of less than 40,000.

'While we felt instinctively that we could go much bigger than Goodison and beyond 50,000, we were also getting advice from some specialist consultants who were advising slightly less than 50,000. All in all, I think we got it right in the end.'

In terms of Kenyon's final thoughts on the finished project and the process, there is a key Goodison Park factor that convinces him that Hill Dickinson Stadium has been a triumph.

He said, 'Despite some challenges along the way, it was an amazing project to be part of, and an incredible stadium has been created, nothing less than the Evertonians deserve.

'I feel so privileged to have been given the opportunity to play a part in something so special and proud to have been the only senior executive to work on the project from the initial concept through to completion.

'I love going to the games there now with my family and friends and I've not really missed Goodison Park which says a lot given how much that place has meant to me over the last 45 years or so ... that in itself says to me that we got it right.'

2

# From Newcastle to Windsor Castle – early summer 2025

A WEEK on from Everton's emotional final fixture at Goodison Park after 133 years at the first purpose-built football ground in England, the Blues' 2024/25 season ended in surreal fashion in the north-east.

Once again, Jordan Pickford was the centre of attention against Newcastle United, but the goalkeeper controlled the narrative against his Geordie baiters and haters.

As the final whistle blew at St James' Park and Eddie Howe's side clinched a place in European football's elite competition – despite their 1-0 defeat to Charly Alcaraz's goal – all you could hear around the ground was the jubilant travelling Blues supporters whose chants drowned out a recording of the Champions League anthem on the hosts' public address system.

Tucked away 'up in the gods' in the higher reaches of the giant Leazes End, Evertonians hailed their hero with a full-blooded rendition of his new anthem, 'He hates Newcastle, he hates the shite, Jordan Pickford is dynamite.'

The Toon puppet master who these days seems to have the Geordie home fans on strings and controls them at will produced another masterclass, playing his pantomime villain role to perfection.

As a younger man, and less-experienced performer, the former Sunderland player was guilty of letting the pressure-cooker atmosphere at their local rivals get to him, most infamously the 2019 visit when his wild display enabled Rafael Benítez's hosts to recover from 2-0 down to triumph 3-2.

Those days are long gone it seems though, and Pickford led by example from the start here, puffing out his chest and nonchalantly making his way to the centre circle at a leisurely pace when called to perform his pre-match captain's duties by referee Tony Harrington.

He promptly won the toss and made the sides switch ends so the hosts were made to play towards the Gallowgate End, the first of numerous occasions that he would frustrate them.

England's number one produced a mature and masterful performance, confident on the ball and then once again at the top of his game with a string of spectacular saves to repel everything Newcastle threw at him, including a couple of stinging efforts from their talisman Alexander Isak.

The Swede would soon turn his back on the Magpies in controversial fashion to force through a transfer to Everton's local rivals for a British record £125m fee, in what was the most expensive purchase by anyone other than petrodollar-fuelled Paris Saint-Germain, not that Newcastle's backers, the sovereign wealth fund of the House of Saud, needed the cash.

Yet here was another world-class performer at the peak of his powers and while they might be at pains to admit it, even the most die-hard fan in black and white could see that.

Speaking after the final whistle, Pickford told me how he was a fan of his new chant, which had debuted in the 3-1 comeback win at Fulham a fortnight earlier, 'It's a really good song, it's got a good bounce to it shall we say. As a football fan to have your own chant is mega. It's what football is all about, you're doing something right if the fans are buzzing off you.'

Meanwhile, after leading his side to a fifth away victory since his return in January, manager David Moyes was coy when asked by my *Liverpool Echo* colleague Joe Thomas whether match-winner Alcaraz, on loan from Flamengo, had done enough to secure a part in Everton's future, replying, 'Well, you'll need to wait and see like everybody else.'

Just six days later, the club triggered an option to turn the Argentinian midfielder's move into a permanent deal as he became the Blues' first signing of what would prove to be a busy summer.

Less than a week after Alcaraz's acquisition, Everton were named as bookmakers' favourites to sign Jack Grealish who, despite having become the first £100m English footballer a full four years before Liverpool would seal a brace of nine-figure acquisitions in the same transfer window, had become surplus to requirements at the Etihad Stadium with Pep Guardiola about to leave him out of Manchester City's squad for the FIFA Club World Cup.

As we all know, the bookies seldom get it wrong, and although it took a while, this would be no such occasion.

On 11 June, over three months before US President Donald Trump was invited there as part of his second UK state visit, David Moyes had a trip to Windsor Castle to pick up the OBE for services to football he had been awarded in the King's New Year Honours List.

It was perhaps apt then that the boss collected his gong from the Prince of Wales, who until the previous year had served as president of the Football Association from 2006, and who, as a match-going Aston Villa supporter – subsequently taking in their Europa League Final triumph against Freiburg in Istanbul – follows the game more closely than any other major royal.

Moyes revealed that the pair of them chatted about football after his investiture, remarking, 'He [Prince William] actually congratulated me on Everton and was praising us for the way things have turned around in the second half of the season. I had said that I thought his side were doing remarkably well.'

With the club announcing 48 hours earlier that they were offering new contracts to Séamus Coleman and Idrissa Gueye, while continuing to liaise with representatives of Michael Keane and Dominic Calvert-Lewin, Evertonians were focusing more on news about their out-of-contract stars rather than their manager's pleasantries with the future sovereign.

On that score, Moyes added, 'I think we'll secure the ones that we really want to secure and make sure they're here.'

The next day it emerged Moyes was bringing Manchester City's director of scouting and recruitment James Smith back to Everton having first attracted him to Goodison Park in 2003 with Smith then following him to Manchester United a decade later.

Six days after that – as the 2025/26 Premier League fixtures were announced and Everton found out they were starting the season at Leeds United before hosting Brighton & Hove Albion in their inaugural competitive match at Hill Dickinson Stadium – the Blues' raid on Manchester United for academy director Nick Cox came to light.

Cox, who took up a new role as technical director at Everton, had his appointment confirmed by the club along with Smith, Chris Howarth and Nick Hammond, who was CEO Angus Kinnear's transfer guru at Leeds United, a further 48 hours later on 20 June.

With the Blues having struggled for several years to bring in a suitable long-term successor for club captain Coleman – widely regarded as being their best right-back of the Premier League era and certainly a player who, in following Tony Hibbert, revolutionised the position at a time when full-back play was changing rapidly – word got out that an early target for the new-look recruitment team was Fulham's Kenny Tete, who was on the verge of becoming a free agent.

In 2017, while playing for Lyon, the Dutch international was in the thick of a mass brawl in front of the Gwladys Street – sparked by home captain Ashley Williams shoving opposition goalkeeper Anthony Lopes – which included a spectator carrying his young son under his arm; the fan was later jailed for assault.

Tete is also the son of a former Thai kick-boxing champion, so as well as a potentially prudent move to acquire an experienced Premier League performer for nothing in a summer when they knew they had to attract both quality and quantity to their squad, perhaps he also possessed the fighting qualities that many Evertonians like to see in their players.

However, they were soon to become moot points as, despite earlier reports that the Amsterdam-born player had reached a verbal agreement to join the Blues, on 1 July, it was announced that he had instead agreed a new three-year deal at Craven Cottage after improved terms were offered.

Ultimately there would be no new right-back through the door, ensuring that the 6ft 6in Jake O'Brien, naturally a towering central defender, would continue to be deployed in the role.

In the meantime, while Everton had been sweating on Tete, on 24 June, two days before the club launched their 2025/26 home kit with a 'wave design' to reflect their relocation to the banks of the Mersey, it was confirmed that the capacity of Hill Dickinson Stadium, which from the offset had been billed as 52,888, was in fact to be 119 seats fewer.

Instead, the Blues' new waterfront home would hold 52,769 with the club insisting that following a thorough post-construction audit and review of the seating configuration, factors such as segregation lines between the home and away section and the compliance and provision for media facilities and camera positions had played a part in the original maximum capacity being reduced by 0.2 per cent.

That still didn't prevent local woman Cathy Clarke, a season ticket holder for 30 years, from having the shock of her life when she arrived for the Brighton game to sit together by her husband, son and nephew, only to discover a metal panel and railing in the space where her seat should have been.

Thankfully, after she raised the issue online, Everton officials were able to give the family a private tour of the stadium with Cathy saying the club 'redeemed themselves' by offering them an alternative four seats together in a comparable area.

The final days of June then brought alternative outcomes for a couple of Blues players whose contracts were due to expire.

On 27 June, as expected, Séamus Coleman signed a new one-year deal as David Moyes said, 'Séamus is more than just a player at Everton. He offers so many different qualities.'

And 48 hours later, Dominic Calvert-Lewin announced he would leave Everton after nine years. Explaining his decision, the Sheffield-born player said, 'This isn't something I chose lightly. Everton has been my home since I was 19. It's the place that saw potential in me, challenged me to grow, and shaped me both as a footballer and as a man.'

On 2 July, the Blues confirmed arguably their biggest signing of the summer and it was a player who still had another two years to run on his existing deal.

Jarrad Branthwaite, the club's most valuable asset, penned a new five-year contract to commit himself until 2030.

The ball-playing defensive colossus, who this author has dubbed 'The Carlisle Kaiser', had signed his previous deal in October 2023 shortly after he had initially become a first-team regular in what proved to be a breakthrough season for him which culminated in an England cap, having returned from his loan spell in the Netherlands at PSV Eindhoven.

However, Branthwaite's basic wages were understood to be still lower than the likes of Mason Holgate's.

Goodison Park's top brass had dismissed a brace of offers from Manchester United (first £35m plus add-ons, then £45m plus add-ons) out of hand the previous summer when they were determined to hang on to the player.

They based their valuation on the £80m fee that United paid for Harry Maguire in 2019, the £75m Chelsea spent on Wesley Fofana in 2022 and the £77m sum that Manchester City laid out for Joško Gvardiol in 2023.

The 23-year-old was rewarded with fresh terms to better reflect his status as a potentially generational talent, and remarked, 'Obviously, with the new stadium we've got here, the new ownership and the new manager, it's an exciting project and it's something I want to be part of.'

The following day though, Merseyside was rocked by a tragedy that stunned the football world.

Liverpool striker Diogo Jota – who had scored the winning goal in the previous Merseyside derby on 2 April – was killed in a car crash in Spain along with his brother André Silva, when driving to catch a ferry for the start of pre-season training, having been advised by doctors not to fly after undergoing recent lung surgery.

Born in Porto on 4 December 1996, the Portuguese international, who scored 14 goals in 49 games for his country, had revealed that during David Moyes's first spell in charge he'd been an Everton fan growing up before he signed for the Reds.

In April 2020, some six months prior to joining Liverpool from Wolverhampton Wanderers, Jota told *The Guardian*, 'I loved to watch Everton play, especially when they were playing at home. It was not a club that fought for the title but that always made life very complicated for the big teams. And I loved that drive and competitiveness. They were relentless.'

In an echo of the aftermath of the Hillsborough disaster in 1989, Liverpool was a city united in grief following the death of

Jota, who had married high-school sweetheart Rute Cardoso, the mother of his three children, a mere 11 days before the fateful accident.

Just 24 hours later, Everton's Portuguese-born players Beto and Youssef Chermiti joined club ambassador Ian Snodin outside Anfield to lay wreaths for the siblings. A card on Beto's wreath contained the message 'With heartfelt condolences', in English and Portuguese.

The following day, David Moyes and his assistant Alan Irvine went to Liverpool's ground to lay flowers and other Everton personnel are also known to have gone to the site to pay their respects.

Ahead of the next Merseyside derby at Anfield in September, Beto was asked about the visit and revealed the kind gesture that Jota paid to him when he signed for the Blues, 'We were not friends, but you know, when you play against Portuguese players and everything, we normally stop, we speak a little bit.

'You have Bernardo Silva, Bruno Fernandes, these guys, but when I signed for Everton, he was the first guy who texted me. He just texted me and said, "I'm happy for you. If you need anything on the city, everything, I can help you, just give me a shout."'

Back at Hill Dickinson Stadium, Everton's last two out-of-contract players both signed new deals.

On 4 July, Michael Keane committed himself to a ninth season with the Blues and said, 'I love Everton and have been massively proud to play for this club since the day I joined so I'm delighted to extend my stay here.

'We've got a world-class new stadium to play in, and our form under the manager last season shows there's a lot of reasons to be positive. I'm looking forward to being part of it.'

Three days after that, Idrissa Gueye also signed on for another year with the option for a second, remarking, 'Everyone knows what Everton means to me and my family. After six seasons here, this club is more than just a place I play, it's part of who I am.

'With our beautiful new stadium and a real sense of momentum throughout the club, this season feels like a turning point, the chance to build something big and lasting.'

Before the friendlies began, there was also time to get a deal for the first new face of the summer over the line following on from Charly Alcaraz's loan being turned into a permanent switch.

Fresh from turning out for France at the UEFA European Under-21 Championship, which was retained by former Blues favourite Lee Carsley's England, striker Thierno Barry completed a £27m move from Spanish side Villarreal.

The 6ft 5in prospect, who once got sent off in both of his first two matches for Swiss outfit Basel, proclaimed, 'I think the fans here are, like, crazy people ... I like this!'

## Tuesday, 15 July 2025: Accrington Stanley 1 Everton 1, Wham Stadium Attendance 3,875 (2,336 Everton)

Mention the words 'Accrington Stanley' to football fans, or probably most people in the UK over the age of 40, and they'll think of milk, given the iconic advertising campaign that name-checked the boyhood Blue turned Everton nemesis Ian Rush.

Originally made in 1989, it proved so popular that the Milk Marketing Board continued to show it for six years.

At the heart of the campaign were a couple of young, aspiring Scouse footballers, and a generation later Blues' homegrown hero Harrison Armstrong – from West Derby – was the latest prospect coming out of England's most passionate football city looking to make his way in the professional game.

It was in another friendly against League Two opposition almost 12 months earlier, a 2-1 defeat to Salford City under Sean Dyche, that the then 17-year-old midfielder had played his first senior minutes for the club he'd been with since the age of five.

In between, Armstrong, who was looking to follow other academy graduates from the city such as Michael Ball, Ross Barkley, Tom Davies, Anthony Gordon, Tony Grant, Tony Hibbert, Francis Jeffers and Wayne Rooney into the first team, had played competitively for Everton on half a dozen occasions before proving a big hit on loan with Derby County fans in the second half of 2024/25 as he helped the Rams to avoid relegation in their first season back in the Championship.

Operating on the right wing in the first half and then as a deeper, central midfielder after the break, the local lad was the Blues' most polished performer at Wham Stadium in the first pre-season friendly of the summer.

His display highlighted the dilemma that David Moyes faced over whether to use him as a squad player in the upcoming campaign or farm him out again to gain more first-team experience.

Other than Jake O'Brien and Beto, who both played the entire second half, Moyes went with his strongest available side against an Accrington outfit managed by another boyhood Blue, John Doolan, who had been Alan Stubbs's assistant when Hibernian lifted the Scottish Cup for the first time in 114 years in 2016.

Therefore, after wasting several good chances, it was something of an embarrassment to Everton when Ben Ward put Stanley ahead five minutes into the second half and it took a penalty 13 minutes from the end to spare their blushes.

It was another Blues prospect who earned their share of the spoils as under-21 player of the year Isaac Heath – who impressed sufficiently for Accrington to subsequently take him on a season-long loan six weeks later – won the spot kick by being brought down by Liam Coyle.

Fellow substitute Beto made no mistake from 12 yards by converting in front of the Coppice Terrace, open to the elements, where the majority of Evertonians were situated on what was a night of torrential rain.

The goal ensured Moyes's men survived intact, but the author's laptop computer did not.

It's not often that Stanley's modest 5,450-capacity home, traditionally known as the Crown Ground, gets compared to its more illustrious neighbour Old Trafford some 30 miles to the south, but like Manchester United's supposed 'Theatre of Dreams' it also possesses a leaky roof.

Accrington officials were clearly already aware of this as a towel was handed to those of us in the press box before kick-off which because of my particularly unfortunate 'spec' I ended up commandeering.

It was something of a light-hearted novelty for most of the contest but just after the Blues drew level and the heavens opened again, the waterfall that suddenly started gushing down was as if one of the urchins from the aforementioned advert had got that pint of milk and poured its entire contents on to my keyboard.

Suffice to say, that's not what I wanted a week before heading to the USA to cover the Premier League Summer Series and a replacement had to be ordered before I crossed the Atlantic Ocean and only arrived the day before I flew out.

*Line-up*: Harry Tyrer; Nathan Patterson; Vitalii Mykolenko (William Tamen 46); Michael Keane; Jarrad Branthwaite (Jake O'Brien 46); James Garner (Beto 46); Tim Iroegbunam; Harrison Armstrong; Charly Alcaraz (Isaac Heath 62); Dwight McNeil; Youssef Chermiti (Justin Clarke 62).

## Saturday, 19 July 2025: Blackburn Rovers 1 Everton 0, Ewood Park

## Attendance: 11,399 (4,541 Everton)

The enduring image of Everton's 1-0 defeat at Blackburn Rovers was a scene that most of the spectators who went to Ewood Park did not see, as most of them had departed by this point.

Although the travelling Blues supporters did not outnumber their hosts like they had done less than ten miles away just four days earlier, they still took their entire allocation as always, filling the lower tier of the Darwen End as 4,541 made the relatively short trip from Merseyside to take in the action.

What they witnessed left them with more questions than answers though, as having fallen behind to a sloppy goal early on with Dion De Neve left unmarked in acres of space at the back post just seven minutes into the contest, Everton were unable to hit back against their Championship opponents.

The display, which was neat at times but still lacking in sharpness, certainly left them with plenty of food for thought.

However, after most of the paying customers were on their way home, some players were conducting post-match interviews and substitutes finishing their warm-downs, a couple of high-ranking figures from the visitors were deep in conversation in the Ewood Park tunnel.

David Moyes was spotted talking to chief executive Angus Kinnear with both men acutely aware of the task at hand for each of them.

While the Blues had already conducted some astute business, with a significant overhaul of the squad required in terms of additional acquisitions, there was still plenty of work to do and it's doubtful that the CEO was enquiring about what Broadway shows the Glaswegian gaffer might be taking in.

*Line-up:* Mark Travers; Nathan Patterson (Michael Keane 59); Vitalii Mykolenko; Jake O'Brien; Jarrad Branthwaite; Idrissa Gueye (Harrison Armstrong 59); James Garner; Dwight McNeil (Jenson Metcalfe 79); Charly Alcaraz (Justin Clarke 70); Iliman Ndiaye (Isaac Heath 59); Beto (Youssef Chermiti 70).

3

# American dream – the trip that forged a landmark season

EVERTON'S OVERSEAS jaunts under Sean Dyche had amounted to me being the only UK journalist reporting on a solitary game with Swiss second-tier side Stade Nyonnais across the road from UEFA's headquarters by the shores of Lake Geneva in 2023, and Séamus Coleman's homecoming to his first club Sligo Rovers in 2024 – on the day that the Friedkin Group (TFG) pulled out of takeover talks with Farhad Moshiri (only to go back in of course) – so a proper long-haul tour restored a sense of adventure for many at the club after the years of austerity.

David Moyes loves visiting the USA and as well as taking the Blues there on no fewer than half a dozen separate occasions during his first spell in charge, a seventh trip for 2013 was set up under his watch and would ultimately see rookie defender John Stones – the Scot's final signing from Barnsley and parting gift – win a shoot-out against Juventus in San Francisco for Roberto Martínez's side with a 'Panenka' penalty.

That would be part of a competition called the International Champions Cup with Everton going on to face eventual tournament winners Real Madrid in Los Angeles' Dodger Stadium before finishing against Valencia in Miami Gardens.

The Blues' 2025 return would be their most substantial and high-profile visit to the country since, after trips under Rafael Benítez in 2021 and Frank Lampard the following year.

Many of Everton's early visits to the USA under Moyes had seen them face Major League Soccer opponents but this was for the Premier League Summer Series that pitted them against regular domestic rivals.

These included his previous employers, West Ham United, who he steered to UEFA Europa Conference League success in 2023 for their first major trophy in 43 years, plus Manchester United, the team he quit the Blues to join a dozen years earlier when hand-picked by fellow Glaswegian Sir Alex Ferguson to be his successor at Old Trafford.

It was Bournemouth first up though at the MetLife Stadium which earlier that month had hosted Chelsea's 3-0 win over Paris Saint-Germain in the FIFA Club World Cup Final and would also stage the World Cup Final the following year.

With space at a premium on the island of Manhattan, the MetLife Stadium, built on the site of the old Giants Stadium that witnessed the Republic of Ireland's shock 1-0 victory over Italy in the 1994 World Cup finals, has – like its predecessor – long been the base for New York's two NFL teams, the Giants and Jets, despite being across the Hudson River in the borough of East Rutherford, in the neighbouring state of New Jersey.

Although the city's basketball team the Knicks and ice hockey outfit the Rangers share the iconic indoor arena Madison Square Garden in the heart of Manhattan, both of New York's Major League Baseball sides are situated in the outer boroughs with the Yankees in the Bronx and Mets in Queens, close to the Flushing Meadows-Corona Park complex where tennis's US Open is held.

Trips to the USA provide Premier League players with a degree of anonymity they don't enjoy back in the UK though and Everton's squad based themselves close to the Empire State Building which they visited together.

It might have been very much a working 'holiday' but in order to get the balance right, the Blues also enjoyed some precious downtime to relax.

Jordan Pickford and Michael Keane donned the iconic pinstripe jerseys when visiting Yankee Stadium but their presence couldn't prevent the home favourites from losing 12-5 to Philadelphia Phillies.

Senegal international pair Iliman Ndiaye and Idrissa Gueye enjoyed Central Park, with the former revealing, 'We saw the bridge where *Home Alone* was!' while the latter remarked, 'It's a nice place to be and it's natural.'

Charly Alcaraz, who was making his first visit to the Big Apple, thought Times Square was 'very nice' after looking around with Beto, and wanted to go back and explore the city with his girlfriend. Meanwhile, Thierno Barry explained he had already been with his partner the previous December and that Times Square was also his favourite spot 'because it's like a film'.

Training took place in a lesser-known location in one of the world's most iconic cities, as Everton started their first full day in the USA with an open session on Randall's Island, a corner of the country's largest metropolis that a Blues staff member described as New York's 'hidden gem', but this quiet section of the city has played host to some truly gigantic sporting names.

The smart but modestly sized Icahn Stadium, a multi-purpose track and field facility, opened on 23 April 2005, the day that David Moyes's Everton drew 1-1 at home to Birmingham City with Duncan Ferguson equalising in the 86th minute to snatch a precious point on their way to their highest Premier League finish of fourth.

However, it was a case of 'After the Lord Mayor's Show' somewhat given that the Scottish centre-forward had also scored the winner at Goodison Park against Manchester United just three days earlier.

The biggest football draw here these days is usually MLS side New York City FC's second team but in its previous incarnation, the site's original ground, Downing Stadium, played host to Pelé's first game for New York Cosmos and Jesse Owens qualifying for the 1936 Olympic Games.

That venue also staged a couple of Everton matches under the guidance of their newly appointed chief coach Ian Buchan – the club would never give the former Loughborough University PT lecturer the title of manager. They played there twice in 1956, defeating American Soccer League All Stars 7-0 on 22 May and Scottish side Aberdeen 6-3 on 17 June.

Fast forward to 2025 though and having taken the subway to 125th Street station, and walked through Harlem on to the pedestrian section of the Robert F. Kennedy Bridge, I'm joined by a select but eclectic group of other onlookers for the open training session.

Everton's former USA international goalkeeper Tim Howard, who had just sent me a WhatsApp message in reply to an online link I'd forwarded to him of his exclusive *Liverpool Echo* interview to launch the tour – in which he reveals that it was a trip to the aforementioned Giants Stadium with his mother that sparked his passion for football as a boy – watches on, alongside club ambassadors Graham Stuart and Leon Osman.

I ask Tim, who has now relinquished the record for the most Premier League appearances for the Blues to Séamus Coleman but has still played more matches for the club than any other player from outside the British Isles, to pose for a photograph with his former team-mate Osman (847 games for Everton between them) and we share a joke about me not realising he was only a couple of hundred yards away when we just communicated by phone.

As I make my way to my vantage point to observe proceedings, new chief executive Angus Kinnear, who was spotted deep in conversation with David Moyes at Ewood Park after the Saturday's 1-0 defeat to Blackburn Rovers, was on this occasion chatting with Graeme Le Saux who, along with Howard, was present as part of ESPN's broadcasting team, alongside John Champion, Peter Drury, Robbie Earle and Rebecca Lowe.

Later on, I go over to speak to Mr Kinnear himself, and by this point he is joined by Brian Walker, one of the first representatives of the Friedkin Group to attend a game at Goodison Park following the completion of their takeover, having been present for the goalless draw with Chelsea on 22 December 2024.

Joining in 2018, TFG's vice-president of strategy previously served seven years in the United States Marine Corps between 2003 and 2010.

Although the club's most valuable asset, Jarrad Branthwaite, has stayed back in the UK to try and shake off his injury picked up at Blackburn, Moyes – wearing dark sunglasses to protect those piercing blue eyes in the July sun – and his staff and players all look relaxed as they put on a show for an enthusiastic crowd of several dozen Evertonians who had made their way to get a close-up view of their heroes from across the Atlantic.

After the session, I catch up with man of the moment James Garner, who just three days earlier had scored Everton's winning goal with a long-range free kick in the 2-1 comeback victory over League One Port Vale in a behind-closed-doors friendly at Hill Dickinson Stadium – the senior side's first match at their new home.

For the second season out of three so far with the Blues, the midfielder drew a blank in the scoring stakes in 2024/25, so I ask him if he feels his strike might lead to more.

Garner tells me, 'I hope I'm able to do that a few more times this season, that's the plan. I'm half-decent at free kicks, so hopefully I get to take a few in the league and hopefully they go in. It's a little bit of history, even though it was a pre-season game. I just hope I can do it in a game that matters now.

'It's not like I've been putting the extra effort in because it's something that is hard to replicate. You can practise all you want but in a game scenario, it's tough. It's something that I definitely feel I've got in my locker, but I just need to show it.'

It must be pointed out that although the temperatures are in the mid-30s Celsius in New York, for the first two nights I was still wearing the same outfit I left my house in.

Along with some lads from Formby who were also here for Everton and share a mutual friend with me in Danny Prentice, there were initial fears when we landed at JFK that our suitcases had been swiped from the carousel, but after inputting our data into a computer it transpires our luggage has been inadvertently left by Aer Lingus at Manchester Airport.

The lack of fresh clothes is bad enough – my suitcase finally makes it to my hotel almost 48 hours late – but although I've got my laptop which was in my carry-on backpack, for a working journalist the real killer is not having my UK-to-USA plug adapters to charge my computer and phone.

I won't make the mistake of putting them in the check-in bag again as I quickly realise you cannot buy them in the USA, only the other way around of course.

After using Google Maps on my phone to guide me to the training session, it's on one per cent battery by the time I get there and huge thanks must go to the club's head of media Andy Neild and head of engagement Mo Maghazachi for lending me some replacements which enable me to get some essential top-ups.

That's just as well as I had a hectic first full day ahead of me. After a quick pit stop to eat, I'm off to Dan Meis's Third Avenue office for a recorded chat and exclusive interview featured in chapter 20 of this book, then it's on to the Turnmill bar, home of NYC Evertonians, for a special fan edition of the *Royal Blue* podcast.

I get to the 27th Street venue early to try and set up before the crowds arrive, but after a chat with its Irish manager Peggy it becomes clear that with the throngs already packing the Everton-decorated interior and a pleasant but noisy 1980s disco blaring out from the sound system, we're going to have to record outside.

That's unless we want to head down to the basement by the gents where bizarrely there is a sticker next to the urinals with the slogan 'Skelmersdale – world-class for business'.

We duly opt to go outdoors and in the words of my producer Ian Croll back in Liverpool, who is always a stickler for production values, the decision proves to be 'a masterstroke'.

Recording on the streets of New York gives our chat a lively authenticity. It was salty at times but it was most definitely real.

I'm joined by native New Yorker Stephen Neave, who nevertheless is at pains to differentiate his Brooklyn roots. The borough was begrudgingly absorbed into a 'Greater' New York City in 1898, and still has over a million more residents than Manhattan, ensuring that had the merger not taken place then it would now be the third-largest city in the USA after Los Angeles and Chicago.

The other two members of the panel are NYC Evertonians co-chairs Michael Setterberg (originally from Arizona) and James Rogers – a diamond who also lent me an adapter as well as organising the whole interview – who hails from Huyton but is now a neighbour of Stephen's across the Brooklyn Bridge.

We're also periodically joined by the Turnmill's larger-than-life doorman, who is particularly chatty for someone who insists he likes to 'fly under the radar', but it proves to be one of my all-time favourite episodes, so give it a listen online if you haven't already.

You can't buy moments like when James was discussing the merits of Branthwaite's new contract only to be met by one of the seemingly ever-present honking car horns in the background followed by a distinctly New York accent being heard telling the driver to 'shut the fuck up!' (The finger is pointing firmly at you, Stephen.)

After the mayhem of Thursday, Friday at least starts with me being reunited with my luggage as my bag is waiting for me in the hotel lobby and resplendent in a clean shirt and having swapped my jeans for my shorts that have now turned up, I head over to New Jersey for the pre-match press conference to preview Everton's opening Premier League Summer Series game against Bournemouth.

Having done a video diary to camera in Times Square, I go to collect my train ticket at Penn Station by Madison Square Garden.

As a long-time Wirral resident, and all the 'dark side' jibes the peninsula receives from many in Liverpool, I can't help but feel New Jersey gets something of a rough ride from New Yorkers. The fictional home of *The Sopranos*, in real life it was the birthplace of Frank Sinatra, who of course was charitable enough to sing 'New York, New York'. There's also Bruce Springsteen, Jon Bon Jovi, Meryl Streep, Joe Pesci, John Travolta, Whitney Houston, Danny DeVito, Shaquille O'Neal and Tim Howard.

In the 2007 film *American Gangster*, when in the city, Russell Crowe's New Jersey-based 'good cop' character Richie Roberts is told when running into corrupt undercover New York police officers, 'When was the last time I was in Jersey? Let me think ... never!'

Even the next day when I was listening to the official tour guide at the observatory at the top of One World Trade Center, we're told New York and New Jersey are 'frenemies', while there were legal disputes continuing until 1998 over which side of the state lines the Statue of Liberty and Ellis Island actually fall under.

As soon as we emerge from the tunnel under the Hudson River, it's clear that this adjoining state is rather different from its more high-profile neighbour. Straight away, we find ourselves in a landscape of fields, reeds and marshes running alongside the tracks and when we do pull into an urban area, it's a world away from the high rises of the metropolis.

Because there are so many other skyscrapers in Manhattan, while on the island itself, you can only see One World Trade Center from certain angles, but out here it dominates the horizon.

I spot the 25,000-capacity Sports Illustrated Stadium, home of New York Red Bulls (whom Tim Cahill joined on leaving Everton in 2012) from my window just before I disembark, which to muddy the waters further is also in New Jersey, in the town of Harrison.

Getting off at Newark's Broad Street Station, it's then a walk of just over a mile to the rendezvous point, Washington Elementary School in the town of Kearny.

Although it's a relatively short distance, in order to go over the Clay Street Bridge to reach the other side of the Passaic River, I have to negotiate McCarter Highway, which, while being in a built-up area, is akin to trying to cross the M6.

Having just about survived that, I pass a boarded-up old mill that looks like it's been dropped straight in from a Lancashire cotton town. Despite its dilapidated nature, it has a poster pinned to the wall emblazoned with 'luxury apartments coming soon'.

As often with these kinds of events, the assembled press pack are kept waiting way beyond the allotted start time and to help fill the void, I pose for a photograph next to the Premier League Summer Series trophy (surely a replica).

However, that doesn't prevent me from posting the picture on social media platform X with the caption, 'Does Arne know this thing is here? Maybe I could take it back to Liverpool for the neighbours, it's not like I've got a track record for my luggage getting lost.'

The sweltering temperatures are again in the mid-30s by this point and not long after arriving with Dwight McNeil, Jake

O'Brien and Tim Iroegbunam in tow and joining some local schoolchildren to go through drills with Daniel McDonough of Everton in the Community, David Moyes makes the sage call to make it an indoor session as everyone heads inside to the school gym. It proves an even more inspired choice just a few minutes later as the stifling heat makes way for a heavy thunderstorm and subsequent deluge.

As I speak to the 62-year-old in the corner of the sports hall, I'm privy to a strong message he will declare in public to a captive audience a few hours later and a theme that will become his mantra for the trip.

With Thierno Barry the only new outfield recruit at this point, Moyes tells me, 'We're waiting on new players coming in. I can sense it from the players as well. Maybe they need the competition?'

While Everton's manager is adamant about such needs, what is less clear are claims from some of the Kearny residents that their local side Thistle once defeated Moyes and his Celtic Boys' Club team-mates when the youngsters from the Glasgow giants visited on tour.

Details appear to have been lost in the mists of time, but Moyes himself shrugs off such suggestions and a photo of him as a teenager in Kearny, holding a large trophy, appears to support his version of events, but I'll leave him to discuss that with them at his next port of call.

It seems that these trips in his formative years helped shape his appreciation for US culture though. He reveals that after this event he's going to put his head through the door at Kearny's Scots American Club, a venue that's been open since 1931 but somewhere he hasn't been for almost four decades.

Moyes adds, 'We were here as 15-year-old boys and stayed with families. We had a brilliant time and the hospitality we got was incredible. It was a big thing. We used to love coming here and we used to get a day's trip into New York.'

One person who is visiting New York for the first time is Dwight McNeil, who I speak to one-on-one in Kearny.

The 2024/25 campaign was a difficult one on and off the pitch for the Rochdale-born star, who was sidelined for four months with a knee injury that required surgery.

Enjoying the change of scenery that the tour brings from the more familiar surroundings of Finch Farm, it's a really candid interview with the soon-to-be 26-year-old who shows an increased maturity that he talks about feeling as he moves towards senior player status.

We cover a range of topics, including his preferred position, his new role in the squad, a major reset in his approach, excitement over moving to Hill Dickinson Stadium, interchanging positions with Iliman Ndiaye and Charly Alcaraz and why he believes it will be a huge season for him.

However, McNeil's status will be rocked in the space of the following three weeks as Everton land a couple of huge recruits in his area of the pitch in the shape of Kiernan Dewsbury-Hall and then Jack Grealish.

Ahead of the Blues getting those deals over the line, there's also something of a 'mic drop' moment from the boss back in Manhattan that evening.

Lifelong Evertonian Roger Bennett, originally from Liverpool but now a US citizen who broadcasts *Men in Blazers* on the NBC network, is the host for a raucous event at Racket NYC entitled 'A night live on stage with Everton Football Club featuring David Moyes'.

Although the Scot is the main attraction, Roger warms up the crowd with some entertaining cameos from James Tarkowski, Iliman Ndiaye and Séamus Coleman.

As well as reliving his wonder strike with what was the last kick of a ball from an Everton player in a Merseyside derby at Goodison, ensuring that after over 130 years of combat Liverpool didn't finish with a winning record in the fixture at the Grand Old Lady, Tarkowski provided insight on what it's like to face Ndiaye in training.

The Senegal international seemed to feed off the crowd's energy and joining in with a rendition of his song, while, as always, skipper Coleman was an exemplary inspiration, explaining how as one of the few Everton players who actually lives in Liverpool, he has always been able to relay the mood within the city to his team-mates.

On what was mostly a light-hearted occasion, there was a touch of humour from Moyes, showing the ready wit he possesses as when presented with comparison photographs of his two unveilings as Everton manager almost 23 years apart, he quipped about his once red hair that inspired a terrace anthem, 'I might dye it back!'

Also, when the 'folically challenged' Bennett rued the Blues' controversial Champions League qualifying exit to Villarreal two decades earlier and brought up referee Pierluigi Collina, Moyes responded with, 'Those baldies, eh?'

With his brother Kenny, a football agent, watching on from the wings, Moyes appeared relaxed and comfortable in his own skin, requiring no gimmicks to work the crowd but almost everything he said seemed to strike the right chord with those watching and there was one line in particular that brought the house down.

With the audience hanging on his every word, the Glaswegian insisted that Everton needed to sign 'nine or ten players before the start of the season', which sparked a roar of approval from many onlookers.

Although Moyes would later qualify the calculation included the three recruits he'd already got through the door at this stage, a second-half collapse in the opening Premier League Summer Series game against Bournemouth the next day only seemed to strengthen his claim.

Ahead of the match, I met up with Simon Kendall, son of the late Howard Kendall, who was of course a legendary Everton player as one third of the celebrated 'Holy Trinity' midfield alongside Colin Harvey and Alan Ball, before going on to become the club's most successful manager and presiding over three separate spells in charge at Goodison Park.

Simon, who works for Colgate, emigrated to the US a few years ago with his Irish wife and their children and the family now resides in New Jersey where he combines his day job with duties as a football coach at a local junior team.

Our encounter is to record a podcast about what it was like growing up with an Everton icon as your father. While that goes really well and I'd recommend all Blues fans seek it out online to listen to, it takes place at a venue that takes us both outside of our usual comfort zones, the American Dream Mall, which I find out is the second-largest in the US after the equally patriotically named Mall of America in Minnesota.

We choose it as our rendezvous point as it's across the road from the MetLife Stadium – where Simon is taking the Kendall clan to watch the game – and the two venues are connected by a raised footpath over the freeway in between them.

However, anecdotes about the Gwladys Street End sucking the ball into the back of the net and team bonding on memorable nights at Chinese restaurants are on this occasion set against the surreal backdrop of children zipping around the mall's polished floors, while riding on the backs of electric-powered toy animals.

I told Simon it was only a matter of time before one of these furry rides collided with someone. And sure enough, one unassuming shopper who had been minding his own business came within inches of doing himself a mischief after being rear-ended by the horn of a 'My Little Pony' unicorn!

## Saturday, 26 July 2025: Everton 0 Bournemouth 3, MetLife Stadium
## Attendance: 10,000

Later that afternoon, Everton's display after the break against the Cherries was also something of a car crash.

Dwight McNeil and James Garner found themselves in unfamiliar if not unprecedented wing-back roles.

Nathan Patterson and Vitalii Mykolenko, who had also joined Garner at the American Dream Mall as part of 'The Goodison Experience', where shoppers donned virtual reality headsets to take them 'inside' Everton's long-time home, were in central defensive positions either side of Jake O'Brien in a back three.

Although centre-back was, on a good day, the most well-stocked area of the squad, this was not one of those days with the Irishman, who spent most of the second half of the previous season at right-back after being brought in from the cold by Moyes, the only available senior player who could be viewed as a natural fit in the heart of defence.

James Tarkowski was finishing his rehabilitation following an operation for a hamstring injury, Michael Keane had been kept out of training with a quad issue and Jarrad Branthwaite was back in England after picking up a thigh injury at Blackburn Rovers.

Other than its geography – New York's great rival for domestic supremacy Los Angeles at the opposite end of the country got the nod the only previous time the USA had the World Cup in 1994 – it seemed to me like something of an odd choice to give the MetLife Stadium the 2025 Club World Cup Final and then the 2026 World Cup Final.

Although it was relatively new when I visited, having opened 15 years earlier, as a spartan, open bowl it seemed no better than Chicago's Soldier Field where Everton played their second Premier League Summer Series game – that stadium staged the opening ceremony in 1994 but didn't even make the cut this time around.

And both were vastly inferior to Atlanta's Mercedes-Benz Arena where the Blues rounded off the tournament.

Another factor I disliked about the first two stadia was that, even though the press boxes were plush and well-stocked in terms of facilities, they were both indoor affairs behind glass windows which not only removed most of the atmosphere but also resulted in some truly terrible sight lines that were even worse than the equivalent obstructed views at Goodison Park.

There was very little to like about Everton's display against Bournemouth and although their makeshift side hung in for the first half to ensure the score was goalless at the interval, as their players started to wilt in the heat after the break, the fresher legs of Andoni Iraola's men put them to the sword.

Two goals in the space of just four minutes early in the second half killed the contest as substitute Philip Billing fired Bournemouth ahead from outside the area before Dango Ouattara doubled their lead as Patterson tried to track his run only to tap the ball back to him.

The *coup de grâce* was actually a self-inflicted blow as, inexplicably in such sweltering conditions, O'Brien appeared to suffer from a brain freeze when being guilty of delivering a sloppy no-look backpass towards Jordan Pickford, only for the far more alert Dan Adu-Adjei to accept this unexpected present gleefully with both hands and add a third.

Pickford pulled no punches after the game when I spoke to him and told me, 'It was a good first half, but they made some changes and we haven't got the squad to be honest.'

*Line-up with player ratings (mine unless stated):* Jordan Pickford 6; James Garner 6; Nathan Patterson 5; Dwight McNeil 6; Jake O'Brien 4; Vitalii Mykolenko 6; Idrissa Gueye 6 (Tyler Onyango 82); Tim Iroegbunam 6 (Harrison Armstrong 75); Charly Alcaraz 7; Iliman Ndiaye 7 (Youssef Chermiti 75); Beto 6 (Thierno Barry 75).

***

Still recovering from my left luggage debacle, there was more travel chaos ahead as my scheduled flight the following evening was cancelled due to storms around the Great Lakes region.

With no availability the next day, I ended up having to stay an extra two nights in New York, although I had several interviews on my pad to write up that kept me busy and I suppose there are worse places to be stuck in.

Thankfully, my journey to Chicago did not take on Steve Martin and John Candy proportions in *Planes, Trains and Automobiles* as although I was forced to miss the Everton fan meet at AJ Hudson's, I touched down in Illinois with a few hours to spare ahead of the pre-match press conference for the West Ham United game at the Westin Hotel Michigan Avenue.

David Moyes remained tight-lipped about reports linking him with a move for Jack Grealish but his frustration was clear over the lack of progress when it came to bringing in new faces. He said, 'We want to get it done. We're desperate to get things moving on. The truth is we're not getting them over the line at the moment, that's a fact. We're not getting a lot of the deals done that we were hoping to do.'

One deal that the Blues had sealed earlier that day was for Bayern Munich's 19-year-old left-back Adam Aznou.

Moyes insisted that the Morocco international was one for the future and said, 'We see a lot of good things in him, technically he's very good and he's athletic, although he might need just a little bit to get himself built up all ready for the Premier League.'

I sometimes used to get the famous 'ferry across the Mersey' from Seacombe to the Pier Head when commuting to the Liverpool Echo office on Old Hall Street – those who embark on the daytime service can now enjoy enviable close-up views of Hill Dickinson Stadium – but in Chicago I joined several hundred Evertonians on a pre-match pleasure cruise around Lake Michigan, including the affable John Lally, originally from Huyton but now a Colorado resident, who asks me to pose for a photograph with him.

On my way to Navy Pier, where our vessel, the luxurious *Spirit of Chicago*, was docked, I spotted three Everton players walking together by the shores of the lake and it was nice to see that fellow francophones Idrissa Gueye and Iliman Ndiaye had seemingly taken new signing Thierno Barry under their wing.

While things would continue to be rather choppy for the Blues on the pitch throughout pre-season, thankfully the waters are calm as a pleasant evening is had by all on board with the sun setting behind the Windy City's skyline.

Chicago boasted the world's first 'skyscraper', the Home Insurance Building, of which construction began in May 1884 – just after Everton won the Liverpool Senior Cup for the first time – but it has long since been eclipsed by the modern monoliths of downtown.

Everything is relative though and the biggest of them all, the Willis Tower (previously Sears Tower) – still the tallest building in the USA outside of New York City – enjoyed a 25-year reign as the tallest in the world from when it was built in 1973 until Kuala Lumpur's Petronas Towers were completed in 1998.

When I went up to the Skydeck in 2001 on my only previous visit to Chicago, it was still the second-tallest building on the planet, but such has been the 21st century reaching for the skies in Asia, it no longer makes the world top 25.

Back on board, my fellow passengers included Séamus Coleman, first-team coaching staff Alan Irvine and Leighton Baines, legendary former player Adrian Heath who led an impromptu sing-song which included 'On the Banks of the Royal Blue Mersey', and Dan Meis, who was presented with his Trailblazer award by North American Toffees chair Tony Sampson.

When receiving his cup, Meis remarked, 'This is going to be the first trophy associated with Hill Dickinson Stadium,' and quipped that all his fellow architects would now be jealous.

It was not all partying though for the Everton contingent during their time in the city: ambassador Graham Stuart was joined by club staff including Andy Neild, Mo Maghazachi and Rob Urbani plus members of the North American Toffees, including Sampson, who lives nearby, in volunteering at the Greater Chicago Food Depository, demonstrating the Blues' long-standing commitment to community values while on tour in the USA.

The Greater Chicago Food Depository supports households across the city, with one in five currently experiencing food insecurity. In its last fiscal year prior to Everton's visit, the organisation provided more than 101 million meals, recorded over 2.4 million household visits to its grocery partners, and helped submit nearly 19,000 public benefits applications on behalf of Chicago residents in need.

The morning after the cruise, matchday in Chicago was also a big moment for me on the tour as David Moyes had accepted my request for an exclusive sit-down interview ahead of his first full season back in charge.

Our meeting takes place in the sumptuous setting of one of the upstairs lobbies at the five-star Ritz-Carlton Hotel where Everton are staying and their presence is marked by a couple of chefs walking by in club livery as I make my way across the huge open-plan area of the floor.

Sinking into one of the giant armchairs and preparing to wait, I see that Moyes is still speaking to someone else.

Even though he was on the other side of the room, I could still make out the shape of his head through a pane of frosted glass.

When they're done, out emerges Andy Mitten, *United We Stand* editor since 1989 and one of the good guys at Old Trafford, and I remark to him how I hope the gaffer isn't 'talked out' after their chat.

There are no such issues on that score, and although Moyes is, as you would expect in the middle of a pre-season tour and a transfer window in which he is hoping and expecting to bring in a large number of new players, a busy man with his phone ringing on several occasions while we're together, he is honest and candid with me as ever.

In a piece which we ran as a two-part special in the *Liverpool Echo*, he lifted the lid on his big Everton ambition of wanting to get the club back into European football, his true thoughts on the transfer situation, working with the Friedkin Group, and his challenge for supporters at Hill Dickinson Stadium.

I'm casually attired here but when I'm more smartly dressed for the office, Moyes often ribs me about my choice of clothing, with one of his long-running gags being an enquiry as to whether I'm wearing my dad's suit. This stems back to when I used to cover Everton for the *Liverpool Daily Post* during his first spell in charge and I was rather more fresh-faced and still in my 20s.

But while I doubt Moyes himself remembers it, I first interviewed him as a teenager after a game when he was Preston North End manager. I was studying at the University of Central Lancashire, volunteering for the student newspaper *Pluto* (named because it was furthest away from the *Sun*) and several years before one of the solar system's more distant natural satellites was downgraded by scientists to being a mere 'dwarf planet'.

One of Moyes's quips about my sartorial sense even made it on camera in our hour-long interview the previous September when I spoke to him as the ninth *Goodison Park: My Home* guest on what proved to be a 20-part series.

He was out of work at the time – if you don't count his responsibilities as a UEFA technical observer, a post he had taken up the previous month – with his previous managerial position at West Ham having ended after the 2023/24 season.

When I ask him in Chicago whether at the time he ever expected to be back where he is, Moyes insists not, but he is also thoroughly convinced that he made the right choice.

With that crucial task in the bag, I leave him to get back to returning his calls and set off on my way towards Soldier Field for the game against his previous employers.

## Wednesday, 30 July 2025: West Ham United 2 Everton 1, Soldier Field Attendance 58,927

The previous month, when I'd interviewed the charismatic former Chicago Bears player Charles 'Peanut' Tillman at a children's American football coaching event in Liverpool at Leisure United Jeffrey Humble on Long Lane; the retired cornerback reckoned that Evertonians attending the game would see a lot of similarities with their own new stadium.

I get where Tillman was coming from in terms of the proximity to a body of water and the shimmering effect around the top of Soldier Field's exterior not being dissimilar to the curved barrel roof at Hill Dickinson Stadium.

However, inside this historic venue of American sport, which first opened over a century ago, is more like MetLife Stadium in that it's a vast but basic open bowl.

What Soldier Field, the stadium where legendary singer Diana Ross infamously shanked her shot high and wide in the opening ceremony of the 1994 World Cup – don't play football in stiletto heels – does have is a grandiose set of imposing mock Roman columns, although it didn't even make the cut for the 2026 tournament. As I observed on my arrival, after 133 years, Everton had only just departed a stadium that was full of pillars.

Once inside, I was greeted by another press box behind glass but at least they opened some of the windows which enabled a bit of the crowd noise to filter through, unlike in New Jersey.

The room also received a visit from a certain Richard Masters, chief executive of the Premier League.

It's fair to say that the Blues haven't enjoyed the easiest of relationships with top-flight administrators in recent years, having originally been given a ten-point deduction, the largest in the competition's history, for a single PSR breach and while an appeal saw that figure reduced to six, a second charge then added another two back on.

In the midst of it all, Masters appeared to refer to Everton, who have spent most seasons in the top flight and are the only founder members of both the Football League in 1888 and Premier League in 1992 to be ever-presents in the latter, as a small club, along with Nottingham Forest, when answering a question at a Culture, Media and Sport Committee hearing in 2024.

This further enraged many Blues already furious by what they saw as draconian punishments while the nature of the rules enabled the division's established elite to continue to lavish huge sums on players. However, this didn't stop him from also attending the final Premier League fixture at Goodison Park on 18 May 2025.

As Everton slumped to a second Premier League Summer Series defeat, the one bright spot in another disappointing outing would be the return to the pitch of James Tarkowski, 103 days after his run of 109 consecutive starts – having joined on a free transfer after his Burnley contract expired – came to an end when he was forced to undergo surgery on a hamstring injury picked up against Manchester City. The centre-back came on for the final 20 minutes but the damage had already been done by that point.

Moyes's men, sporting their new pastel yellow away kit for the first time, started brightly with Idrissa Gueye firing them in front on 17 minutes with a low shot that slipped through West Ham keeper Wes Foderingham's fingers after being set up by a nicely weighted pass by 18-year-old Harrison Armstrong.

Shortly before half-time, the east London outfit were gifted an equaliser as, with regular goalkeeper Jordan Pickford rested, his new understudy Mark Travers made a hash of dealing with a floated diagonal pass into the box from Max Kilman, knocking the ball on to his own head with a scuffed punch and presenting Lucas Paquetá with a tap-in into an empty net.

The turnaround was then completed midway through the second half when substitute Niclas Füllkrug picked his spot to arrow a decisive low shot into Travers's bottom-left corner.

Speaking to me after the game, comeback kid Tarkowski remarked, 'Hopefully, I'm physically good now and can come and perform again. We were always a bit cautious of putting an exact timeline on it really. There were markers we needed to hit over the weeks and as they started to come, I started to progress quite well. I've been around the group for a few weeks now and fitness-wise I feel really good, it's just about getting that match sharpness that will hopefully be there in the coming weeks.'

There was also a sting in the tail on the way back to my hotel as while the heavy rain that had returned earlier in the day had thankfully relented on the whole for fans in the exposed bleachers watching the Everton game, by the time my post-match duties were over a biblical downpour was taking place.

Given that Soldier Field is situated in a park and you have to walk a mile before you can hail a cab or even get to a subway station, I got the first of a couple of soakings I endured on the trip.

*Line-up with player ratings:* Mark Travers 4; Nathan Patterson 5 (James Garner 46 5); Vitalii Mykolenko 6; Jake O'Brien 6; Michael Keane 7; Idrissa Gueye 7 (James Tarkowski 69 7); Tim Iroegbunam 5 (Charly Alcaraz 46 5); Harrison Armstrong 7; Dwight McNeil 5 (Isaac Heath 80); Iliman Ndiaye 6 (Youssef Chermiti 69 5); Beto 5 (Thierno Barry 46 6).

* * *

Thankfully there were no more delays for my second US domestic flight but the temperatures were rising again as I touched down in Atlanta with Everton – who had been based in the unofficial capital of the south since their first game (flying into Chicago for their second fixture) preparing to hold another open training session the following morning.

Their base was Walsh Field, a sports facility located at Pace Academy's Riverview Sports Complex, which is ten miles out from downtown Atlanta, a similar distance that the Blues' Finch Farm training base is from Liverpool city centre.

Pace Academy, a private school, is located eight miles down the road and Walsh Field opened in August 2014, after a capital campaign for a new upper school exceeded $35m, and they used the extra funds to build a new stadium and track.

'They're all billionaires,' claimed one of the USA-based Evertonian observers. There were certainly lots of blue bloods present, but they weren't necessarily the high society type. Plenty of them were chatty and the nature of modern journalism and online podcast exposure ensures that I was already recognisable to many.

This prompted several casual conversations to spring up in between me recording a Facebook Live video of the session that lasted for over an hour.

One of the biggest characters I came across was Paul Cushion, who hails from L4, just a Jordan Pickford punt from Goodison Park, having grown up on Roxburgh Street.

Given his accent, I thought he'd come over from there just days before for the trip like so many other Merseyside-based Blues. However, it turned out he'd lived in the USA for around 40 years and was now settled in Atlanta.

I got to meet his American children, daughter Kendall – named after Everton's most-successful manager, who Paul told me wrote him a lovely letter when informed of the decision – and son Graeme, after legendary striker Sharp, who is second only to Dixie Dean when it comes to the number of goals scored for the club.

Although training started around 10am, temperatures were already well north of the 30-degree mark and several of the squad took advantage of using the on-site ice baths after they had finished.

Once the session was complete, there was another lengthy photograph and autograph session with fans which players, including latest recruit Adam Aznou, and staff embarked upon in a relaxed and enthusiastic fashion.

By the time David Moyes's final pre-match press conference of the tour came around though, both the boss and the weather – the interviews were shifted a mile across the city from 'Soccer in the Streets' to the Mercedes-Benz Stadium itself because of potential inclement conditions – were on the turn.

There was a distinct softening in Moyes's demeanour as he faced the assembled press pack, and his updated message included, 'We will need to get a stronger squad, I've said it and there's no doubt about it. But I'm confident we will do, I really am.'

Afterwards, he stayed chatting for several minutes, revealing that he'd been to the stadium before to watch the Super Bowl in 2019, attending an event where rapper Snoop Dogg was also present, while also delivering some off-the-record briefings to provide context to ongoing situations.

However, on enquiring what we'd all seen of Atlanta so far, he seemed distinctly unimpressed when I told him I'd visited World of Coca-Cola, and as someone who is a connoisseur of fine wines, he rebuked, 'I thought you were going to say World of Lagers!'

Personally, I've always preferred Pepsi anyway, which is handy given Everton's subsequent partnership with Pepsi Max, complete with an advertisement starring Peter Reid.

By his own admission, the former midfielder – who Howard Kendall hailed as being the club's most important signing since the Second World War – also likes a drop of something stronger and there were plenty of alcoholic beverages being consumed that evening, including pints of Guinness featuring the Everton crest in the head, at the Limerick Junction Bar.

The turnout at the venue, which is the base for Atlanta Evertonians, was sensational with possibly the largest numbers of each of the three fan welcomes throughout the trip, all of which were roaring successes.

This time it was the turn of Lyndon Lloyd, who ran the Toffeeweb website for many years and now has a new site, Evertonia, to receive his Trailblazer trophy from Tony Sampson.

But while the royal blue throngs enjoyed the revelry, duty called again for yours truly and it was time to record another live podcast. Although it thankfully didn't possess quite the cutting edge of our X-certificate mayhem on the streets of Manhattan, it was another thoroughly enjoyable chat with some far-flung Evertonians, although as someone who has lived on the peninsula for many years I was joined by Christopher Harding and Bridget Bryson, who both originally hail from the Wirral, along with Ben, who is Bridget's American son.

The forecast rain duly arrived on the morning of the Blues' final game in the USA and with it came my second soaking.

A combination of unreliable trains on Marta – Metropolitan Atlanta Rapid (that's a joke, they give Merseyrail a run for their money) Transit Authority – and traffic along the city's urban freeways had left me sprinting through the concourses of the Mercedes-Benz Stadium to get to the press conference the day before, but now I was picking up the pace again, and this time pounding the pavements.

My hotel was less than a mile from Hudson Grille Midtown, the venue for the Blues Brunch Quiz and Pre-Match Party, so I decided to go by foot. Yes, it was raining 'a bit' but I thought I wouldn't get too wet. I was wrong.

In an attempt at some damage limitation, I started to break into an increasingly rapid jog, while wearing the heavy laptop backpack I'd had on my shoulders for the whole trip. When I got there, I told those who commented on my sodden appearance that over the previous 24 hours I'd done more running around Atlanta than Michael Johnson at the 1996 Olympics, and there was that much water on the streets by the end, I think I more or less ended up swimming the last few yards.

Using interactive technology on phones, this was more akin to *Who Wants To Be A Millionaire?* and a far slicker-run affair than the infamous quiz on *Phoenix Nights* – there was no Japanese lager to be won either – with the club's media and publications manager Darren Griffiths taking on the role of master of ceremonies along with US 'soccer comedians' the Cooligans.

Once I had quickly dried off, I was invited to have a go myself, and competing under the pseudonym 'Tarky's Big Tackle' I was initially hesitant to reveal my identity, but then won the first round and decided to give my prize of a big bag of Everton toffees to the runner-up.

In the end, despite answering the most questions correctly (25 out of 32) – I was in a bit of a no-win situation given that if I'd triumphed, then people would say, 'You should do,' and if I didn't they'd say, 'You should have done.'

Ultimately, I had to settle for second place overall anyway behind 'Yer Da Sells Avon', which indicated that my main competition was coming from closer to home rather than one of the many American contestants. It turned out to be Peter McPartland of YouTube channel Toffee TV who, in what was a timed competition, must have been a bit quicker than me in the double points round.

Anyway, with the fun and games over, it was time for the serious business of the Blues' final Premier League Summer Series fixture and thankfully, despite their two previous defeats in the competition and Manchester United's brace of wins, they at least bowed out with a much-improved display.

## Sunday, 3 August 2025: Manchester United 2 Everton 2, Mercedes-Benz Stadium
## Attendance: 47,330

A $1.6bn facility completed in 2017 with air conditioning and retractable roof (which was closed), the Mercedes-Benz Arena was, in my eyes, in a different class to the other two stadia that had hosted Everton in the USA that summer and finally us reporters were not having to watch the action from behind glass.

James Garner got the action under way, kicking off against the backdrop of a train horn sound effect that reflects the city's heritage as a railroad town and is also played when local Major League Soccer side Atlanta United find the net or NFL outfit Atlanta Falcons score a touchdown.

The Blues did well not to find themselves coming off the tracks completely after a shocking decision went against them in the 19th minute.

James Tarkowski – back starting his first game since suffering a hamstring injury in April and captaining the side – applied as much force to United winger Amad Diallo as a maitre d' might be expected to use when guiding you to a seat in a restaurant yet referee Thomas Bramall pointed to the spot.

When I was interviewing him after the game, Garner would tell me that the official from Sheffield had apologised to Everton's players at half-time for the decision and admitted he had got it wrong. But Bruno Fernandes still subsequently sent Jordan Pickford the wrong way from 12 yards to put Ruben Amorim's side ahead.

The Blues were good value for their 40th-minute equaliser though and it was a combination of endeavour and nice passing that saw them back on level terms as Vitalii Mykolenko did well to win back possession just outside the United area before Idrissa Gueye guided a clever diagonal ball that Iliman Ndiaye calmly finished at the back post.

Pickford appeared furious, waving his arms around in frustration, when substitute Mason Mount restored United's lead in the 69th minute but in truth it was a smart finish from a talented player who, like so many at Old Trafford, has lost his way in recent years.

Despite their own lack of options in reserve, it was a couple of players coming off the bench who helped secure a deserved draw for Everton.

Tyler Onyango is a rangy central midfielder by trade who had been loaned to League One Stockport County during the previous campaign – and would subsequently be farmed out again to Edgeley Park on a season-long loan on transfer deadline day – but he did well to burst down the right and pick out Dwight McNeil in the centre.

Just as the former Burnley player was about to pick his spot, a couple of United players stepped in and did the rest for him as Amad and Ayden Heaven got in a mix-up with the latter putting the ball past his own keeper in calamitous fashion.

Garner told me that the air conditioning in the stadium had helped produce a better tempo for the game. However, when it came to the penalty gaffe – following on from VAR reversing a decision to give Everton a stoppage-time spot kick in their final Goodison Park match against Manchester United the previous February despite Ashley Young almost having the shirt ripped off his back – he said, 'It's a bit too late to be honest, isn't it? It's a pre-season game, so hopefully it doesn't happen in the Premier League.'

Look what then transpired at Elland Road in Everton's first game later that month.

*Line-up with player ratings:* Jordan Pickford 7; Jake O'Brien 7; Vitalii Mykolenko 7; James Tarkowski 7 (Tyler Onyango 61 7); Michael Keane 7; Idrissa Gueye 7 (Adam Aznou 61 6); James Garner 7; Charly Alcaraz

6 (Dwight McNeil 61 7); Tim Iroegbunam 6 (Harrison Armstrong 84); Iliman Ndiaye 8 (Youssef Chermiti 84); Beto 7 (Thierno Barry 61 6).

***

Before all of that, there was another of those signings that Moyes had said he was confident of getting through the door.

Three days after the game in Atlanta, Kiernan Dewsbury-Hall joined from Chelsea for an initial £25m. The midfielder had been to the USA himself that summer, winning the FIFA Club World Cup. Dewsbury-Hall had only fulfilled a bit-part role in the west London club's previous Premier League campaign after following head coach Enzo Maresca from Leicester City. However, he was their only player to turn out in all of the matches as they lifted the UEFA Conference League.

On signing, he said, 'You look at the stadium – it's incredible. I've played in all of the Premier League stadiums, and this is one of, if not the most impressive, so that in itself is a major, major exciting factor for wanting to join.'

4

# Previous plans – 1960s 'super stadium'

THE IDEA of a new stadium for Everton to succeed Goodison Park stretched all the way back to the 1960s.

When it was completed in 1892, Goodison Park was the first purpose-built football ground in England; Everton had already won their first league championship the previous year playing at Anfield but back then the venue that would become Liverpool's home was still pretty basic and the famous Spion Kop wouldn't be constructed until 1906.

A couple of months after Everton's first game after crossing Stanley Park, a publication entitled *Out of Doors* would proclaim, 'Behold Goodison Park!

'No single picture could take in the entire scene the ground presents, it is so magnificently large, for it rivals the greater American baseball pitches.'

In 1913 it became the first Football League ground to host a reigning monarch when King George V and Queen Mary watched a display by local schoolchildren on the pitch and by the time of another royal visit in 1938 by King George VI and Queen Elizabeth – the grandparents of our current King Charles III – it had become the only ground in Britain to have double-decker stands along all four sides.

When England hosted the World Cup in 1966, Goodison, as the pre-eminent club ground in the country, was chosen not only to host reigning champions Brazil's three group games but a semi-final, alongside Wembley, although the two matches were controversially switched at the last moment with Everton's home originally scheduled to welcome Alf Ramsey's side for their last-four encounter with Portugal.

The 100,000 capacity of the national stadium in London compared to Goodison's, listed as 50,151 for the tournament, was supposedly a key factor in the decision to keep the host nation down south, and during the 1960s some Merseysiders were already clamouring for a larger 'super-stadium' to be built in the north-west considering its de facto status as the capital of English football.

Given that Goodison and Anfield were both fairly landlocked at the time, surrounded by densely packed Victorian terraced housing, much of the talk about new grounds tended to regard the idea of a shared venue.

The clamour grew as early as the 1962/63 season – when Everton secured their sixth league championship while enjoying their record average attendance over the course of a campaign of 51,603, topping 50,000 for the only time before their move to Hill Dickinson Stadium.

The *Liverpool Echo*'s Leslie Edwards revealed on 28 February 1963 that a visionary businessman 'not particularly interested in football' had visited his office with a revolutionary scheme to construct a 100,000-capacity stadium which actually sounds like he was almost predicting a hybrid between the Premier League and Liverpool One several decades before their time.

He wrote, 'The plan calls for a completely new stadium to be sited in the Custom House area, capacity 100,000-plus, with restaurants and shops incorporated and an underground car park capable of taking the bulk of the thousands of cars which bring fans to the ground.

'This super stadium, with running track and facilities for field events, is to be used by both clubs, thus halving the overheads at Anfield and Goodison Park, and more important, drawing revenue six days a week from the parking space available to lorries on non-matchdays.

'The proposer of the plan suggests that the ground should include every comfort, every facility and that charges should be increased to meet all these costs. He says that the majority of people will pay almost anything to see football if they get comfort and safety. The stadium could be used throughout the summer for "spectacle" promotions, including athletics, and it would be paid for not by the clubs, but financed by land developers.'

However, Edwards revealed that having spoken to John Moores, the Everton chairman poured cold water over the idea.

He wrote that Moores thought the plan had possibilities but feared that the cost of erecting such a stadium would run into many millions, the rent to Everton and Liverpool would be in the region of £60,000 to £70,000 a year and he did not see this sort of money 'in football'.

It seems a seed had been sown though in the minds of *Echo* readers and just six weeks later, Brian Holder of Bampton Road, Childwall, wrote a letter calling for the building of a 'super stadium' with a six-figure capacity, stating, 'Liverpool is being favourably compared with Italian cities for football fanaticism. This is true, but Italian spectators can watch their football comfortably, in modern super-sized stadiums with seats for most people.'

Back in 1966 with the championship at Anfield and the FA Cup at Goodison, Liverpool secretary and later chief executive Peter Robinson suggested to the *Echo* that neither ground was big enough and the local rivals should construct a purpose-built arena for them both to use with a larger capacity.

Despite receiving support for the idea from high-profile MPs in the area, such as Prime Minister Harold Wilson and Bessie Braddock, Robinson would later admit, 'I was pilloried on the letters page the following Saturday.'

Others would make the call though and the following year, Liverpool forward Ian St John penned a column in the *Echo* insisting that a new 'Wembley' should be built in the north.

Later in 1967, a letter with no fewer than eight signatures on it from J. Bews, D.B. Lyons, P. Johnstone, J. Driver, A.B. Collins, E.J. Caldwell, W. Taylor and G. Bathurst, again proposed that 'Liverpool needs a super stadium' on the back of a proposal from Alderman Sir Joseph Cleary.

It read, 'The correspondence suggested, "The most effective way to finance the running of such a stadium would be to enlist the support of both the Liverpool and Everton clubs who between them attract over a million supporters yearly to their home games."

'We are disgusted and yet not surprised to read the short-sighted comments of the chairmen of the respective clubs regarding even the possibility of such an idea for the reasons that the clubs would lose their individual identities.

'The jealously guarded identities of the two clubs would not be jeopardised, and it is about time the respective boards showed consideration to their supporters who after all are their very existence.'

# 5

# We never shone so brightly – a new dawn

**Saturday, 9 August 2025: Everton 0 Roma 1, Hill Dickinson Stadium**
**Attendance: 50,837**

It was a day that started like a lot of days for me, with a run, and that provided me with an early glimpse of Everton's new home.

I could never claim to be a passionate runner, and while those marathon men and women who pound the pavements over huge distances have my utmost admiration, that's not for me, especially as someone who has always been so susceptible to blisters on my feet; just walking around the streets of New York City for work a couple of weeks earlier had left me with a fresh batch that I'd had to tape up with plasters.

However, when the global coronavirus pandemic of 2020 forced gyms across the country to close – including the one I'm a member of in Liverpool city centre – a morning circuit around New Brighton was hastily devised in order not just to keep fit but also get some valuable time outside of the house.

Although society is now thankfully back to normal on that score, on days I'm not in the office, I still like to stretch my legs and ever since my much-loved long-time former *Echo* colleague Dan Kay tragically passed away at 45 (the same age as myself as

I write these words) in 2023, I have devised a 5km route, a legacy of lots of Dan's friends such as myself taking part in the 5KAY initiative to raise money for food banks in his memory.

People often say nice things about others after they're dead but for those of us who knew him while he was with us, in this modern age of division and intolerance of others who do not share your point of view, Dan was a terrific, but all-too-rare example, of a football supporter who, without diluting the intense passion for his own team (Liverpool, who he followed home and away for many years), also possessed a genuine respect, and to a degree, affection, for local rivals.

Make no bones about it, he had a fervour and a knowledge base to top most Kopites, but we called him 'Purple Dan' (with the colour being a mix of blue and red, 'purple' articles at the *Echo* are relevant for Everton and Liverpool).

He was never bitter towards the neighbours, having been taken to his first football match at Goodison Park by his Evertonian father. Also, having been mostly raised in New Brighton by his grandparents, there was a soft spot for Wirral-based Tranmere Rovers too and symbols from all three clubs were included in the 'Dan flag' which was created to celebrate his legacy.

Dan probably did far more jogging than I have ever partaken in, but what he and I have been privileged to experience are the incredible views when trotting along New Brighton promenade, which, extending for over two miles, is the longest in the United Kingdom.

As you get towards the bottom end of Victoria Road, there are a couple of glimpses between the side streets of the New Brighton Lighthouse on the confluence of the River Mersey and Liverpool Bay, but after then spotting the giant cranes of the Port of Liverpool 'across the water' in Bootle, as you reach the 'prom' itself, the full incredible maritime cityscape opens up.

To your right you can see all the great buildings of Liverpool city centre: the Three Graces (also built on filled-in docks), the two cathedrals, the West Tower, St Johns Beacon, the Museum of Liverpool, Albert Dock and M&S Bank Arena, the latter on the site where Everton's previous riverside stadium project on King's Dock was proposed over two decades earlier.

Ahead though, there is something truly unique – the only natural vista on the planet that takes in three major football stadia.

Given its position on the waterfront, Hill Dickinson Stadium is by far the most prominent building presented to your eyes.

However, thanks to a decision confirmed by the Blues' American owners the Friedkin Group, announced just five days before the final Premier League fixture in 2024/25, Goodison Park has – for now at least – been given a reprieve as the new venue for the women's team.

Also, up on a hill you can spot the place where the senior club in the city celebrated their first league championship in 1891 (Anfield, the base of Liverpool FC since they were formed in 1892 for those who really need it spelling out for them).

As I told Dan Meis when we spoke in his New York office a fortnight before the grand opening, over in New Brighton we've got the view, and in that respect at least, are Brooklyn to Liverpool's Manhattan as it were.

Whatever your football allegiances – or lack of them – given the entire cornucopia of amazing sights to take in, it always perplexes me when I see some other people running in the opposite direction down the prom, with their backs to the city.

There's a lyric in the popular terrace anthem 'Spirit of the Blues' that proclaims, 'Everton – we never shone so brightly,' and that's how it felt looking across to Hill Dickinson Stadium on the morning of its inaugural first-team fixture in front of fans.

The waves on the Mersey were lapping and the reflection of the summer sun ensured they were gleaming too, along with the roof on Everton's new home.

Here was a fresh dawn that, depending upon how far back you wanted to trace it, went four years (the time it took to construct); nine years (from the time the site was initially identified); 28 years (the period the Blues had been actively looking to relocate) or even 133 years, from when they built Goodison Park.

For most of her existence, the Grand Old Lady was the leading club ground in the country but she fell woefully behind so many of her rivals in the modern era.

A paragraph contained within the Appeal Board's full written reasons in February 2024 when Everton got four of their initial ten points back after being hit by what was at the time the most severe sporting sanction in 135 years of English top-flight football the previous November is an explanation as to why Goodison had become a financial millstone around the Blues' neck. Along with all those pillars obstructing views, the written reasons pointed out that Goodison ranked 18th in the Premier League for generating matchday revenues.

Although it can take some 40 minutes or more to fight through the traffic back to some outlying environs of Liverpool from L4, Goodison Park and Anfield are just a quick 15-minute drive from New Brighton for me through the Wallasey Tunnel. But after emerging out on to Scotland Road, from now on it would be a sharp left down Boundary Street where the stadium immediately comes into view.

Matchday routines for all Evertonians had changed for ever, but whereas the move from Walton to Vauxhall was a mere couple of miles in distance, in terms of what it represented, this was a giant leap forwards.

Having parked up – still over two and a half hours before kick-off – I was soon on Regent Road, where the party for True

Blues was already in full swing and appeared to be carrying on from where the early morning festivities had left off ahead of Goodison's farewell when Everton had beaten Southampton 2-0 on 18 May.

It was a hive of activity and anticipation in every direction, but nowhere more so than what has surely become Liverpool's happiest pub, the Bramley Moore Hotel. The owners must feel like they've won the lottery having been transformed overnight from being a sleepy backstreets boozer on the dock road to a lucrative matchday hub in the shadow of an arena that will regularly attract crowds of over 50,000.

At this point, spare a thought for Dave Bond, general manager of the Winslow Hotel, across the road from Goodison Park, an affable host and gentle giant originally from County Clare, Ireland, plus an Evertonian from childhood to boot, who I met earlier in 2025 when filming in his hostelry with Dr David France.

After being open for 140 years – a period pre-dating Everton Football Club, let alone their time at Goodison Park – the departure to Hill Dickinson Stadium ensured it was no longer economically viable for the Winslow to continue and it closed its doors for the last time on 24 January 2026, going out with a bang by holding a raucous farewell party.

Back on the waterfront, having entered through the dock wall, like when initially stepping inside the completed site for the first test event back in February, the scale of the construction starts to hit you.

Up close, the stadium itself is considerably larger than its storied predecessor and even at this time while stood in the vast fan plaza that we're told can accommodate up to 17,000 people, it felt busy. There was an eager line stretching back towards the enclosure's boundaries forming as excited Evertonians queued up to splash their cash in the new flagship official store which the previous month had replaced Everton One opposite Goodison Park.

I was then joined by Tony Scott, a long-time contributor who produces video content for the *Liverpool Echo*, and whose links with the newspaper go back further than my own to when he used to work in the staff canteen at the office.

We duly recorded a piece to camera together ahead of the historic day, which was immediately uploaded, and then we set off together over to the far side of the complex to the West Stand by the river where the press box is located.

En route we passed through the shadow of the immense South Stand, already dubbed 'The Blue Wall', where Everton Way is located, containing 36,000 personalised granite stones where supporters have paid to have their individual messages included alongside tributes to the club's playing greats of the past.

It was chock-a-block by this point with thousands of spectators no doubt viewing their own slabs, but among the throng, I am able to spot stones for some true legends such as Dixie Dean, Neville Southall, Kevin Ratcliffe and the Holy Trinity of Colin Harvey, Howard Kendall and Alan Ball.

By the time we get to the West Stand, access to our turnstile is blocked off as fans eagerly fill either side of the players' entrance where the team bus will pull up so, despite our own entry point being only a few yards further, we have to step outside to the Western Terrace and go the long way around along the perimeter of the stadium footprint.

After a quick glance of the new media workroom, we're then whisked up to our new 'specs' in the press box and although a lift takes us as far as the third floor, there are still plenty of steep steps to negotiate before we reach our seats 'at the top of the shop'.

They have a similar set-up at Sunderland where the press box is at the back of the stand, but while you feel somewhat 'up in the gods' at the 1997-built Stadium of Light, despite it containing almost 4,000 fewer seats than Everton's new home, the design of Hill Dickinson Stadium enables you to retain that intimate feel.

I discuss with Patrick Boyland of The Athletic how the lofty spot actually gives you a clear tactical view of the game and we joke about how it compares to the 'anti-football' converted Olympic bowl of the London Stadium where we wouldn't be as high but would be much further back.

We speculate where exactly we might be if West Ham United's ground was plonked on Bramley-Moore Dock. I guess at halfway across the Mersey, while Patrick quips that I might be closer to my living room back in New Brighton.

It all brings back memories of what Dan Meis told me during our recent New York interview, 'Even if you're in the highest seat, and I've done that myself, you still feel like you're right on top of the pitch because it's so steep. Not everyone is going to love it because it's a little scary, but you feel like you're in the game, even when you're the furthest away.'

Perhaps it will be somewhat dicey for those who don't have a head for heights, but as someone who loves to take in the view from elevated platforms wherever I am in the world – the observatory at One World Trade Center was a big improvement on the observation deck at Shanghai Tower where we could barely see more than a mile in all directions – I lapped it up, as, after all, I've already watched my fair share of games from Goodison Park's Top Balcony over the years.

While Evertonians all loved the Grand Old Lady, the press box was not one of her beauty spots. There was a huge pillar obstructing views which meant the ball would often disappear into a momentary 'Bermuda Triangle' when it got close to the corner flag between the Main Stand and Park End, while during the 2008 UEFA Cup penalty shoot-out between Everton and Fiorentina I had to choose whether to watch the taker or the goal as I couldn't see both at the same time.

Built when most reporters were seemingly just 5ft 6in tall and armed with a notepad rather than a laptop, you often had to stand your ground with Marouane Fellaini-esque sharpened elbows in order to type when the press box was full.

In those latter seasons, which were some of the most traumatic in the club's history, the wifi signal would often have the dubious honour of being even less dependable than the team on the pitch.

With those days now behind us, my fellow *Liverpool Echo* Everton writer Joe Thomas and I take in the magnificent panorama in front of us but before the game kicked off, I was heading back down those steps having been invited by the club's Darren Bentley to be the first ever guest on the Village Street stage.

I talk to compère Jamie about Everton's summer, the move to the Mersey waterfront, covering the team in the USA, a potential Jack Grealish transfer and my book *Spirit of the Blues* which had been published earlier that week.

Then it was up again in time for kick-off with the sights now being combined with sounds as the theme from *Z-Cars* – which seems to have a greater oomph behind its clarity and bass thanks to the enhanced speaker systems – greeting the entrance of the teams.

Along with his frustrations over incoming transfers, David Moyes had been candid about his feelings that his side have not played well throughout pre-season but with main men returning to fitness, this looks more like a proper team.

James Tarkowski, their on-field leader and de facto skipper in the absence of club captain Séamus Coleman, made just a second start after being sidelined following hamstring surgery, while his usual centre-back partner Jarrad Branthwaite was also back alongside him having not travelled to the USA and stayed home to work on his fitness.

Meanwhile, the Blues' latest acquisition, Kiernan Dewsbury-Hall – match fit after helping previous club Chelsea to win the

FIFA Club World Cup the previous month – made his debut in the 'number ten' role as the hosts' most advanced central midfielder.

Despite only putting pen to paper three days earlier, the Nottingham-born player was Everton's star performer, especially in the first half as he drove forward with purpose on several occasions, creating some inviting openings.

Arguably the best fell to the feet of another summer signing making his first start, Thierno Barry, but the £27m purchase from Villarreal appeared to tread on the ball as he shot when it was slipped through to his feet.

After the break, Barry then turned provider, picking out Iliman Ndiaye, but the scorer of Everton's final two goals at Goodison Park fired his shot wide from 12 yards out.

Such was the hosts' profligacy, as Roma then started to turn the screw with Ndiaye almost gifting them an opener with a wild backpass intercepted by Wesley, Mr Boyland turned to me and declared that this game had started to reek like a 1-0 win for the visitors; he was proven correct.

Jordan Pickford had already been forced into several smart saves but with 20 minutes remaining, centre-back Gianluca Mancini drove forward and took out rookie left-back Adam Aznou – who had entered the fray after just ten minutes when Vitalii Mykolenko went off injured – with a threaded pass that enabled Matías Soulé the opportunity to curl a shot around Branthwaite and beyond his goalkeeper's grasp for what was the only goal of the contest.

Although Hill Dickinson Stadium had lived up to all expectations for its first full house and Everton's biggest home attendance in over 38 years since 53,323 watched a League Cup quarter-final against Liverpool on 21 January 1987 (the only three bigger crowds for Blues' Goodison Park 'friendlies' were for Merseyside derby Floodlit Cup and Liverpool Senior Cup matches against the Reds), it remained clear that on the pitch Moyes's men remained a work in progress.

Despite the Scot steering a team who had won just one Premier League away game across the previous year to five successes on the road after his return in January, Goodison's final season had produced just five home league victories in total, the joint-lowest in the club's history, along with 1957/58.

Everton's old boys fared better against their Roma counterparts, triumphing 2-0 in a 25-minutes-each-way 'legends game' after the main event, thanks to goals from Moyes signings Phil Jagielka and Steven Naismith. It was also a contest that saw the home team's boss Peter Reid, 69, come on as a late substitute for his first appearance in a royal blue jersey since 1989.

However, Moyes recorded in his programme notes, 'I am incredibly privileged and honoured to be the manager who is taking us into this new stadium. I am excited about the future which looks so much brighter for Everton Football Club as we move away from some dark days in the past. We are starting from a blank page. We have built the stadium, and we are starting to rebuild the team.'

***Line-up with player ratings:*** Jordan Pickford 7; Jake O'Brien 6; Vitalii Mykolenko (Adam Aznou 10 4; Séamus Coleman 79); James Tarkowski 6; Jarrad Branthwaite 6 (Michael Keane 79); Idrissa Gueye 6 (Tim Iroegbunam 61 6); James Garner 6; Kiernan Dewsbury-Hall 7 (Dwight McNeil 61 5); Charly Alcaraz 5 (Youssef Chermiti 79); Iliman Ndiaye 5; Thierno Barry 5 (Beto 61 6).

# 6

# Ili starts where he left off at Goodison – the rest of August

A WEEK before Everton kicked off their 2025/26 Premier League campaign, they bagged the marquee signing they'd been chasing all summer. The Blues had been installed as bookmakers' favourites to land Jack Grealish in early June but now the two-month chase was complete.

Although the man who had become the first £100m English footballer in 2021 when he departed boyhood club Aston Villa had played an integral role in Manchester City's Champions League, Premier League and FA Cup 'treble' in 2023, he had found himself surplus to requirements at the Etihad Stadium and had been left out of Pep Guardiola's squad for that summer's FIFA Club World Cup in the USA.

There had been plenty of Evertonians working on the charm offensive to land the Brummie ace in the meantime, including one of David Moyes's ex-captains, Alan Stubbs, who revealed he'd given Grealish the spiel when they bumped into each other on a night out while holidaying in Marbella. The Kirkby-born former centre-half admitted, 'I tried my best to get him to Everton. I was telling him how much he'd be loved.'

Moyes himself is understood to have dined with Grealish ahead of sealing the deal, outlining how he would fit into his team's system and how the Blues could revive his career to get him enjoying his football again.

Although the confirmation of the England international's season-long loan deal was embargoed until 4.30pm on Tuesday, 12 August, photographs of the player posing in an Everton shirt showed the clock in the gym at the club's Finch Farm training complex displayed the time 22.08, proving it must have been done on the previous day at least and highlighting how choreographed agreements over these announcements are.

On completing his move, Grealish said, 'As soon as I spoke to the manager, I knew there was only one place that I wanted to go. On social media, I've been flooded with messages from Everton supporters, so there's that side of it as well and that's another reason why I chose Everton.'

An hour before the 2025/26 Premier League season kicked off, the Blues confirmed a rather more low-key signing at 7pm on Friday, 15 August as they snapped up Tom King from Wolverhampton Wanderers for their third-choice goalkeeper role.

Despite coming from Plymouth, King had been capped once by Wales as a substitute against Gibraltar the previous summer, having qualified through his Cardiff-born mother.

The 30-year-old also held the Guinness World Record for the longest goal having netted for Newport County against Cheltenham Town on 19 January 2021 with a wind-assisted goal kick measuring 105 yards, usurping the previous best held by another former Everton understudy keeper, Asmir Begović, who scored from 97.5 yards for Stoke City against Southampton on 2 November 2013.

On signing a two-year deal, King said, 'We have two extremely good goalkeepers here in Jordan [Pickford] and Travs [Mark Travers] and a young keeper in Harry [Tyrer]. My job is to push them as far as possible. The chance to learn off someone like

Jordan, who has been England's number one for so many years, is a really big thing for me.'

## Monday, 18 August 2025: Leeds United 1 Everton 0, Elland Road
## Attendance 38,820 (2,916 Everton)

One place where Grealish, Everton, or indeed this author, weren't feeling the love was at Elland Road for the opening fixture the following Monday.

Given the timing of the match, which had been picked for live Sky Sports coverage, the rest of the top flight – including neighbours Liverpool some three nights earlier – had all played their first game by the time Moyes's men crossed the Pennines.

The slot would become a major bugbear for Evertonians, as despite Sky supposedly picking individual clubs a maximum of five times a season on Monday or Friday nights, the Blues would end up with seven bookings in the former over the course of the campaign.

Making our way to the game, Joe Thomas and I passed the M62 Summit sign that proclaims it is the highest motorway in England at 372 metres (1,221 feet) by Junction 22 at Windy Point.

Given that Joe was driving, soon afterwards I prepared my phone to take a photograph of the White Rose boundary stone that marks where Lancashire turns to Yorkshire.

Joe, who likes to regale me on our lengthy away days with geographical nuggets like boasting that his native Shropshire is England's largest landlocked county (take that, Staffordshire!) seemed underwhelmed and complained, 'Is that it?' I'm not sure what the self-confessed *Lord of the Rings* aficionado was expecting, perhaps a real-life Gates of Argonath?

What we were met with though was something resembling a football version of Mordor when we pulled up at Elland Road.

First of all, the car park attendant claimed he couldn't see my name on the list, and he'd have to call his gaffer, but we'd need to wait because he in turn had gone for something to eat.

The list was arranged in alphabetical order, so given that it read 'Christopher Beesley', not 'ZZ Top', I was therefore one of the first names on there when Joe quickly inspected the sheet of paper himself and pointed this out to our new friend who had perhaps forgotten his reading glasses.

That first hurdle jumped, we then passed through what can only be described as a cage before making our way to the accreditation point inside the ground.

This was also something of a kerfuffle as the staff fumbled their way through a myriad of passes before eventually finding the correct ones, but to give them the benefit of the doubt, perhaps this was first-night nerves and teething problems with the system as the club adjusted to life back in the big time.

The next issue was self-inflicted, but we can pin that one on Joe.

Having up until this point been the biggest venue on my list yet to be ticked off, Elland Road was the only Premier League ground in 2025/26 I was visiting for the first time.

However, instead of making our way into the main media room, we took our pre-match meal in a smaller room which, it turned out, was the preserve of photographers rather than the written press. We felt the glare from the assembled pack of snappers as we quickly ate up and moved on to our correct position, although at first we weren't sure whether this was just a typical Yorkshire 'welcome'.

Apart from when Everton triumphed spectacularly against Tottenham Hotspur in the 1995 FA Cup semi-final, denying the London-based national scribes a Wembley showdown against Manchester United and prompting Blues boss Joe Royle to declare 'Sorry about your dream final lads, but bollocks to it and that's with a double l!', Elland Road had seldom been a happy hunting ground for the club.

When Wayne Rooney came off the bench to net the winner there for David Moyes's side on 3 November 2002, just five days after his 17th birthday, it was Everton's first league victory at Elland Road for 51 years, and the only one they have enjoyed since was in 2021 behind closed doors because of the pandemic.

At first glance it looked like the ground hadn't changed much in the 30 years since Daniel Amokachi wrote himself into Blues folklore by coming off the bench, wandering on to the pitch and netting twice as the best substitution that Royle 'never made'.

However, we could only see the playing surface and very little of the rest of our surroundings from our dark spec on the benches at the back of the John Charles Stand with a view that was like peeking through a letter box.

Then one of the aforementioned staff members who had made such heavy weather of handing out our lanyards proceeded to distribute a team sheet to virtually everyone else in the press box other than ourselves.

I had to chase him halfway across the stand and after catching up with him, only to be told he'd just given his last copy to the public address announcer, my paranoia had peaked.

I was starting to believe these were all dark arts being deployed by 'Dirty' Leeds, a moniker the club have possessed for over six decades, going back to the start of their first golden era under Don Revie.

You couldn't say we hadn't been warned as under the lights and a white-hot atmosphere which exemplified all that you didn't want from an opening fixture against a newly promoted club, Everton wilted with a tame performance.

Vitalii Mykolenko's injury in the final friendly against Roma left Moyes with a major problem at left-back which he chose to fill by deploying midfielder James Garner as a square peg in a round hole.

While the right-footer looked awkward in that area, especially in the early exchanges, he settled down and was not the reason for the visitors' downfall.

While Leeds' display wasn't high on quality, it was high on energy and they threw the kitchen sink at the Blues in the first half, only for the away side to cling on.

Grealish spent most of the evening on the bench, on the receiving end of repeated barracking from home fans, one of whom told him to 'get his hair cut'. This seemed rich, given that it feels like Leeds have had more players with man buns than anyone in recent years (their own new acquisition, former Everton striker Dominic Calvert-Lewin, who also used to possess one, had joined too late to be eligible for this match).

Grealish finally entered the fray for his debut with just under 20 minutes to go and despite their deficiencies, it looked like the Blues were going to hold out for a point until they were done by yet another piece of controversial refereeing with a mere six minutes left on the clock.

Captain James Tarkowski, in typically fearless fashion, flung himself at Anton Stach's shot, only for referee Chris Kavanagh to point to the spot. There was no outstretched arm from the centre-back and the ball appeared to strike him on the upper part of his limb. Perhaps predictably, unlike when Manchester City's Rodri attempted to play a bit of basketball at Goodison Park in 2022, there was no reprieve here from the supposed 'T-shirt' line.

Despite VAR official John Brooks taking a look down at Stockley Park, the original decision stood and the game was lost as Lukas Nmecha converted from 12 yards.

Afterwards, I asked Tarkowski about the crucial moment and he told me, 'It's not a penalty. I leaned into the ball, and it hit my arm. I was confident when he was giving the decision that it was going to get overturned. I asked the question to the referee, "If my arm is by my side, is it a penalty?" to which he said "no", so I don't understand how it's been given.'

*Line-up with player ratings:* Jordan Pickford 7; Jake O'Brien 6; James Garner 6; James Tarkowski 6; Michael Keane 7; Idrissa Gueye 6; Tim Iroegbunam 5 (Jack Grealish 70 6); Charly Alcaraz 5 (Thierno Barry 86); Kiernan Dewsbury-Hall 6; Iliman Ndiaye 6; Beto 5.

## Sunday, 24 August 2025: Everton 2 Brighton & Hove Albion 0, Hill Dickinson Stadium
## Attendance: 51,759

The Roma friendly 15 days earlier had been like a dress rehearsal where the stage and theatre were both magnificent only for the actors to fluff their lines, but this opening night – or Sunday matinee given the 2pm kick-off – proved a roaring success.

There were lots of occasions on which it could have gone horribly wrong for Everton in their first competitive match at their new home.

For the visitors, Kaoru Mitoma volleyed against the crossbar when the game was still goalless, Danny Welbeck missed a sitter before being denied from the penalty spot, and Matt O'Riley was handed a golden opportunity by Tarkowski's calamitous no-look backpass only for Jordan Pickford to come to the rescue.

But ultimately it was all's well that ends well on a historic occasion for the club and the dawn of what will hopefully be a bright new era after years of turmoil and strife, on and off the pitch.

While their own footballing journey is a very different one than the Blues, given that they are not trying to live up to numerous past glories, they have never won a major honour and the current era is the most illustrious in their history, Brighton were still something of an apt selection from the 'fixture computer' when it came to providing the first opponents.

The Seagulls endured their Gillingham exile when, after their long-time home, the Goldstone Ground was sold, they were forced into a 150-mile round trip for home games over two years, and then the wilderness at the Withdean Stadium, a converted athletics venue, before the Amex Stadium, a financial game-changer, was built.

But whereas that 31,876-capacity venue is six miles inland from Brighton Pier in suburban Falmer by a university campus, Everton are now, as the title of this book states, on the Mersey waterfront in a building that has taken its prominent place among Liverpool's iconic maritime cityscape skyline.

Indeed, when the Blues took to the field for this momentous occasion, video footage taken in the Wirral showed that *Z-Cars*, the roar of the crowd and fireworks could all be heard on the other side of the river, a phenomenon I've been told by neighbours has continued all season (I'm always in the stadium itself).

Having been invited to be a guest on the stage in the fan zone – where Giulia Bould kindly told the crowd how much she was enjoying my first book, *Spirit of the Blues* – I quickly realised gazing out at the audience how much grander the scale was here than in the Park End car park at Goodison.

I was then taken through the bowels of the stadium, including concourses packed with away supporters (to be fair, there are plenty of other fanbases where it could have been much worse) back to the media area and then it was up to the press box, which is the highest seat in the house, to work on the game.

Writing in his programme notes, David Moyes declared, 'The move here wouldn't be worthwhile if we didn't bring the soul of Goodison Park with us to Hill Dickinson Stadium. We know we have to earn your support and we understand that watching a winning team is really important to generating that atmosphere.

We hope to make this a stadium which is difficult for our visitors to play in, a phrase which so many said about Goodison.' The boss needn't have been concerned on this score as a deafening wall of noise greeted the teams on their arrival.

After years in purgatory, Everton came perilously close to football hell but here their passionate supporters enjoyed a royal blue heaven by the banks of the Mersey and when it came to 'souls' there were also over 12,000 more than Goodison Park could hold in recent years: the 51,759 attendance was Everton's biggest for an opening league game of a season for 52 years.

It was the 20th time in their history that the Blues have had a crowd of more than 50,000 for their first home league fixture, but their first since 52,348 watched them defeat Manchester United on 16 August 1972.

Having survived their early scares, Everton scored the first goal in a competitive game at Hill Dickinson Stadium with a well-worked team move on 23 minutes.

Thierno Barry started the passage of play by winning possession with his back to goal, just inside his own half, enabling Iliman Ndiaye to beat two men before laying the ball back for Idrissa Gueye to feed Kiernan Dewsbury-Hall, who in turn picked out Jack Grealish on the left wing. The on-loan man, making his first start, drove forwards to the edge of the six-yard box before firing in an inviting cross to the back post which Ndiaye attacked and met with a decisive first-time finish.

Home supporters erupted in delight and for the Senegal international, it completed a unique hat-trick given that Ndiaye's double strike against Southampton 99 days earlier were Everton's last two goals at Goodison Park.

There was added poignancy soon after as Evertonians marked the 26th minute with a period of applause for one of their own, Michael Goodison Jones from Kirkby, who had died two years ago that month aged 26, while working on the stadium construction site.

The victory was secured seven minutes into the second half with another Grealish assist and an even more spectacular finish to mark the occasion. Grealish picked up the ball just outside the Brighton area and patiently waited to lay it off to James Garner – who again was operating as an auxiliary left-back – to run on to it and dispatch an emphatic 20-yard howitzer on his right foot through Yankuba Minteh's legs and beyond keeper Bart Verbruggen's reach.

It could have been a nervous finish for Moyes's men but after they conceded a second penalty in as many games for handball with Minteh's shot being blocked by Dewsbury-Hall, the instructions of taker's techniques displayed on Pickford's trusty water bottle helped the England number one to guess right when keeping out Welbeck's 77th-minute effort from the spot.

Indeed, on 1 June the following year, Pickford won the inaugural Microsoft Goalkeeper Performance of the Season award for his display that day.

Afterwards, I reminded Iliman Ndiaye that his infant daughter Ayla had predicted he would write himself into history on this landmark occasion when he first signed for the club in July 2024 and he dedicated the goal to her. Ndiaye said, 'Yeah, it means a lot. Obviously when you play football you want to create history, so it felt good. The question was asked to me about "who's going to score the first goal at the new stadium?" and my daughter just said "Dada" so that goal was for her. It was amazing.'

***Line-up with player ratings:*** Jordan Pickford 9; Jake O'Brien 7; James Garner 8; James Tarkowski 5; Michael Keane 8; Idrissa Gueye 7; Tim Iroegbunam 6 (Dwight McNeil 73); Iliman Ndiaye 8 (Charly Alcaraz 64 6); Kiernan Dewsbury-Hall 7; Jack Grealish 9 (Harrison Armstrong 90); Thierno Barry 7 (Beto 64 6).

***

Grealish's arrival and deployment on the left wing meant that Ndiaye, who had operated there for most of his first season at Everton, moved over to the right but the very next day the club announced their biggest signing of the summer in terms of a transfer fee when they confirmed Tyler Dibling's move from Southampton.

The 19-year-old Exeter-born prospect had played for the Saints in Everton's last game at Goodison and the move, for what these days is an all-too-common undisclosed fee but understood to be in the region of £35m, made him their most expensive sale for a homegrown player.

A patient approach from the Blues had nevertheless forced a significant climbdown from St Mary's chiefs, who less than a month earlier had been demanding £50m plus a 20 per cent sell-on fee for their prize asset.

While it was Southampton's prerogative to set the valuation of one of their players, just as Everton had done when Manchester United came calling for Jarrad Branthwaite the previous summer, the major difference was that Sir Jim Ratcliffe's penny-pinching Red Devils had not come close to a price that would have forced the hand of Goodison Park top brass.

On joining, Dibling said, 'I think it's the perfect match because of where the club is right now. Obviously with the new stadium, the fans here are unreal and it has a family feel to it. I think it was the perfect fit and was a no-brainer to join.

'I think I've come to Everton at the perfect time and hopefully I can be here for many years. [The Brighton win] gave me a feel for the club. It looked unbelievable. I also played in the last men's game at Goodison. It was so loud. I was looking around and thinking, "This is quality." That was a really good insight for me into what it's like here with the fans and the atmosphere they can create.'

## Wednesday, 27 August 2025: Everton 2 Mansfield Town 0, Hill Dickinson Stadium
## Attendance: 48,583

If Brighton were something of a fitting choice for the first Premier League opponents at Hill Dickinson Stadium, then what of Mansfield Town for the first club to arrive for a cup tie?

Although officially named the One Call Stadium at the present for sponsorship reasons, the Stags' Field Mill home is the oldest ground in the Football League having hosted football since at least 1861 – some 36 years before the current club were formed – with some reports claiming it goes back as far as 1850.

When I travelled there on 7 November 2023, to cover Everton under-21s' 1-0 win in the EFL Trophy thanks to a last-minute penalty from Youssef Chermiti, the Mansfield fans who were occupying the club bar at the ground where I was filing my post-match copy were curious about Goodison Park's successor that was being built at Bramley-Moore Dock and were asking me lots of questions.

That was a night for the die-hards, with just 819 in attendance, but 21 months later over 5,000 travelling supporters made the trip from Nottinghamshire with the scheduled 7.45pm kick-off delayed by 15 minutes to allow spectators 'safe access' into the stadium.

As reported in the *Liverpool Echo* by my colleague Joe Thomas, a technical problem for home fans with physical season ticket cards was one setback, with many of those possessing them needing to visit the ticket office after problems at the turnstiles.

Separately, logistical issues in relation to Mansfield's ability to distribute tickets to travelling supporters led to around 700 needing to pick them up from the club before queuing for turnstiles.

When the action finally got under way, there were still a large number of empty seats visible on a night when the official attendance was 48,583, and it also proved to be a game of patience for Everton on the field.

Led by the experienced Nigel Clough, who first entered management 27 years earlier and by this point was 59 and over a year older than his legendary father Brian when he retired from the dugout at Nottingham Forest, Mansfield were no mugs having gone into the tie on the back of four consecutive victories.

Although 18-year-old Harrison Armstrong ran the show from a deep central midfield position – giving David Moyes more food for thought ahead of the transfer deadline, with the Scot ultimately deciding to send him back on loan to the Championship again – it took the hosts until six minutes into the second half to break the deadlock and even then it was through a stunning strike by Charly Alcaraz.

Picking up the ball in the area, Armstrong used some quick feet to open up some space before laying off to the Argentinian, who let fly with a curling effort from just outside the D.

The Blues brought on Tyler Dibling – whose move had been confirmed 48 hours earlier – for his debut on the hour mark, but it was Beto, who entered the fray just moments later, who sealed their passage in the 89th minute.

James Garner, who was being deployed back in his favoured role in the engine room, threaded a ball through to Armstrong, who squared it to the Guinea-Bissau international at the back post who was presented with a simple tap-in into the empty net.

*Line-up with player ratings (by Joe Thomas):* Mark Travers 6; Seamus Coleman 7; Vitalii Mykolenko 6 (Jake O'Brien 86); James Tarkowski 6; Michael Keane 6; James Garner 7; Harrison Armstrong 8; Dwight McNeil 5 (Tim Iroegbunam 77 6); Charly Alcaraz 8 (Iliman Ndiaye 77 6); Jack Grealish 6 (Tyler Dibling 59 6); Thierno Barry 6 (Beto 59 6).

## Saturday, 30 August 2025: Wolverhampton Wanderers 2 Everton 3, Molineux Attendance: 30,271 (3,010 Everton)

This was a pivotal game for Everton's early season momentum as after starting with the lacklustre display in the opening-day defeat at Leeds, they secured a third consecutive win in the space of a week before going into the first international break of the campaign.

The victory also provided a welcome birthday present for yours truly on what was the 11th occasion that the Blues have played on the date since I've been following them.

Fittingly, my boyhood favourite Kevin Sheedy netted for Everton on the first such occasion after my football consciousness had been awakened in a match at Hillsborough in 1989, but Sheffield Wednesday's Dalian Atkinson proved to be a party pooper with a last-minute equaliser.

The first time I saw the Blues play on my birthday was in 1994, and while I have vivid memories of new signing Daniel Amokachi being paraded to the Goodison Park crowd to the strains of the Elton John song 'Daniel', there was no jelly and ice cream with Mike Walker's men beaten 2-1 by Nottingham Forest.

After that, it's been a real mixed bag with a 2-0 win at Manchester City in 1995, a 3-0 home defeat to Liverpool in 2003 (the only Premier League derby in August and one of just five league derbies ever in August just to spite me?), a 0-0 draw away to Manchester United in 2004, a 3-0 home defeat to Portsmouth in 2008, a 2-1 home win over Wigan Athletic in 2009, a 6-3 home loss to Chelsea in 2014, a 1-1 draw at Leeds in 2022, a 2-1 win at Doncaster Rovers in 2023 and now this latest fixture which restored parity to bring an overall record of won four, drawn three and lost four.

Returning to the bigger picture though, not only was this an important result – a sixth Premier League away win since Moyes returned for an Everton side that had triumphed just once on their travels in the previous 12 months – but the swashbuckling style in which it was achieved hinted at the more expansive style of play they were deploying with the pair of attacking midfielders they had acquired earlier that month from a couple of clubs among the division's established elite at the heart of their success.

In truth, the Blues' victory should have been more emphatic but at the other end of the pitch, some defensive frailties also reared their head.

Vitalii Mykolenko, who had missed the opening two Premier League fixtures before returning against Mansfield, had more joy going forward than defending as the left-back started the move for the opening goal just seven minutes in, lofting a pass to Jack Grealish, whose header in turn picked out Beto at the back post to nod in.

With Everton still reeling from referee Michael Oliver's decision to penalise their goalscorer after a tangle with Emmanuel Agbadou, they were caught cold on 21 minutes after a lapse at the back.

Marshall Munetsi's low right-wing cross enabled Hwang Hee-chan to get between the Blues' centre-backs and equalise with a first-time finish past Jordan Pickford.

The visitors restored their lead a dozen minutes later though as Grealish slipped the ball through to Kiernan Dewsbury-Hall, who squared for Iliman Ndiaye – with Beto dummying – to curl in a left-footed finish at the back post.

Ndiaye celebrated by seemingly mimicking a wolf, a week after he reprised his 'seagull' gesture when netting against Brighton, but this time he avoided a booking unlike when referee Tim Robinson had shown him the yellow card for flapping his arms like wings after scoring what proved to be the winner from the penalty spot at the Amex Stadium back on 25 January in Moyes's first away match since returning.

Everton extended their advantage ten minutes into the second half as Grealish nonchalantly threaded a pass to Dewsbury-Hall, who hammered a left-footed shot into the roof of José Sá's net for his first goal for the club with what was the on-loan Manchester City player's fourth assist in two starts.

The final 11 minutes proved to be a bit nervier than they needed to be though as a hopeful left-wing cross from David Møller Wolfe – following in the tradition of the hosts signing players with names like the club after John de Wolf in the 1990s – was allowed to bounce in the visitors' area before fellow substitute Rodrigo Gomes, who had got between Michael Keane and the ponderous Mykolenko, crashed past Pickford.

The Blues held out for the three points though and afterwards, Moyes was humble when it came to new star Grealish, 'It's nothing to do with me, let me tell you, it's all to do with Jack and his own mentality to be better ... there's a wee bit to prove, I'm sure. I think we all have, I think in life you've always got to keep something you have to strive to do and I think Jack wants to show that he's a good player.'

***Line-up with player ratings (by Joe Thomas):*** Jordan Pickford 6; Jake O'Brien 6; Vitalii Mykolenko 4; James Tarkowski 5; Michael Keane 7; Idrissa Gueye 7 (Tim Iroegbunam 75 5); James Garner 7; Iliman Ndiaye 8 (Séamus Coleman 90); Kiernan Dewsbury-Hall 9; Jack Grealish 9 (Charly Alcaraz 88); Beto 7 (Thierno Barry 75 5).

7

# Merlin magic then thrown to the Wolves – September

FIVE WEEKS earlier, David Moyes had declared in New York that he needed to sign 'nine or ten players before the start of the season', and it ultimately took a bit of 'Merlin magic' to get the Blues there.

Everton had already played four matches by this point as the fledgling campaign had moved into the first international break, and two of the new recruits were backup goalkeepers, but then again, two backup goalkeepers had left.

However, the ninth new face arrived through the door on 1 September – transfer deadline day – with Merlin Röhl's capture not announced until 9.10pm, over two hours after the window 'slammed shut' as Sky Sports News like to say on a date that used to be all their birthdays and Christmases rolled into one before PSR punishments to the likes of the Blues spooked spending.

Röhl, a 23-year-old central midfielder from Germany – who, like fellow new boy Thierno Barry, had played in the UEFA European Under-21 Championship earlier that summer – joined on a season-long loan from Bundesliga club Freiburg with an obligation to buy the following year so long as relegation was avoided.

Although later that week West Ham United's 30-year-old Czechia captain Tomáš Souček – who had been brought to the Irons on David Moyes's watch in January 2020 and had been pictured talking to each other, while arm in arm after their Premier League Summer Series game in Chicago on 30 July – told a media outlet called *Idnes* in his homeland that there was interest in him from Everton late in the window, but Röhl was a player who had been on the Blues' radar for over 12 months.

Initially considered as a potential replacement for Amadou Onana ahead of the Belgium international moving to Aston Villa for £50m in July 2024, Röhl was born just outside Berlin in Potsdam, the city where the 'Big Three' of British prime minister Winston Churchill, US president Harry Truman and Soviet general secretary Joseph Stalin held their 1945 conference to plan the post-Second World War peace.

Moyes had personally watched him up close on several occasions with West Ham facing a Freiburg side containing the 6ft 3in prospect in the Europa League on four occasions in 2023/24.

On signing, Röhl declared, 'The Everton fans are passionate and demand hard work and that's what I like as it matches what I can bring,' while adding on a clip released on the club's social media channels, in a thick Teutonic accent, 'Up the Toffees.'

Before competitive action resumed, I joined a clutch of other guests on an invite to the Blues' Mersey waterfront home for a sneak preview of the new Hill Dickinson Stadium Tours experience alongside my youngest daughter Jemima.

Kicking off at Beyond – which Everton bill as being a tunnel club experience like no other – we found ourselves in one of the stadium's most sought-after premium spaces and from there we followed in the footsteps of Everton heroes by undertaking the tunnel walk and then spectacular pitchside views from the touchline.

Gazing up from pitch level, I was able to point to show Jemima where my own usual 'spec' is, in the press box, up at the top of the West Stand, on the back row, and from this vantage point we were able to spot ourselves on the giant 32m x 9m screens behind each of the goals and also pose for photographs in the home dugout, which we were told is different to the away one as David Moyes insisted the bottom row be taken out because he felt it was too low.

We were then given access to the first team's circular dressing room, complete with giant club crest on the ceiling, where Moyes prepares his squad on matchdays, before a swift journey upwards in one of the stadium's lifts, to the South Stand's upper concourse to take in the stunning panoramic views of Liverpool's skyline where I was able to point out to my daughter the West Tower, the city's tallest building, and how the *Echo* office is situated just behind it.

Ahead of Everton's return to action at Hill Dickinson Stadium, Michael Ball revealed in his *Echo* column how he'd heard whispers from Finch Farm that Röhl had impressed, had adapted really well to the sessions and was impressing with his performances in training and the former Blues defender added, 'That's fantastic to hear he's showing so much quality already as you don't often get such glowing praise so soon.'

The deadline-day signing would promptly come on as a substitute for his debut at the next possible opportunity, but then not play again for over a month.

## Saturday, 13 September 2025: Everton 0 Aston Villa 0, Hill Dickinson Stadium
## Attendance: 52,114

The most-played league fixture in England – this was the 215th meeting – has been a long-standing clash since these two clubs were founder members of the Football League in 1888, so it was perhaps apt that it provided the first traditional Saturday 3pm kick-off at Hill Dickinson Stadium.

There will be far more memorable meetings between the sides though, as Unai Emery's men, who arrived by the Mersey as the only team in the top seven divisions of the English pyramid not to have scored a goal that season, came for a stalemate and got one with Everton unable to break down their stubborn resistance.

After being linked with a move away before the transfer window closed, Argentina's World Cup-winning goalkeeper Emiliano Martínez returned for Aston Villa and denied a winner for Michael Keane when tipping the centre-back's header over the bar following a pinpoint cross from Jack Grealish.

However, while the hosts bossed the play and finished 20-7 ahead on the shot count, it was perhaps tellingly only two to one when it came to shots on target and Brummie Grealish's personal battle against the club he played for from the age of six to when he joined Manchester City became the main sideshow to events.

Earlier that year, David Moyes proclaimed Grealish to be the best player in the Premier League. But for all his dazzling displays at Villa Park and then the Etihad Stadium, playing a starring role in Pep Guardiola's side's treble season of 2023, Grealish went into this fixture having been named Premier League Player of the Month for the first time and it took him until the week of his 30th birthday to receive the honour, the day before the game.

In the end it was team-mate Kiernan Dewsbury-Hall who handed over the trophy to him, which was fitting given the way the two summer signings had dovetailed on the pitch in their attacking midfield roles and the former Chelsea man pledged to keep helping Grealish – who picked up the gong on the back of four assists from his first two Premier League games – on his way.

Not that he seemed to be receiving much encouragement from his former adoring public at Villa with significant sections of the away end booing him here and chanting, 'You're not super any more.'

What was somewhat poignant after the final whistle though – once most fans had cleared out – was the sight of Grealish walking over to that corner of the ground, alongside another Villa old boy in the home line-up, Idrissa Gueye, and the pair of them clapping and being applauded back by those who were still in their seats.

Moyes, who was beaten 1-0 in the corresponding fixture the previous season at Goodison Park for what was his first game back as Everton manager, tried to put a positive spin on proceedings when I asked him about the game afterwards.

He said, 'It was a really good performance. It was intense, a good Premier League game. I thought we had the best of it to be honest. I feel we were a bit unlucky not to come away with all three points.'

*Line-up with player ratings (by Connor O'Neill):* Jordan Pickford 6; Jake O'Brien 8; James Garner 7; James Tarkowski 7; Michael Keane 7; Idrissa Gueye 7; Tim Iroegbunam 6 (Merlin Röhl 66 6); Iliman Ndiaye 8; Kiernan Dewsbury-Hall 6; Jack Grealish 7; Beto 5 (Thierno Barry 75).

## Saturday, 20 September 2025: Liverpool 2 Everton 1, Anfield
## Attendance: 60,342 (3,052 Everton)

For the first time in over 130 years of Merseyside derbies, the visitors did not 'cross Stanley Park' for a league fixture, but whereas James Tarkowski had saved face for Everton on the final occasion that the Reds journeyed in the opposite direction, it was the same old story for the Blues at Anfield.

Although it's been completely reconstructed since then like Trigger's broom in classic sitcom *Only Fools and Horses*, which the slow-witted road sweeper revealed has had 17 new heads and 14 new handles, Anfield was once Everton's base before their rivals even existed and as well as starting out there as founder members of the Football League in 1888, they celebrated their first league championship at the ground in 1891.

Despite being just 800 yards at its closest point from Goodison Park, it's felt anything like home for Evertonians for a very long time now.

The artificial empty surroundings of behind-closed-doors football during the coronavirus pandemic produced Everton's last win at Anfield – 2-0 on 20 February 2021 – but their most recent triumph in front of fans came over a quarter of a century ago.

That was thanks to the late Kevin Campbell's fourth-minute strike in front of the Kop on a tumultuous night that saw home keeper Sander Westerveld and Francis Jeffers sent off for fighting (quite the catchweight contest), forcing defender Steve Staunton to go between the sticks for the final 16 minutes, with a teenage Steven Gerrard also dismissed in stoppage time for a horror challenge on the match-winner.

There has been plenty of derby controversy and crazy moments from both sides across the generations since, but while it took Liverpool 87 years to move ahead on derby victories with a 3-1 success at Anfield on 7 November 1981, in a fixture in which they're now over 30 wins ahead, this was in many ways just another routine outing.

Indeed, while David Moyes possessed the tactical acumen to hold his hosts to a goalless draw here on 3 February 2007, following on from a 3-0 home success earlier that season, prompting opposite number Rafael Benítez to churlishly make his 'small club' jibe towards Everton, a remark he was forced to do some serious back-pedalling over when controversially taking the reins at the Blues himself in 2021, the Scot extended his winless record at Anfield with all teams he has managed to 23 matches.

In truth, Moyes's Everton side started lamentably slowly this time around, against a team that, after dispatching Championship Southampton in the EFL Cup next time out, would subsequently lose their following four matches.

Ryan Gravenberch fired Liverpool ahead just ten minutes in with a clever lofted finish, and when Hugo Ekitike doubled their lead on 29 minutes with a low shot, it looked like it was going to be a long afternoon for the Blues.

Moyes responded by swapping Beto for Thierno Barry up front at half-time and after the interval Everton looked much better, pulling a goal back through Idrissa Gueye on 58 minutes with a powerful, rising drive after being teed up by countryman Iliman Ndiaye for what was his first assist for the club.

However, on a day that derby debutant Kiernan Dewsbury-Hall – who had fired over the bar in front of the Kop when played through in the first half – was booked by referee Darren England for taking a free kick 'too quickly' and a mere three minutes of second-half stoppage time was played (not that the visitors were knocking at the door), a much-improved second-half display was not enough.

Afterwards, Dewsbury-Hall was disappointed by what felt like a passive start from Everton in the first half an hour and said, 'I feel we gave them too much respect. Yes, they're champions but we're trying to do something this year as well.'

*Line-up with player ratings:* Jordan Pickford 6; Jake O'Brien 6; Vitalii Mykolenko 5 (Charly Alcaraz 86); James Tarkowski 6; Michael Keane 6; Idrissa Gueye 7; James Garner 7; Iliman Ndiaye 6 (Tyler Dibling 86); Kiernan Dewsbury-Hall 5; Jack Grealish 7; Beto 6 (Thierno Barry 46 6).

## Tuesday, 23 September 2025: Wolverhampton Wanderers 2 Everton 0, Molineux
## Attendance: 18,758 (3,010 Everton)

Unlike Liverpool, who have now won the competition a record ten times, the EFL Cup in all its various guises (Carabao is the latest in a long line of drinks sponsors, having started with the Milk Marketing Board and going on to Coca-Cola, Worthington and Carling), has been a cruel mistress for Everton.

It's now 65 years since the competition first started but the Blues have still never lifted the trophy and the two occasions that they have reached the final have both ended in heartbreak.

In 1977, it took three games – the only time a second replay has been required – played over a month to separate Everton and Aston Villa, whose managers Gordon Lee and Ron Saunders both had playing spells at the opposition club, before Brian Little's goal two minutes before the end of extra time secured a 3-2 victory for the West Midlanders.

Just ten days after that, the Blues' hopes of reaching a second domestic final that year were robbed by a decision that still rankles with their supporters as controversial referee Clive Thomas inexplicably disallowed substitute Bryan Hamilton's late winner against Liverpool in their FA Cup semi-final at Maine Road and, after a 2-2 draw against their neighbours, who would lift their first European Cup the following month, they lost the replay 3-0.

It was a similar story when the Mersey rivals met again for the first time at Wembley for the 1984 League Cup Final. For Everton, it was another goalless stalemate beneath the Twin Towers, and also a familiar tale of woe with the man in the middle as Alan Robinson refused to award them a penalty when Liverpool centre-back Alan Hansen used his hand to steer a goal-bound shot by Adrian Heath off the line. The Blues would lose the replay 1-0, while for his part Robinson showed that lightning can strike twice in the same place.

He failed to point to the spot when Blues centre-forward Graeme Sharp was clipped in mid-air by Steve Nicol when preparing to dispatch a header into the net in their 3-1 loss to their local rivals in the 1986 FA Cup Final.

However, in between, his decision to disallow Kevin Sheedy's free-kick goal against Ipswich Town in 1985 only for the player to curl his retaken effort into the opposite corner, produced one of Goodison Park's most iconic moments.

Talking of 1984/85, the League Cup even saw Everton on the receiving end of a giant-killing in what proved to be their most successful season as Grimsby Town triumphed 1-0 at Goodison Park and it was far from an isolated incident.

The Blues actually bowed out of their first foray in the competition 2-1 at Shrewsbury Town in the quarter-finals in 1961 and that's only one of 18 occasions that they have been knocked out by lower-division sides.

This trip to Molineux wasn't that but facing the Premier League's bottom club, who they had defeated at the same ground less than a month earlier, it felt like the Blues had thrown their chance away.

Ahead of the game, James Tarkowski insisted that, inspired by Crystal Palace and Newcastle United, there was an emphasis on Everton doing well in the cups that season and declared, 'It's massive.'

Nevertheless, David Moyes made seven changes for the game (Wolves, whose priority was staying in the division, made nine) and a lacklustre display against a side who had lost their opening five Premier League games saw the Blues – who were wearing black armbands following the death of club life vice-president Keith Tamlin, a long-serving director – dumped out.

Wolves went ahead just before the half-hour mark as Everton's veteran captain Séamus Coleman – the club's best right-back of the Premier League era but no more a left-back than when Moyes played him there for a baptism-of-fire debut in a 5-0 Europa League drubbing at Benfica almost 16 years earlier – failed to judge the flight of a ball into the box and Wolves' Jhon Arias struck it wickedly on the volley.

In the second half, James Garner hit the crossbar with a free kick from a wide angle but the hosts sealed their passage into the last 16 with a clincher a couple of minutes before full time when substitute Tolu Arokodare latched on to a pass over the top and coolly dinked the ball over advancing understudy keeper Mark Travers.

Moyes, who felt heat from the fanbase for the first time since returning due to his selection policy following the defeat, admitted he was 'disappointed' but insisted, 'We were coming to another Premier League team, so I don't think you can say it's a missed opportunity.'

For his part, when I asked Garner in the tunnel about what had unfolded, he acknowledged, 'I think any tournament or cup you enter, you want to go as far as you can so to go out now, playing against a team who we probably thought we're in a better place than at the moment form-wise, and going in the right direction, so to lose is a big disappointment.'

*Line-up with player ratings:* Mark Travers 6; Jake O'Brien 6; Séamus Coleman 5 (Vitalii Mykolenko 78 5); James Tarkowski 6; Michael Keane 7; James Garner 7; Tim Iroegbunam 5; Tyler Dibling 5 (Iliman Ndiaye 59 5); Charly Alcaraz 6 (Kiernan Dewsbury-Hall 46 5); Dwight McNeil 5 (Jack Grealish 59 6); Thierno Barry 5 (Beto 46 5).

## Monday, 29 September 2025: Everton 1 West Ham United 1, Hill Dickinson Stadium
## Attendance: 51,890

For the second time since returning to Everton, David Moyes hosted his previous employers West Ham United, and having never got the chance to face his successor Julen Lopetegui, who had been sacked on 8 January, three days before he came back to the Blues, he was coming up against a second Irons boss in six months.

When the Hammers made what was their final trip to Goodison Park on 15 March, it was Graham Potter – who replaced Lopetegui and had also held talks with representatives of Everton owners the Friedkin Group before Sean Dyche's exit – who was in the opposition dugout, just as he was when the sides met again for their pre-season clash in Chicago.

Potter had been put through the wringer to face the press by conducting his pre-match media duties when he was quizzed not just about results and his future but a gallery of 'face-swaps' featuring his image that went viral that week online, a 'ridicule' he described as 'just the environment we are in' and something that made his 15-year-old son 'laugh a lot'.

However, the former Brighton and Chelsea boss was then axed by West Ham's owners the next day as just 48 hours before the fixture, Nuno Espírito Santo replaced him.

This was the first Premier League night game at Hill Dickinson Stadium and the crowd were treated to a light show before kick-off, but it was Michael Keane who shone brightest at both ends of the pitch.

An arcing header from Keane, who was the Blues' most impressive performer on the night, put the hosts deservedly in front on 18 minutes but despite a promising start to the second half, they were unable to add to their advantage and survived a self-inflicted scare when Jake O'Brien's back-header almost played in Crysencio Summerville and despite Jordan Pickford's save, the Hammers had soon restored parity.

Jarrod Bowen, who was Moyes's match-winner to end West Ham's trophy drought when they lifted the UEFA Europa Conference League in 2023, picked up the ball in his usual right-wing berth, cut inside and fired his side level on 65 minutes to leave Evertonians frustrated.

Despite being unable to hold out for the three points, the Blues boss insisted, 'I've taken lots of positives from the game.'

One of them wasn't referee Sam Barrott's late booking of Kiernan Dewsbury-Hall for a challenge on Kyle Walker-Peters, his fifth yellow card in as many Premier League fixtures, which ensured the midfielder would serve a one-match suspension. Moyes lamented that it was 'a really shabby decision'.

***Line-up with player ratings:*** Jordan Pickford 6; Jake O'Brien 5; Vitalii Mykolenko 6; James Tarkowski 6; Michael Keane 8; Idrissa Gueye 6; James Garner 7; Iliman Ndiaye 7 (Tyler Dibling 81); Kiernan Dewsbury-Hall 6; Jack Grealish 7; Beto 5 (Thierno Barry 69 6).

# 8

# Previous plans – a 'third cathedral' post-Hillsborough

TRAGEDY BROUGHT the idea of a 'super stadium' for Everton and Liverpool back into fruition after a couple of decades in hiatus but ultimately the two rivals from either side of Stanley Park opted to go it alone.

Football was blighted by hooliganism problems for significant portions of the 1970s and 80s and with a major economic downturn and mass unemployment across Merseyside, attendances could fluctuate wildly so ground improvements weren't typically high on the agenda of either club during the era.

All that changed overnight though after the Hillsborough disaster on 15 April 1989. At the same time that Everton were defeating Norwich City 1-0 in one FA Cup semi-final at Villa Park, Liverpool fans were being crushed in the Leppings Lane end of Sheffield Wednesday's ground, causing the abandonment of their tie against Nottingham Forest and 94 deaths on the day, a total that has since increased to 97.

The tragedy would revolutionise British football stadia, prompting the Taylor Report to call for the removal of fencing and the implementation of all-seater grounds, while on Merseyside the idea of a large, shared venue was back on the agenda.

Just a week after the tragedy, the *Liverpool Echo*'s Ian Hargraves examined the logistics behind a new shared ground and wrote, 'The finest memorial that the city of Liverpool could possibly erect to the victims of Hillsborough would be the construction of Britain's first purpose-built sports stadium on Merseyside.

'A stadium capable of seating some 60,000 people in comfort and safety, a stadium with a track that could be used for cycling or running, a stadium linked to the city by rail and possessing parking for at least 10,000 cars, a stadium capable of taking Merseyside and Britain proudly forward into the 21st century.

'Such a stadium could be used by both Everton and Liverpool in turn, could be made available for international matches and cup semi-finals, and could even be used to stage events like pop concerts and the like to augment its income.'

A generation on, we know that such a stadium was never built but at least Everton's new Hill Dickinson Stadium home at Bramley-Moore Dock is greater than anything envisaged in the late 1980s and far more appealing as a football-specific venue.

Hargraves acknowledged that the idea of a super stadium was not a new one and referenced the debate back in the 1960s.

He pointed out that Merseyside County Council even drew up detailed plans for such a stadium in Aintree, but they had been abandoned and were no longer practical as a large, permanent structure would obscure views of the racing.

Curiously enough Hargraves also stated that a similar fate had befallen a project in the North Docks, prompting him to speculate on a potential new venue for such a venture.

While the North Docks got another mention – somewhere between Sandhills and Seaforth – Aintree also remained in the mix while the Garden Festival site in Aigburth 'would have also been a credible choice, although much of it has been gradually whittled away for housing'.

There was no indication of Everton chairman Philip Carter's thoughts on such a project but Hargraves claimed 'reaction to thoughts of a super stadium is generally favourable', with Liverpool chief executive Peter Robinson, who had floated the idea privately for many years, quoted as saying, 'It would cost a great deal of money and require a great deal of thought but I believe it would confirm Liverpool as the soccer capital of England with a stadium worthy of our two fine teams.'

Six days later, John Byrne from Great Crosby, an Evertonian who said he hadn't attended a match for over 20 years, wrote in a letter to the *Echo*, 'I believe the time is now right to resurrect the idea of a super sports stadium – a third Merseyside "Cathedral" dedicated to sport, friendship and the fans who died at Hillsborough.

'Let the councils of Merseyside join with Liverpool and Everton football clubs in designing and building a stadium that could safely accommodate 100,000 people. The colours for the stadium: red, white and blue. Red for Liverpool's end, blue for Everton and white for peace and unity.'

On 8 May, under the headline 'Turning a golden vision into reality', Ian Hargraves was back on the case but conceded that while he believed the idea of a shared super stadium was 'an attractive thought' it was 'complicated by the fact that almost everyone who talks about the project has his or her ideas about what should be done'.

He also cautioned, 'One of the main stumbling blocks is likely to be the reluctance of Everton and Liverpool to abandon their existing grounds, on which both have lavished a great deal of money.'

In reality though, many fans of both clubs had little appetite for sharing a venue with their rivals and while the idea was rekindled at a time of great solidarity, as Mr Byrne also pointed out in his letter, he felt the people of Merseyside were more united at the time than at any point since the Second World War, an artist's impression published in the *Echo* of what the stadium might look like now seems staggeringly simplistic almost four decades on.

# 9

# The house that Jack built – October

**Sunday, 5 October 2025: Everton 2 Crystal Palace 1, Hill Dickinson Stadium**
**Attendance: 51,770**

Jack Grealish needed that. Evertonians needed that. Hill Dickinson Stadium needed that.

There were a trio of official 'test events' before the Blues' new 52,769-capacity home received its safety certificate.

However, those foundations that were piled into the filled-in Bramley-Moore Dock and the stunning barrel roof that covers this already iconic venue were given their sternest examination yet as the ground shook to its core following the stoppage-time winner that brought Crystal Palace's six-month unbeaten run to a grinding halt.

Before this game, David Moyes revealed that he'd told Grealish he wanted him to shoot more but surely even the Blues boss wasn't expecting a moment like the on-loan star netting with moments remaining to complete a dramatic comeback for his side and stop Crystal Palace making it 20 matches without defeat.

It was a simple instruction but in truth this game hinged just as much on a second-half sliding doors flashpoint which exemplified another Moyes request and could go down in Everton folklore alongside Phil Neville's bone-crunching challenge on Cristiano Ronaldo in front of the Bullens Road Stand during the Glaswegian's first spell in charge.

When Everton moved to Hill Dickinson Stadium, Moyes said he wanted them to bring 'the soul' of Goodison Park with them; the Grand Old Lady was more belligerent battleaxe than sweet grandmother and hell hath no fury like a woman scorned.

Blues fans are often galvanised into life when a decision angers them and the momentum in this game turned when Palace's Yéremy Pino refused to withdraw when the hosts had a free kick by the centre circle.

James Garner – who shoved the Spaniard – and Moyes got a yellow card for their troubles but Everton got their cue for a comeback.

It had all seemed so unlikely as the Blues were largely overrun for over an hour by their opponents who possessed the confidence of a side who hadn't lost a game since April.

With Adam Wharton pulling the strings in midfield, Oliver Glasner's men dominated proceedings in the first half, as Jordan Pickford – making his 300th Premier League appearance for Everton – had to showcase his ability to deny Pino, Marc Guéhi and Jean-Philippe Mateta with a string of smart saves before Palace broke the deadlock on 37 minutes.

The Blues' defence parted like waves on the Mersey for Ismaïla Sarr to run towards goal and he picked out the overlapping Daniel Muñoz with a smart pass for the Colombian to fire past Pickford.

Things still had to get worse before they got better for Everton and Jake O'Brien was the last man when he headed a dinked goal-bound effort from Mateta away against his former club and the big French striker was left to rue a shot that went wide at the back post after Sarr had carved open a home rearguard that lost Michael Keane to injury soon afterwards.

The Blues survived though and spurred on by their anger, on and off the pitch, they triumphed against adversity.

Referee Michael Salisbury had a straightforward decision to award the hosts a penalty on 76 minutes when Maxence Lacroix brought down substitute Tim Iroegbunam in the area; Iliman Ndiaye was the coolest person among over 51,000 in the stadium when he rolled the ball into the net and sent Dean Henderson the wrong way.

The stunning comeback was completed three minutes into the allotted eight extra as Beto's header was saved by Henderson but among the hectic goalmouth scramble, Muñoz touched the loose ball on to Grealish's boot for Hill Dickinson Stadium to erupt.

After breaking his duck, the Brummie ace said, 'Do you know what's mad? The last games we've played here we've been drawing and I keep saying to myself in the 85th minute, "Come on Jack, go and score. Imagine if you scored now."

'I did it against Villa, I did it against West Ham and I didn't score, so today I actually said the same thing again and I scored and I ran to where my mum and dad were, so it was nice. That goal goes to all the Evertonians for making me feel so welcome here.'

*Line-up with player ratings (by Connor O'Neill):* Jordan Pickford 9; Jake O'Brien 6; Vitalii Mykolenko 6; James Tarkowski 6; Michael Keane 7 (Tim Iroegbunam 65 7); Idrissa Gueye 6; James Garner 7; Tyler Dibling 4 (Charly Alcaraz 46 8); Iliman Ndiaye 6 (Séamus Coleman 90); Jack Grealish 7; Thierno Barry 4 (Beto 46 7).

***

The October international break would see a couple of Everton's key players sign new contracts but not before one of them was caught up in yet another brouhaha about his commitment to the club.

First up was James Tarkowski, with an announcement made less than 72 hours after the Crystal Palace comeback. The 32-year-old centre-back had entered the final 12 months of the three-year deal he signed when joining from Burnley on a free transfer in the summer of 2022, but penned an extension until 2028.

Tarkowski said, 'I'm super excited and proud to be an Everton player and to continue this journey. It's been a crazy few years with some big lows and some massive highs. We've managed to get through those tough times and hopefully now we're on to more positive and exciting times ahead.'

But while tying up Tarkowski's deal was typically no-nonsense, there was the usual furore around Jordan Pickford ahead of his announcement nine days later.

It's been a sore point for Evertonians for a long time that their goalkeeper often doesn't seem to get the credit that his performances merit from many other corners of the country, something Neville Southall and the late Kevin Campbell both dubbed 'a witch hunt'.

Second only to Peter Shilton – who holds England's all-time appearance record of 125 – as the Three Lions' most-capped goalkeeper, Pickford has also already broken Shilton's record for the most clean sheets for his country in major tournaments and in the 2026 finals would surpass him for the most England World Cup appearances.

Also, unlike the then 40-year-old custodian at Italia 90 who didn't get close to any of West Germany's efforts as Bobby Robson's side missed out on a place in the World Cup Final, the Everton man has saved at least one penalty in each of four shoot-outs on international duty, including two in the European Championship Final against Italy in 2021, and he even scored the pressure fifth kick in a 6-5 victory over Switzerland in the UEFA Nations League in 2019.

In all of this lengthy tenure, Pickford officially hasn't been at fault for conceding a single goal in a competitive match according to statisticians, with Opta deeming that the only such mistake came on his 60th appearance on 24 March 2024, in a friendly against Belgium.

Five days before England became the first European nation to qualify for the 2026 World Cup finals, Pickford's shut-out in the 3-0 friendly win over Wales at Wembley ensured he broke Gordon Banks's 59-year-old record for consecutive clean sheets.

However, when Thomas Tuchel's side secured their place in the following summer's tournament with a 5-0 romp over Latvia in Riga, Lee Dixon, who was part of the England squad that failed to qualify for the 1994 World Cup, questioned why Pickford hadn't joined 'a bigger club' while on commentary duty alongside Sam Matterface for ITV's live broadcast of the game.

In response, Everton's official account posted on X to set the record straight with a message that read, '9 top-flight titles, 5 FA Cups, 1 European title, one of football's most-passionate fanbases, a world-class new stadium. Everton FC – a big club: past, present & future', tagging in Dixon's account.

Pickford, as always when others are critiquing him, seemed totally unfazed by the whole rumpus though and declared himself to be 'over the moon' with 'the opportunity to build a legacy for myself here', when his extension to 2029 was confirmed on 16 October.

Remarking that it had 'been a mega journey so far', he echoed Tarkowski's sentiments by adding, 'I think the dark days are behind us and it's about building that momentum as a team and the club now.'

## Saturday, 18 October 2025: Manchester City 2 Everton 0, Etihad Stadium
## Attendance: 52,498 (3,065 Everton)

The benchmark of how far Everton still had to go with the team-building Pickford referenced was displayed here, but their issues were at the other end of the pitch.

The best centre-forwards have always cost the big money so despite breaking Everton's transfer record three times during his first spell on frontmen and the Blues' rich tradition for number nines, a hallmark of David Moyes's sides has often been having the most potent performers in the attacking midfield areas. That remained the case as despite having two clear options vying to spearhead the attack, the squad continues to feel light on polish up front.

For almost an hour, Everton's stubborn resistance had their hosts getting increasingly frustrated and it wasn't just a rearguard action with Moyes's men being more than a match for Pep Guardiola's side.

However, while striker Beto had netted just once all season – and his backup Thierno Barry, who replaced him with 15 minutes to go, had yet to find the net – City's Erling Haaland continued to be prolific with this brace taking his tally for club and country to 23 for this term alone, a total that many frontmen would be proud of come May, never mind before the clocks go back.

Moyes, now the Premier League's oldest and most-experienced active manager – only serial title winners Sir Alex Ferguson and Arsène Wenger have taken charge of more games in the competition – is long enough in the tooth to have been in the dugout before City's petrodollar-fuelled revolution began.

When Sheikh Mansour first took over, Moyes compared trying to compete against their new-found wealth to 'taking a knife to a gunfight'.

But while he was still able to give them a bloody nose back then, with a dozen wins during his first spell at Everton including five at the Etihad, the momentum has long since shifted in this fixture with City now unbeaten in their last 19 head-to-heads in all competitions.

And here, the Blues' attack, led by Beto, wouldn't cut through butter, while Haaland, heading in with his first chance on 58 minutes and then confidently sweeping in a shot from the edge of the area that went through James Tarkowski's legs to seal the win five minutes later, remained razor sharp.

Iliman Ndiaye twice put chances on a plate for Beto only for the striker to fluff his lines on both occasions.

Firstly, he failed to make a clean connection on an inviting low cross from Ndiaye, who was sensational in the first half, and then, when picked out by a threaded pass, the assistant referee's flag going up for offside spared his blushes as his shot went wide.

Speaking in his pre-match press conference, Moyes backed Beto's attitude, remarking, 'The boy is mad to do the work. He's a brilliant, brilliant lad and his dedication to try and improve himself is second to none, so you can only praise him for that.'

The Scot also admitted that the team had perhaps not been playing to the 27-year-old's strengths, but here when he had the opportunities, just like when on international duty for Guinea-Bissau the previous week in Ethiopia, allowing the ball to slip through his legs and go out for a goal kick in a 1-0 loss, he was unable to take them.

When I spoke to Tarkowski after the game, he bemoaned how easy Haaland's opener had been after Everton had kept him quiet for almost an hour.

He said, 'I thought we made it pretty difficult, so it's just a shame the way they got in behind us so easily in the start of that second half. Any player in the world is going to fancy that chance, especially him from six yards out.'

*Line-up with player ratings:* Jordan Pickford 6; Jake O'Brien 6; Vitalii Mykolenko 6; James Tarkowski 6; Michael Keane 6; Idrissa Gueye 6 (Tim Iroegbunam 70 6); James Garner 6; Iliman Ndiaye 7 (Tyler Dibling 86); Kiernan Dewsbury-Hall 5 (Dwight McNeil 86); Charly Alcaraz 5 (Merlin Röhl 70 6); Beto 4 (Thierno Barry 75).

***

While the trip to Manchester City and subsequent defeat was always unlikely to shape Everton's season, the rumours spreading like wildfire through the away end at the Etihad Stadium were rather more alarming.

The Blues' most-valuable player, Jarrad Branthwaite, who had penned a new five-year deal in the summer but hadn't kicked a ball all season, had gone from being on the cusp of making his long-awaited comeback to suffering another injury setback.

The defensive colossus had been photographed training with his team-mates ahead of the clash with Pep Guardiola's side and Moyes had been hopeful of integrating him back into the team, but by the time we were back in Merseyside that evening, the bad news had been confirmed to my colleague Joe Thomas.

At 3pm the following Monday, Everton announced Branthwaite had 'experienced a complication in his recovery from a hamstring injury' and added that following specialist consultation he would undergo a surgical procedure the next day.

If 23 goals from Haaland before the clocks went back was some going, then how about three managers from the start of the season for Nottingham Forest? And they would of course go on to have four.

Three days after Everton's defeat at the Etihad Stadium, their previous boss Sean Dyche was back in the Premier League at the club where he started his career as an apprentice under Brian Clough.

Although he came in at the Blues when they were at their lowest ebb, the job was still a huge opportunity for Dyche.

But like Sam Allardyce before him, in landing a position at the most-successful club of his career, he was unable to demonstrate a more expansive playing style, even if he insisted, 'Why fight the box you're put in?'

There are three distinctly different acts when it comes to Dyche's reign and after all he was the longest-serving of the eight managers in as many years under Farhad Moshiri's ownership – a boast akin to being the tallest of Snow White's Seven Dwarfs – even though it was Everton's late chairman Bill Kenwright, rather than Moshiri, who pushed to bring him in.

Moshiri himself preferred Marcelo Bielsa, who flew in for talks, only to be told that the former Leeds United boss wanted to work with the under-21 squad for the rest of the season before taking charge of the senior side.

It would have been a hare-brained scheme worthy of the maverick Argentinian's *El Loco* nickname and by which time the Blues would have been in the Championship because make no mistake, they were going down under Frank Lampard.

Therefore, having taken over on 30 January 2023 with Everton second-bottom of the table, Dyche deserves considerable credit for keeping them up, even if they posted the lowest equivalent points total in the club's history and avoided a first relegation in 72 years by a single goal, scored by Abdoulaye Doucouré, a player brought in from the cold after his fall-out with Lampard, on the final day against Bournemouth.

Ditto in 2023/24, Dyche's only full season in charge, which saw the Blues face an unprecedented brace of points deductions for PSR rule breaches – punishments that would have condemned them to the drop if inflicted 12 months earlier – but still he kept their heads above water.

It wasn't pretty and it certainly wasn't painless with Everton failing to win a Premier League game between Christmas and Easter, a run that ended with Dyche admitting he'd deliberately asked his team to play ugly to beat his previous employers Burnley.

Even then, the 6-0 shellacking at Chelsea followed next up, and I stuck my neck out with a very public declaration in a *Liverpool Echo* opinion piece that yet another change in the revolving door of the dugout was not a prudent move when it came to the club's already fragile stability.

While I could feel swiftly vindicated with the hat-trick of home wins that followed in the space of a week to guarantee the Blues' Premier League safety, all bets were off when it came to Everton's historic final season at Goodison Park.

The momentous campaign started badly with a 3-0 home defeat to Brighton & Hove Albion on the opening day, the first of four consecutive Premier League losses, a run that included back-to-back 3-2 reversals in games that Dyche's side were leading 2-0, the former against Bournemouth until the 87th minute.

Although the Kettering-born gaffer always insisted he was respectful to the supporters, other than that aforementioned seven-day spree that included a first home victory over Liverpool for 13 and a half years, he struggled to harness the power of Goodison.

He would often harp on about how it being the final season at the club's home since 1892 didn't make his players better, but ultimately 17 points from 19 games with just two home wins in that time wasn't good enough.

In an ideal world, nobody wanted to change partners halfway through 'The Last Dance with the Grand Old Lady', but when the time came, Dyche seemed to have thrown in the towel, telling new owners the Friedkin Group he felt he'd taken the team as far as he could.

Many have observed that in the fullness of time, he will come to be respected as the tough guy leader that Everton needed to guide them through a time of crisis on and off the pitch, yet in the face of an 'us against the world' siege mentality as they were hit twice by sporting sanctions, he seemed unconcerned with making new friends.

Dyche was always cordial and polite towards myself – which is only fair given that I must have written more words of support for him than anyone in my profession during his tenure – but while he was jocular and matey with time-served reporters who he knew from almost a decade in charge at Burnley, several senior members of the Merseyside press pack quickly became exasperated by the figurative wall he put up around himself.

Anyway, having enjoyed the increased profile that came with the job which enabled him to play golf with Tommy Fleetwood in Dubai and for someone who has always been heavily into his music to appear in a video with indie rock band Blossoms, Dyche's career came full circle to the City Ground.

However, he would find Evangelos Marinakis rather different from the regime under Clough, who once remarked that, '85, perhaps 90 per cent of football chairmen bring the game into disrepute'.

This was the owner who, having already dismissed Nuno Espírito Santo – the manager who guided Nottingham Forest to Europe for the first time in 30 years – gave Ange Postecoglou his marching orders after 39 days a mere 18 minutes after the final whistle on the 3-0 home defeat to Chelsea. And there was more of that ahead.

## Sunday, 26 October 2025: Everton 0 Tottenham Hotspur 3, Hill Dickinson Stadium Attendance: 52,501

Whether it was Daniel Levy negotiating Richarlison's transfer for £20m less than the selling club's valuation in the elegant surroundings of Scott's in Mayfair or the various on-the-pitch thrashings, Everton have struggled in head-to-heads with Tottenham Hotspur in recent years and so it proved here with the Lilywhites making history by becoming the first visiting side to triumph in a competitive game at Hill Dickinson Stadium.

Plush seafood restaurant Scott's sells caviar and boasts an oyster and champagne bar, but the late former chairman Bill Kenwright still left with a bad taste in his mouth given he felt that Levy had the Blues over a barrel in the summer of 2022 as they needed to sell their Brazilian ace to satisfy PSR issues.

To add insult to injury, Everton ultimately were still deemed to have breached that financial year and a subsequent brace of points deductions loomed for that and the following 12 months.

This was just the latest in a line of heavy defeats though.

Under Farhad Moshiri's ownership, the Blues went down in the capital eight times, including 4-0 on 13 January 2018, 5-0 on 7 March 2022 and 4-0 on 24 August 2024, while they even suffered a 6-2 reversal at Goodison Park on 23 December 2018, a result to ruin Christmas for thousands of Evertonians.

But whereas many of those chastening days were inflicted through the intricate, passing football that Spurs are famed for, this came through the rising Premier League trend of exploiting dead-ball situations.

David Moyes was blunt about Everton's set pieces in the previous season when he came back to the club, describing them as 'rubbish', but when it came to keeping them out at the other end the Blues were the last men standing in 2025/26.

But just as Everton's praises were being sung for being the only Premier League team who had not been breached by a set piece, lightning struck twice in the same place against Tottenham Hotspur, whose captain Micky van de Ven headed in from a brace of corners in the 19th and 45th minutes.

In between, the Blues were denied an equaliser from one of their own as Jake O'Brien's header was ruled out after Craig Pawson checked the pitchside monitor and deemed that Iliman Ndiaye and Jack Grealish, standing in offside positions, were impeding opposition goalkeeper Guglielmo Vicario.

It was a brutal lesson for Moyes's men who, in chasing the game, conceded again a minute from full time as Richarlison – who has netted five times against Everton in opposition colours

– crossed to fellow substitute Pape Matar Sarr, who, unmarked in the area, dispatched a third headed goal of the evening.

Afterwards, I interviewed Merlin Röhl who said, 'We had good control over some parts of the game but of course, in the important situations we didn't make the right moves and conceded goals after set pieces. We need to get better on this.'

*Line-up with player ratings:* Jordan Pickford 6; Jake O'Brien 5 (Merlin Röhl 66 6); Vitalii Mykolenko 5; James Tarkowski 5; Michael Keane 5; Idrissa Gueye 6 (Charly Alcaraz 86); James Garner 6; Iliman Ndiaye 7; Kiernan Dewsbury-Hall 6; Jack Grealish 7; Beto 5 (Thierno Barry 66 6).

# 10

# Manchester United slapped down – November

NOVEMBER KICKED off at Hill Dickinson Stadium with an oval ball rather than a round one as Everton's new home staged its first major non-football event.

It was announced back in March that England would host Australia in the first rugby league Ashes Test series in 22 years and the second match took place on 1 November in front of a 52,106 crowd as the Kangaroos triumphed 14-4 to go 2-0 up overall ahead of them completing a whitewash at Headingley the following week.

Goodison Park had hosted four rugby league matches involving Antipodean sides during its early years. Australia defeated a Northern Union XIII 10-9 on 18 November 1908 with England beating Australia 14-7 on 3 March 1909, while Australasia (a combined team of Australians and New Zealanders) overcame a Northern League XIII 16-3 on 25 October 1911 and later had a 29-6 victory over Lancashire on 30 November 1921.

While the general response from the rugby league community was overwhelmingly positive over the experience on the Mersey waterfront – less than a month later on 25 November it was announced that Hill Dickinson Stadium would be hosting more rugby league with the following July's Magic Weekend of six Super League matches – there was an embarrassing security breach.

A pitch invader, who had already gained notoriety for getting on to the playing areas at other major sporting events, donned an Australia kit to line up with his arm around stand-off Cameron Munster during the national anthems. It was an act for which, when pleading guilty to trespass the following April, he was given a ten-week sentence suspended for 12 months while also being handed 20 days of rehabilitation along with 150 hours of unpaid work and ordered to pay £500 in damages and a £154 court surcharge.

## Monday, 3 November 2025: Sunderland 1 Everton 1, Stadium of Light
## Attendance: 41,476 (3,086 Everton)

He'd suffered back-to-back defeats, but David Moyes had been in tighter spots than this going to Sunderland as Everton manager and emerged stronger.

One game in particular proved to be a watershed moment in his lengthy first spell in charge and it remains particularly poignant for the author given that it was the first Everton match I reported on, so while driving up to Wearside I was going back to where it all began for me almost 20 years earlier on New Year's Eve 2005.

My 11-word appraisal of why goalkeeper Nigel Martyn was the man of the match hardly did justice to the magnitude of the veteran Cornishman's herculean efforts between the sticks, though, as I remarked that he 'kept Everton in the game during a sustained period of pressure'.

The game was set against the backdrop of unused Sunderland substitute Alan Stubbs being cheered by the away fans as he warmed up. After captaining his beloved Blues to fourth the previous season, Stubbs had quit the club because Moyes wouldn't offer him a longer new contract, but he would end his nightmare spell in the north-east less than a month later, returning to Goodison.

Mick McCarthy's men threw the kitchen sink at the visitors to no avail but the decisive moment came from a corner in the 92nd minute in what was the ultimate smash-and-grab raid by the Blues.

My match report at the time read, 'In what must have been a nightmare combination for Sunderland, former Black Cats boo-boy victim Kevin Kilbane provided the cross for Tim Cahill, who famously nodded in the goal that beat Sunderland in an FA Cup semi-final two seasons ago. Cahill rose majestically in typical fashion and delivered a bullet straight into Sunderland hearts and the back of the home net.'

This time around, Everton would start strongly before fading.

As well as being Moyes's first match back at the Stadium of Light since his spell in charge of the Black Cats, it was an even more emotional homecoming for local hero Jordan Pickford, playing against his boyhood club where he launched his Premier League career – after half a dozen loan spells – before making his £25m transfer to Goodison Park in 2017 and becoming England number one.

In the build-up, I tracked down Jim Welch, his old PE teacher at St Robert of Newminster Catholic School in his home town of Washington.

Recalling his former pupil, the 71-year-old, who worked alongside Pickford's mother who was school secretary, told me, 'I played him in midfield. You could get away with it in schoolboy football and put anyone in goal as he would have been wasted in goal and he wanted to play out as well. He's calmed down a lot though because when he was younger, he used to tackle knee height when he played for me. In fact, in his last game for me, the referee told me that I'd have to take him off otherwise he'd send him off.'

With Pickford given a suitably warm reception by all sides of the Stadium of Light before kick-off, Everton – wearing their third kit despite there being no clash of colours – bossed the early exchanges and took a deserved lead on 15 minutes.

Thierno Barry won the ball from Noah Sadiki, who fed Iliman Ndiaye on the right wing with the Senegal international slaloming past several Sunderland players before planting the ball into the roof of the net for what was a wonderful solo goal of pure genius.

At this point Moyes's men had the newly promoted hosts on pins, but after Jack Grealish struck a shot against the foot of the post and then Barry failed to hit the target from his inviting cross, blazing over from close range at the back post, the belief seemed to be sapped out of them.

Having come up from the Championship via the play-offs under Frenchman Régis Le Bris, Sunderland, who had won 2-1 at Chelsea in their previous fixture – Everton hadn't picked up three points at Stamford Bridge for 31 years – appeared game but technically limited, but having hung in the contest they became increasingly dangerous, forcing Michael Keane into a string of well-timed interceptions.

Their pressure finally told just moments after the second half kicked off as home captain Granit Xhaka's shot deflected off James Tarkowski and past Pickford via the crossbar.

Pickford then did well when wrong-footed moments later to claw away another deflected effort from Enzo Le Fée, but in the end a share of the spoils was a fair result as Everton concerned themselves with the fitness of star man Ndiaye, who had been forced off through injury just after the hour with eyebrows being raised over Moyes's choice of Dwight McNeil over his most expensive summer signing, and more natural right-sided option, Tyler Dibling to replace him.

Afterwards, the goalkeeper – who had taken to the field with his son wearing a half-and-half Sunderland/Everton shirt

– admitted he'd been praying for a good reception from home supporters, 'I grew up as a Sunderland fan in the crazy corner watching games. I gave that passion when I played for Sunderland. I've been at Everton for nine seasons, and I think I've got a great relationship with both sets of fans. That's just what type of lad I am, and I'll never change who I am.'

*Line-up with player ratings:* Jordan Pickford 6; Jake O'Brien 6 (Tim Iroegbunam 83); Vitalii Mykolenko 6; James Tarkowski 7; Michael Keane 8; Idrissa Gueye 6; James Garner 7; Iliman Ndiaye 8 (Dwight McNeil 62 6); Kiernan Dewsbury-Hall 6 (Charly Alcaraz 83); Jack Grealish 7; Thierno Barry 6 (Beto 56 6).

## Saturday, 8 November 2025: Everton 2 Fulham 0, Hill Dickinson Stadium
## Attendance: 52,491

Despite having three goals disallowed for offside, Everton got back to winning ways and following his Sunderland return with Jordan Pickford, David Moyes went back to where it all began for him as Blues boss with a home victory against Fulham.

Having not tasted victory for over a month, Moyes decided to mix things up at right-back and replace natural centre-back Jake O'Brien in the role with James Garner, whose preferred position is central midfield.

Moyes pulled off arguably the best pound-for-pound signing of the Premier League era when he plucked Séamus Coleman from Sligo Rovers in January 2009 for his fabled '60 grand fee' but with his 37-year-old captain by this point in the autumn of his career, the boss could not turn back the clock.

Garner started the season at left-back, but here it was once more his turn to move from the engine room to the other side of defence. In that respect, the Birkenhead-born player's versatility is reminiscent of another solid citizen Everton acquired from

Manchester United, Phil Neville, who served Moyes with such distinction during his first spell in charge.

While Neville was more of a natural vocal presence, Garner leads by example and possesses better technique – as displayed by his curling free kick here that almost put his side ahead.

Of course, it might not have been an issue if, as mentioned earlier in the book, Kenny Tete hadn't turned his back on a move to Everton over the summer and decided to sign a new deal at Fulham.

On this occasion, the Dutchman fell out with someone who might have been one of his team-mates, James Tarkowski, who threw Tete to the ground and then grabbed Calvin Bassey by the neck, earning a yellow card from referee Andrew Madley for his troubles.

The skipper made light of the incident when talking to *Match of the Day* that evening though, revealing that the Cottagers defender had tweaked him in the chest, 'He gave me a nipple cripple I think, which I've not had in a while!'

The incident, in first-half stoppage time, would be followed moments later by the opening goal, after Tarkowski and Thierno Barry had earlier seen efforts ruled out for offside.

A lofted left-wing cross from Vitalii Mykolenko was headed against the crossbar by Tarkowski, and after Tim Iroegbunam's initial swipe of a shot from the rebound had been blocked, Idrissa Gueye slammed the ball in from the edge of the six-yard box.

After the break it was the turn of Kiernan Dewsbury-Hall to have a goal ruled out for offside but with nine minutes to go he delivered the corner for Michael Keane, who was also colossal again at the back, to seal the three points with a 'header'. The ball was nodded towards goal by Keane but when I interviewed him after the game, he admitted, 'It was a great shoulder.'

However, that didn't dampen his spirits as they all count and Keane added, 'To score in front of those fans in that stand is a great feeling – it's the best feeling ever.'

***Line-up with player ratings:*** Jordan Pickford 7; James Garner 7; Vitalii Mykolenko 6; James Tarkowski 7; Michael Keane 9; Idrissa Gueye 8; Tim Iroegbunam 7 (Merlin Röhl 67 6); Iliman Ndiaye 7; Kiernan Dewsbury-Hall 7 (Jake O'Brien 89); Jack Grealish 7; Thierno Barry 7 (Beto 78).

***

During the final international break of the calendar year, thoughts turned to a tournament of the future with the announcement of the match schedule for the 2028 European Championship as it was confirmed that Hill Dickinson Stadium – or 'Everton Stadium' as it will be known for the duration of the finals due to the ban on using sponsors' names – will be hosting five matches.

Four group games will be coming to the Mersey waterfront plus a last-16 knockout clash that could potentially feature England if they were to finish runners-up in their group.

Goodison Park staged five fixtures in the 1966 World Cup, with holders Brazil, featuring the likes of Pelé and Garrincha, playing all their group matches there; Golden Boot winner Eusébio netting six of his nine goals, including four in Portugal's 5-3 comeback win over North Korea; and Franz Beckenbauer coming up against Lev Yashin in the semi-final, only for many angry fans to boycott West Germany's 2-1 victory over the Soviet Union after it was switched with England's last-four encounter less than 48 hours before.

## Monday, 24 November 2025: Manchester United 0 Everton 1, Old Trafford
## Attendance: 74,158 (3,099 Everton)

Richard Jolly of *The Independent* best summed this game up when he wrote, 'A slap in the face from Idrissa Gueye became a kick in the teeth for Ruben Amorim ... the team that fought each other beat the team with no fight.'

The match took place on Amorim's first anniversary as Manchester United manager with the Portuguese coach, subsequently sacked little over a month later on 5 January, just the latest of successors to follow David Moyes in what has become the poisoned chalice of attempting to replicate the title-winning days of Sir Alex Ferguson, a challenge that even Louis van Gaal, José Mourinho and Erik ten Hag had all failed in, despite delivering silverware.

Repeatedly reminded that for all the good he did during his 11-year first spell at Goodison he had never won away at Arsenal, Chelsea, Liverpool or Manchester United, Moyes got the first of these monkeys off his back.

Another statistic that had been trotted out whenever this fixture was played was the fact that other than when the Glaswegian himself was in charge of the Red Devils, Everton's most recent Old Trafford triumph had come in their very first Premier League away game, Howard Kendall's side securing a 3-0 victory on 19 August 1992 when 'Rhythm Is a Dancer' by Snap was at number one in the UK charts.

Tempers would snap here but the Blues would go on to win the hard way having already suffered a setback before the sending off with Séamus Coleman forced out of the action after just ten minutes.

The 37-year-old had not started a Premier League game for Everton since leading them out for their 2-0 win over Southampton on 18 May in their final match at Goodison Park – he only lasted

18 minutes that day before succumbing to injury – but having been deployed as a wing-back and played the full 90 minutes in the Republic of Ireland's 2-0 victory over Portugal and then an hour in the 3-2 comeback success in Hungary in World Cup qualifiers the previous week, Moyes felt it was the right time to select his veteran skipper.

On what was his 433rd Everton appearance, Coleman entered the club's all-time top ten for number of matches as he went level with former team-mate Leon Osman and legendary leading goalscorer Dixie Dean, but was soon left hamstrung and replaced by compatriot Jake O'Brien.

As Everton – who had started refreshingly on the front foot – were still adapting to their early enforced switch, the big flashpoint left everyone inside Old Trafford stunned.

There was a defensive mix-up as following James Tarkowski's challenge in the area to deny Bryan Mbeumo, Gueye attempted to lay the ball off to Keane but the centre-back failed to read the pass, allowing Bruno Fernandes to fire a shot across the face of goal.

It was a let-off but seemingly there was no harm done, so it seemed extraordinary that just seconds later, following an angry exchange between Gueye and Keane, the former was shown the red card by referee Tony Harrington for slapping the latter in the face.

The unseemly fracas was not a good look for either player, but while the letter of the law would say that Gueye was guilty of violent conduct, many within the game commented on how if the match official had just taken a 'common sense' approach and spoken to the colleagues and asked them to calm down then there would have been few complaints.

Instead, the incident seemed to halt the momentum of the early proceedings with a strange atmosphere of disbelief prevailing, but Everton dug in and were well worth the lead they took in spectacular fashion on 29 minutes.

Picked out by James Garner, Kiernan Dewsbury-Hall dribbled forwards to ride challenges from Fernandes and Leny Yoro before curling a shot on his weaker right foot from the edge of the area into the top corner of Senne Lammens's goal before racing towards the jubilant away supporters, celebrating with a knee slide and salute.

For the final hour the Blues defended doggedly and kept United at arm's length, with Jack Grealish particularly intelligent in his play, tracking back and then winning free kicks to help alleviate the pressure.

While Jordan Pickford had to make a clutch of smart saves in the second half, including a particularly impressive one at full stretch to keep out a Joshua Zirkzee header, it never felt like Moyes's men were under the cosh as they pulled off a famous triumph on their travels against the odds.

When asked about the sending off – which in the pre-match press conference for the next fixture he revealed they'd unsuccessfully appealed – Moyes insisted, 'I like my players fighting each other, if someone didn't do the right action. If you want that toughness and resilience to get a result, you want someone to act on it.'

Pickford had been the team-mate who got between Gueye and Keane to split them up and when I asked him in a post-match interview what had gone on, he told me, 'Initially I didn't see what happened. I just saw them arguing. But the main thing is that Idrissa has come in and apologised. It doesn't look nice ever, but we move on from it, and the main thing is we've got the win.'

*Line-up with player ratings:* Jordan Pickford 9; Séamus Coleman (Jake O'Brien 10 7); Vitalii Mykolenko 7; James Tarkowski 8; Michael Keane 8; Idrissa Gueye 1; James Garner 8; Iliman Ndiaye 7 (Beto 81); Kiernan Dewsbury-Hall 10 (Charly Alcaraz 87); Jack Grealish 8 (Dwight McNeil 87); Thierno Barry 7 (Tim Iroegbunam 81).

***

After the game, Gueye would follow up his face-to-face apology to his Everton team-mates with a statement online. The 36-year-old said, 'I want to apologise first to my team-mate Michael Keane. I take full responsibility for my reaction. I also apologise to my team-mates, the staff, the fans and the club. What happened does not reflect who I am or the values I stand for. Emotions can run high, but nothing justifies such behaviour. I'll make sure it never happens again. UTT [Up the Toffees].'

Then, three days after the game, Gueye and Keane appeared together in a light-hearted video posted on Thierno Barry's Instagram account to show they had made up with each other.

The footage showed the duo stepping into a makeshift 'ring' at Everton's Finch Farm training complex, each wearing a single boxing glove as Beto stood between them like a referee and told them to 'touch glove'. Keane then pretended to get a first blow in on a giggling Gueye before the pair of them embraced. The footage was also accompanied by the caption 'Only love here', complete with a blue heart emoji.

Less than 24 hours after Gueye and Keane had come to blows, there was a very special evening for me as we held a live event for *Spirit of the Blues* at Waterstones Liverpool.

I was joined by fellow Everton author Steve Zocek, my friend and former colleague Sam Carroll, who acted as master of ceremonies, and ex-Blues player Michael Ball, whose *Liverpool Echo* column I regularly ghostwrite – not that he needs any words putting in his mouth because he's the best in the business in my opinion.

'Bally' as he's known in the game is forthright and never scared to dish out a few home truths. His fellow pros can either like it or lump it because his opinions are always delivered with Everton's best interest at heart and with the insight and tactical understanding of someone who played football for the club he loved before experiencing top-flight football in two other leagues.

It was great to hold our talk on the back of the win at Old Trafford, and I was delighted and humbled that our assembled audience seemed so engaged with what we had to say as family and friends were also present for what felt like a landmark occasion for my efforts.

A hectic week continued on Friday, 28 November as it was announced that Hill Dickinson Stadium had been named as a proposed host venue in the United Kingdom's official bid to stage the 2035 Women's World Cup. Everton's new home is one of 22 UK stadia included in the bid to host what would be, with 48 teams taking part, the biggest single-sport event in the country's history.

Before the home game against Newcastle United and with fan representatives of both clubs present, Everton unveiled a Gary Speed memorial at Hill Dickinson Stadium as a lasting tribute to one of the Blues' most admired former players who died aged 42 in 2011, with what was the club's first talking bench.

Talking benches have been introduced across the UK as a simple but powerful way to encourage conversation, tackle loneliness and isolation, and signpost people to mental health support, offering a space where individuals can pause, speak openly, or simply sit alongside others without judgement.

When attending the event, BBC Radio Merseyside's Giulia Bould and I got to interview Gary's mother, Carol, who laid a bouquet of flowers at the site. She told us, 'I think it's a fantastic idea. We didn't know that Gary was struggling, people don't always know what's going on in people's minds.'

David Wycherley of the Everton Fans' Forum said, 'It's a new stadium but we still have our memories and now Gary's lives on. It's not what anyone would have wanted but hopefully it becomes a real positive influence in the future and gets us talking. Football is sometimes the spark for us to get together, and this can hopefully start some of those conversations.'

## Saturday, 29 November 2025: Everton 1 Newcastle United 4, Hill Dickinson Stadium Attendance: 52,544

While Idrissa Gueye and Michael Keane had made light of their Old Trafford scrap with the mock boxing match, Everton were already on the canvas here by the interval in what was their 5,700th competitive fixture (thanks to Steve Johnson from evertonresults.com for that nugget).

Perhaps David Moyes's men's herculean effort to become the first side to win a Premier League game away to the Red Devils after having one of their side red-carded, digging in against Ruben Amorim's charges with a numerical disadvantage for 77 minutes, left them physically and mentally exhausted because they were sluggish from the start against a Newcastle outfit without a win away from home in the competition all season.

Although Gueye apologised for his actions straight away and neither he nor Keane looked forced in their actions for their joke sketch to show they'd buried the hatchet, nobody among the hosts was smiling here as despite his diminutive 5ft 7in frame he left a gaping hole in the middle of the pitch.

The Blues found themselves on the back foot from the start with Jordan Pickford forced to turn Anthony Elanga's low shot around the post just after the kick-off but then Newcastle opened the scoring from the resultant corner as Malick Thiaw headed in with just 55 seconds on the clock.

If that was disappointing, what followed was even worse; the Magpies doubled their advantage on 25 minutes as, despite Keane cutting out an Elanga cross, a loose touch by Tim Iroegbunam gifted possession back to the visitors and following some penalty box pinball, teenager Lewis Miley's shot through a crowded area seemed to deceive Pickford, bouncing on the turf twice and into the net through his legs.

Eddie Howe's side then moved out of sight in the final minute of the first half as Iroegbunam – who would be hooked at the interval – made a hash of dealing with Tino Livramento's knock up the line towards Elanga, who picked out Nick Woltemade, the £65m striker brought in from Stuttgart to replace Alexander Isak when he forced through a £125m move to Liverpool.

Woltemade – who had been on David Moyes's radar since his West Ham days and was a potential Everton target under him before they got priced out – showed why he is known as 'the two-metre Messi' back in his native Germany as he coolly struck a third goal with a deft chip over Pickford's head.

Charly Alcaraz – who had come on for the out-of-sorts Iroegbunam – had an opportunity to reduce arrears soon after his introduction when the ball fell invitingly for him on the edge of the area following a corner but his powerful effort rattled the crossbar.

Moments after James Tarkowski had blocked another Woltemade effort on the line, Newcastle added a fourth when the ball was swung back into the danger area by Lewis Hall and Alcaraz found himself hopelessly mismatched in an aerial duel with Thiaw at the back post, the Dusseldorf-born defender dispatching his second headed goal of the contest on 58 minutes.

On 65 minutes, Thierno Barry was cruelly denied a first goal in a royal blue jersey when, having brought down Vitalii Mykolenko's left-wing cross and beaten Aaron Ramsdale with a left-footed finish, a VAR check ruled the effort out for an accidental handball by the French striker.

Four minutes later, Everton would complete the scoring with the best goal of the match – and one that Kiernan Dewsbury-Hall would claim was the best of his career at the time – but it was a mere consolation.

Tarkowski spotted the midfielder's run and picked him out with a lofted diagonal pass and the summer signing from Chelsea would net for the second consecutive game by bringing the ball down from behind him – a piece of control that Michael Ball would describe as 'Dennis Bergkamp-esque' – and then slotting in a left-footed finish.

Although his own side have their own share of big units, Moyes admitted afterwards that the muscular Magpies had overpowered Everton on this occasion, 'We beat Newcastle at St James' Park when they had to win to beat us to qualify for the Champions League, so we can go and beat them. But tonight they were far too powerful for us. Maybe the strongest, maybe the most powerful team in the Premier League. Maybe Arsenal might sway them on that. Strong team, big, every player big, physical, hard to play against.'

*Line-up with player ratings:* Jordan Pickford 4; Jake O'Brien 5; Vitalii Mykolenko 5; James Tarkowski 4; Michael Keane 5; James Garner 6; Tim Iroegbunam 3 (Charly Alcaraz 46 5); Iliman Ndiaye 5 (Tyler Dibling 80); Kiernan Dewsbury-Hall 7 (Jake O'Brien 89); Jack Grealish 6 (Dwight McNeil 80); Thierno Barry 5 (Beto 87).

11

# Double over Dyche – December

**Tuesday, 2 December 2025: Bournemouth 0**
**Everton 1, Vitality Stadium**
**Attendance: 11,161 (1,307 Everton)**

Apologies to any readers of a delicate disposition – although what are you doing reading a book about Everton? – but to paraphrase King George V, who is reputed to have uttered 'Bugger Bognor', loyal but long-suffering Blues supporters could be forgiven for declaring, 'Bugger Bournemouth!'

George V, the great-grandfather of our current sovereign King Charles III, actually has a significant Everton connection, as mentioned in *Spirit of the Blues*.

On 11 July 1913, Goodison Park became the first English football ground to be visited by a reigning monarch when George V and his wife Queen Mary – whose statues mark the Liverpool entrance to the Queensway Tunnel underneath the Mersey to Birkenhead after they opened it in 1934 – attended Everton's home on a trip which also saw the royal couple open the Gladstone Dock, the biggest in the world at the time, in Bootle.

George V, who also created the House of Windsor by changing his family's name from Saxe-Coburg and Gotha in 1917 because of anti-German sentiment during the First World War, had benefitted from the sea air at Bognor when convalescing from septicaemia in 1928, a stay that would subsequently prompt town officials to successfully petition him to bestow their 'Regis' suffix.

But the story goes that as the king lay on his deathbed at Sandringham, a well-meaning attendant suggested he'd soon be well enough to go back to the Sussex resort, only for him to retort, 'Bugger Bognor.'

While, like many a good tale, the outburst is now considered apocryphal, in a private journal the king's physician wrote that George V's last words were actually, 'God damn you.' Up until this game, Evertonians could be forgiven for also having a less than enthusiastic appetite for making long treks down to the south coast.

Although Everton had beaten Bournemouth when it really mattered at Goodison Park on the final day of the 2022/23 season to avoid relegation, even at home the following year they somehow conspired to lose despite leading 2-0 going into the 87th minute.

Over a decade of trying, trips to this Dorset Premier League outpost – a world away from professional hotbeds in the industrial north of England – the Blues had been unable to pick up three points.

Other long-standing bogey grounds for Everton such as Stamford Bridge (no Premier League wins since 1994), Anfield (no wins in front of fans since 1999), or at Highbury or the Emirates Stadium against Arsenal (no wins in front of fans since 1996) are all records that are painful and frustrating, but at least they offer some mitigating circumstances in that all of those hosts are established powerhouses of the English game.

Although a long-awaited expansion is now afoot, the Vitality Stadium in contrast is the smallest ground in the Premier League with an overall capacity in 2025/26 of just 11,307, which is less than Tranmere Rovers' Prenton Park (16,587) or even the South Stand alone at Hill Dickinson Stadium which holds over 14,000.

Everton's trail of tears began on 28 November 2015 – I was there – when they raced into another 2-0 lead through Ramiro

Funes Mori (25) and Romelu Lukaku (36), only to be pegged back by goals from Adam Smith (80) and Junior Stanislas (87).

That day, there was enough time for Ross Barkley to restore the visitors' lead in the 95th minute, sparking a jubilant pitch invasion from the away end, but Stanislas equalised again in the 98th minute and Bournemouth even had another chance to pinch all three points against Roberto Martínez's side.

Although the Blues followed that result up with a 2-0 triumph in the FA Cup at Bournemouth later that season, in terms of Premier League fixtures it was just one more draw and six losses plus a seventh defeat in the shape of the 4-1 EFL Cup drubbing when Frank Lampard made an unprecedented 11 changes.

With a 3-0 reversal following in the Premier League at the same venue just four days later, in Everton's final fixture before the mid-season break for the 2022 World Cup, the brace of heavy defeats started a downwards spiral in fortunes for the Londoner from which he could never recover.

Sean Dyche didn't fare any better at the Vitality and the following season, on 30 March 2024, substitute Beto thought he'd snatched a precious point – although it still wouldn't have been enough to halt their winless run between Christmas and Easter – only for captain Séamus Coleman to inexplicably deflect the ball into his own net in stoppage time to bring a 2-1 defeat.

Then, the following year, the 1-0 loss at Bournemouth on 4 January 2025, a result that left his side with just 17 points at the halfway point of the Premier League season, proved to be Dyche's final match as manager.

While the soon-to-depart boss and his players flew back, my *Liverpool Echo* colleague Joe Thomas and I, along with thousands of travelling supporters, had to negotiate the return leg of a 530-mile round trip in treacherous, snowstorm conditions.

So, along with all those beleaguered Blues who had trekked up and down a footballing 'Road to hell' for ten years, this was a watershed moment.

You do at least get a warm welcome from the groundstaff at this diminutive venue, located some three miles inland from Bournemouth Pier and the seafront, on the edge of town in Boscombe's leafy King's Park, who offer you a selection of chocolate biscuits on arrival.

But unlike the Wagon Wheel the author plumped for, there was nothing 'Jammie' about Everton's maiden three points here as, following on from their Old Trafford success, they produced another textbook away-win display.

For the first time all season, Michael Keane, who had been deputising so impressively for Jarrad Branthwaite, was unable to start due to a calf problem.

Therefore, Jake O'Brien, who had been deployed mostly on the right of defence since David Moyes came in, switched to centre-back, which in turn forced James Garner to leave his favoured central midfield position – on a night when the visitors were already without the suspended Idrissa Gueye – and fill in for the Irishman in the full-back berth.

Both excelled though, especially 6ft 6in O'Brien, who produced a colossal display at the heart of the backline to snuff out any threat from the Cherries and provide the Blues with the platform to deservedly hit the winning goal 12 minutes from the end.

Charly Alcaraz drove forward and picked out Jack Grealish, who had moved out from the wing to take up a central position and picking his spot from just outside the area, his right-footed shot beat Đorđe Petrović via a deflection from Bafodé Diakité.

The 30-year-old subsequently raced over to celebrate in that same corner where Barkley briefly thought he was being congratulated on securing a victory ten years earlier.

This time there was no sting in the tail and after having Moyes take to the field after the final whistle to put his arm around him, Grealish remarked, 'I love the manager to pieces,' also adding, 'I have scored two goals now this season, one was a tackle and one was a deflection, but I got hammered for years for not scoring so I am taking both of the goals.'

Grealish's comments had his gaffer on the back foot with the Glaswegian admitting, 'I don't know if I like that because players used to not like me.'

However, Kiernan Dewsbury-Hall, who excelled again in a deeper role, was also full of praise for his central midfield colleague Tim Iroegbunam, who bounced back from his Newcastle United horror show to walk a disciplinary tightrope for 65 minutes after picking up his fifth yellow card of the season that left him facing a one-game suspension.

As well as reiterating to me that he felt his most natural position is a box-to-box number eight, Dewsbury-Hall remarked of Iroegbunam, 'I said to Tim, I've never seen a lad make so many clean tackles on a yellow card in my life. He got a yellow card in the 25th minute and made eight perfect tackles after that. I said, fair play lad. You've got some *cojones* to be able to keep going in when you're on a yellow, but he reacted unbelievably today.'

*Line-up with player ratings:* Jordan Pickford 7; James Garner 7; Vitalii Mykolenko 7; James Tarkowski 8; Jake O'Brien 9; Tim Iroegbunam 7; Kiernan Dewsbury-Hall 8; Iliman Ndiaye 7; Charly Alcaraz 7 (Dwight McNeil 79); Jack Grealish 8; Thierno Barry 6 (Beto 79).

## Saturday, 6 December 2025: Everton 3 Nottingham Forest 0, Hill Dickinson Stadium
## Attendance: 52,501

There was no ghost of Christmas past haunting Everton in their first December fixture at Hill Dickinson Stadium when

Sean Dyche returned, the action on the pitch displaying a sharp contrast with David Moyes being back at the helm for almost a year, and the home fans were finally able to cheer a new hero.

Thierno Barry at long last got off the mark in a royal blue jersey and everyone wanted to wish him well. The relief on the striker's face after breaking his duck some 17 matches, 737 minutes and 19 shots following his £27m transfer from Villarreal was obvious. The Frenchman's team-mates congratulated him heartily, Moyes put his arm around him when he substituted the player and even the stadium staff joined in the congratulations.

As Barry walked down the tunnel following the final whistle, Iliman Ndiaye, who was several paces ahead and had set him up for the goal, pointed in his colleague's direction as Séamus Coleman offered the 23-year-old some words of encouragement before one of the suited and booted security staff made the frontman smile with a quip as he ushered him towards the home dressing room.

After falling behind to Newcastle after just 55 seconds in their previous home game, this time it was Everton who were quick off the mark.

Nottingham Forest right-back Nicolò Savona had already been booked for his first challenge of the match on Grealish when, with two minutes on the clock, Dewsbury-Hall exchanged passes with James Garner down the left wing, cut inside by working some space from Dan Ndoye and curled the ball into the six-yard box and ultimately into the net via a glancing header off Nikola Milenković for what was classed an own goal.

The Blues weathered not so much a storm but rather something of a light breeze from the East Midlanders, a period that would include an unnecessary off-the-ball incident when home skipper James Tarkowski used his torso to bump into Ndoye, an act that prompted Forest to lodge a complaint to the PGMOL.

It was a flashpoint that Dyche, who was given a warm round of applause by home supporters as he made his way in from the car park to the stadium's main entrance, referenced in his post-match press conference.

Making a joke about his microphone not working in the plush media theatre and looking at the bottles that are placed on the desk in front of managers for sponsorship reasons, he quipped, 'Maybe they spent the money on the drinks?'

He then complained, 'I said to big Tarky, just to be clear, and I respect him and like him as a bloke, how he got away with that in the first half, I don't know what's going on there.'

Bizarrely, Dyche baffled most observers, by, in his own words, 'really crying it in', with moans about the ball hitting referee Chris Kavanagh in the build-up to Everton's second goal in first-half stoppage time.

Regardless of gripes over the match official's supposed touch, which took place over 70 yards from the visitors' goal, it proved a decisive moment for both the Blues and their scorer.

Picking up the ball in a central position, just inside his own half, Iliman Ndiaye burst forwards and within seconds the break saw three Everton attackers against just one Forest defender, Milenković.

Charly Alcaraz, to Ndiaye's right, might have seemed the easier option, but instead Ndiaye rolled a pass to Barry on his left and for a player who had still been waiting to get off the mark, it was a cool finish that prolific former Blues Gary Lineker and Andrei Kanchelskis – both making their first visits to Hill Dickinson Stadium – would have approved of, and the outpouring of relief around the ground was palpable.

Forest's best chance of pulling a goal back in the second half came when Jordan Pickford, who had done well to save a low Elliot Anderson shot seconds before Everton had doubled their lead, failed to claim a cross and in a penalty box scramble, Tarkowski blocked an effort from Nicolás Domínguez.

Nottingham-born Dewsbury-Hall finally got the goal his efforts deserved on 80 minutes to seal the points as Forest struggled to clear Garner's inswinging corner from the left and Jake O'Brien knocked the ball out to his midfield colleague, who drove a right-footed shot through a mass of bodies to beat Matz Sels.

Having mentioned Tim Iroegbunam's *'cojones'* at Bournemouth four days earlier, Dewsbury-Hall was at it again in the mixed zone. Praising Barry, who had to wait until after the turn of the calendar year to net his first league goal for Basel before becoming a prolific scorer for the Swiss club, he said, 'I'm so happy for him. I think it's probably one of the loudest [cheers] you've heard the stadium all season, and he deserves that. The last five or so games, he's absolutely worked his nuts off for us, he works all the time, and you deserve good rewards when you work hard. Hopefully now that can kick-start him and he can go on and score as many as he wants.'

The 27-year-old had a glint in his eye when I asked him what happened when he found himself in an altercation with Forest captain Morgan Gibbs-White late on. He replied, 'I don't know, I mean, you know what it's like when the temperature gets a bit hot. It's all handbags. But look, I feel like if you play for this club, you've got to show a bit about you. It is what it is, but I enjoyed that.'

Evertonians did too.

***Line-up with player ratings:*** Jordan Pickford 7; Jake O'Brien 7; Vitalii Mykolenko 6; James Tarkowski 7; Michael Keane 7; James Garner 7; Kiernan Dewsbury-Hall 9; Iliman Ndiaye 7; Charly Alcaraz 6 (Dwight McNeil 73 6); Jack Grealish 6 (Tyler Dibling 85); Thierno Barry 7 (Beto 62 6).

## Saturday, 13 December 2025: Chelsea 2 Everton 0, Stamford Bridge
## Attendance: 39,552 (3,083 Everton)

After failing to win away at Arsenal, Chelsea, Liverpool or Manchester United during his first 11-year spell as Everton manager, David Moyes had enjoyed a breakthrough moment at Old Trafford some 20 days earlier, but once again the trip to this corner of west London proved a (Stamford) Bridge too far.

To be fair to Moyes, Everton's long wait for three points at Chelsea goes back further than him and even than the club's record-breaking trophy drought, which has now extended to 31 years.

You have to go back to 26 November 1994 for their last Premier League win there, courtesy of Paul Rideout's 39th-minute header past Dmitri Kharine in what was Joe Royle's first away game in charge.

The world was obviously very different back then with Baby D's 'Let Me Be Your Fantasy' at number one in the UK charts (it would eventually be knocked off top spot some three weeks later by East 17's Christmas smash 'Stay Another Day'). John Major was prime minister; Charles and Diana were still married. The first National Lottery draw had taken place the weekend before the Blues' triumph at Stamford Bridge while that month the *Daily Telegraph* became the first national newspaper in Britain to launch an online edition although only 600,000 people – little more than one per cent of the population – had access to the internet in their homes at this point.

In football terms, Chelsea's neighbours Fulham were languishing in the Football League's basement division, finishing three places below Preston North End, who had a certain centre-back called Moyes among their ranks, while other current Premier League clubs Bournemouth, Brentford and Brighton & Hove Albion were all in the third tier.

Some 11 of the 15 players Everton used in this game – Jake O'Brien, Vitalii Mykolenko, James Garner, Iliman Ndiaye, Kiernan Dewsbury-Hall, Jack Grealish, Thierno Barry, Tim Iroegbunam, Charly Alcaraz, Tyler Dibling and Beto – had not yet been born.

Just who has picked up three points in the Premier League at Stamford Bridge since? Well, Brighton and Sunderland earlier in 2025/26 for starters.

Although Chelsea went over four seasons unbeaten at home between 2004 and 2008 under José Mourinho and Avram Grant, and then again throughout the 2014/15 season during the Portuguese manager's second stint in charge, they have still suffered 80 home defeats in the competition since Everton's last victory.

While Enzo Maresca's side were reigning FIFA Club World Cup champions they were without a win in their previous four games while Moyes's men went into this fixture in fine form with victories in their previous two away from home and four successes from their previous five matches.

However, their plans were scuppered early on in the contest when their most consistent performer of the previous month, Dewsbury-Hall, a £25m summer signing from Chelsea, was forced off injured a mere 15 minutes into his Stamford Bridge return.

He had been relishing going back to his old stamping ground and when asked by the author about the prospect after his star performance against Nottingham Forest the previous weekend, he said, 'I had a great year there, winning two trophies, but of course I'm going there wanting to show what I can do for the opposition, and I'd be lying if I said I wasn't thinking about that and there's no reason why I can't.

'I'm probably feeling the best I've ever felt and the way I'm playing is up there with the best I've played. I'll be honest, I'm confident going against anyone in the Premier League at the moment and it's a nice place to be.'

It was such a shame then for the player and his team that Dewsbury-Hall was unable to show his previous employers what they were missing.

But Chelsea possess an embarrassment of riches in the attacking midfield areas that show why it was so hard for the former Leicester City man to hold down a regular place there. That was exemplified on 21 minutes when, after what had been one of Everton's best spells of the game, the hosts broke upfield.

Nobody could get between Idrissa Gueye and Michael Keane at Old Trafford but with the midfielder returning from suspension for this one match before heading to the Africa Cup of Nations with Senegal team-mate Iliman Ndiaye, Chelsea right-back Malo Gusto played a pinpoint pass to split the pair and Cole Palmer did the rest with a cool left-footed finish from just outside the six-yard box.

With England manager Thomas Tuchel watching in the stands, Grealish – who Moyes later revealed was nursing a hamstring issue – missed three decent chances to score while Ndiaye struck the foot of the post late on.

However, by that point the contest was out of sight with Gusto's decisive first-time strike with his left foot on the stroke of half-time having doubled Chelsea's lead after right-winger Pedro Neto had taken Mykolenko to the cleaners when one-on-one with the left-back to set him up.

Asked in his post-match press conference whether the defeat had been down to fine margins, Moyes baulked, 'Maybe a billion-pound difference? Possibly, you know what I mean?' He then added, 'I thought we played well today.'

Meanwhile, despite his side's return to winning ways, opposite number Maresca stunned reporters with his cryptic remarks.

The Italian, who subsequently departed the club on New Year's Day, said, 'The way the players want to learn has been fantastic and this is the reason why I praise them – because with so many problems, they are doing very well after a complicated week. Since I joined the club, the last 48 hours have been the worst because many people didn't support us.'

Asked what he meant, he responded, 'Worst 48 hours since I joined the club because people didn't support me and the team.'

Another curious response came in the mixed zone where James Garner – whose existing deal was due to expire at the end of the season – was asked about a new contract. The 24-year-old claimed, 'I haven't thought much about it, no. I am just touching in week in, week out.'

*Line-up with player ratings:* Jordan Pickford 5; Jake O'Brien 6; Vitalii Mykolenko 4; James Tarkowski 6; Michael Keane 6; Idrissa Gueye 5; James Garner 6 (Tim Iroegbunam 84); Iliman Ndiaye 7; Kiernan Dewsbury-Hall (Charly Alcaraz 15 5); Jack Grealish 6 (Tyler Dibling 84); Thierno Barry 6 (Beto 68 6).

## Saturday, 20 December 2025: Everton 0 Arsenal 1, Hill Dickinson Stadium
## Attendance: 52,513

There were two dramatic raisings in front of the South Stand as Everton faced Arsenal – one was sublime, but the next was ridiculous.

Before kick-off, fan group The 1878s produced their most spectacular showing yet.

Having found that the flags and banners that had helped the Grand Old Lady to put her best face on during her latter years were now dwarfed by the steep bank of almost 15,000 Evertonians in the 'Blue Wall', a giant tifo was produced for their inaugural display in the final fixture of the first calendar year at their new waterfront home.

An imposing rendering of the Everton Tower was hoisted aloft, complete with the 'On the banks of the Royal Blue Mersey' slogan (great minds think alike?), and the stage was set.

As David Moyes had remarked in his programme notes, 'It's a Saturday night under the lights, and I hope you can all make this place as noisy and ferocious as possible. We all want to see and hear this stadium in full voice and you fans making it as difficult as Goodison was for visiting teams to come.'

However, all that atmosphere was punctuated when Jake O'Brien gave away a needless penalty on 27 minutes with what proved to be the pivotal moment of the match. Just why the giant Irish defender was raising both his arms in the air to handle the ball from Declan Rice's corner when taking part in an aerial duel, only he will know.

Moyes was still fuming about the action the following week in his pre-match press conference for the trip to Burnley when he lamented, 'I was annoyed with Jake, I thought it was a really, unbelievably poor decision he made to put his arms up in the air.'

Referee Sam Barrott missed the incident in real time but was left with a straightforward decision to make when VAR official Michael Salisbury sent him to his pitchside monitor.

In a game of precious few chances, Viktor Gyökeres then smashed the resultant spot kick to Jordan Pickford's right with the England number one going the correct way but unable to keep out his emphatic effort. Afterwards, Pickford remarked, 'I always back myself to save a penalty, so I'm a bit disappointed.'

Leandro Trossard and Martin Zubimendi both hit the woodwork for Arsenal in the second half, but the main talking point from the game was yet another penalty decision not going Everton's way.

While there were no complaints over O'Brien, other than the reasoning behind what he did, given that he was bang to rights, the Blues looked like they should have had a spot kick of their own when William Saliba floored Barry in the area by kicking his foot.

The Premier League Match Centre's explanation merely remarked how the contact 'wasn't deemed sufficient for a penalty', but just 48 hours later, Fulham beat Nottingham Forest 1-0 thanks to a penalty converted by Raúl Jiménez after an almost carbon-copy challenge by Douglas Luiz on fellow Brazilian Kevin.

Moyes claimed watching that incident left him 'half choking' and added, 'It feels like certain clubs seem to get those decisions and other clubs don't – we seem to be on the latter side of that. They [Professional Game Match Officials Ltd, in charge of referees in England] don't make it easy. They will have conversations, but they don't want to because they find it very difficult to explain the decisions.'

However, it emerged on New Year's Eve that the Premier League's Key Match Incidents Panel had subsequently voted 3-2 that the on-field decision by Barrott not to give the foul on Barry was incorrect. They also voted 3-2 that video assistant referee Michael Salisbury should have sent the match official to the monitor to change his decision.

Three panel members noted, 'Saliba carelessly kicks Barry with no contact on the ball' and they felt it was a clear and obvious error, while two panellists supported the no-penalty call because 'there was not enough impact and a delayed reaction'.

Each KMI Panel is made up of five members and three are former players or coaches, plus there is one representative each from the Premier League and Professional Game Match Officials.

At least one person had some dignified words to say following Everton v Arsenal, but then it's easy to be magnanimous when you win.

Gunners boss Mikel Arteta, who, after being brought to Goodison Park by Moyes in January 2005, spent six and a half years in the Blues' midfield before being transferred to Arsenal, took it upon himself to praise his former club's new home.

The Basque said, 'Before I leave, guys, I want to congratulate everybody at this football club at Everton, everybody has contributed to building this amazing stadium, because it was incredible to witness. Not only the way they've done it, the atmosphere that they created, so as an ex-player and someone that supports this club, congratulations to all of them.'

*Line-up with player ratings:* Jordan Pickford 6; Jake O'Brien 4; Vitalii Mykolenko 6; James Tarkowski 7; Michael Keane 7; James Garner 7; Tim Iroegbunam 7; Dwight McNeil 6 (Tyler Dibling 75); Charly Alcaraz 4 (Merlin Röhl 75); Jack Grealish 6; Thierno Barry 6 (Beto 65 6).

## Saturday, 27 December 2025: Burnley 0 Everton 0, Turf Moor
## Attendance: 20,650 (2,450 Everton)

Badge check complete. No penalty.

Like thinking everyone who lives in the neighbouring county, rival city in the same region or even the next town down the road are all crazy, it's part of the English mindset to believe that the football team you support gets the thin end of the wedge when it comes to decisions from referees.

Evertonians are no different in this respect, but what they do have is an increasing portfolio of evidence to support their claims that they're getting a raw deal from officials.

Once the season was complete, Everton became the first Premier League team in seven years of VAR not to get an overturn in their favour, and they also finished joint-bottom of the VAR goals affected table as one of four clubs with a net score of minus four.

Hot on the heels of not being awarded that penalty against Arsenal, the Blues missed out again here. With just four minutes remaining the stalemate could have been broken when Burnley substitute Jaidon Anthony blocked a shot by Everton's Tyler Dibling with his arm.

The Premier League Match Centre vindicated the decision by stating, 'The referee's call of no penalty to Everton was checked and confirmed by VAR – with it deemed that Anthony's arm was in a justifiable position, with the ball coming from close proximity.'

Yet, in the Blues' first competitive game at Hill Dickinson Stadium against Brighton & Hove Albion the previous August, Kiernan Dewsbury-Hall conceded a penalty with the Premier League Match Centre declaring, 'The referee's call of penalty was checked and confirmed by VAR – with it deemed that Dewsbury-Hall had his arm raised and made his body unjustifiably bigger.' Replays have shown that Dewsbury-Hall was closer to the shot than Anthony.

After failing to remove the club who have played more English top-flight seasons than any other from the division despite an unprecedented brace of points deductions in the 2023/24 season for PSR breaches, perhaps Everton don't have many friends at the Premier League headquarters with their supporters continuing to boo the competition's anthem at every game?

It came as no surprise to Blues fans that the on-field referee at the centre of this incident was Craig Pawson given the number of controversial calls he's made when taking charge of their matches. Everton have won just six of their 33 fixtures when the Sheffield-born official has been the man in the middle and he's sent off Allan and Phil Jagielka in dubious circumstances.

He also failed to dismiss Ibrahima Konaté for what looked like a blatant second yellow card in a Merseyside derby at Anfield (opposition manager Jürgen Klopp responded by hastily substituting the player), a game in which he also awarded Liverpool a penalty for good measure.

In this post-Christmas pudding of a game though, the truth was that if the Blues had sneaked a late 1-0 win from the penalty spot then it would have just papered over the cracks for what was a poor display against a side that, until the previous weekend when they battled to a 1-1 draw at Bournemouth, had lost their previous seven matches.

Already without their other two first-choice attacking midfielders, Dewsbury-Hall and Ndiaye, Everton went to Burnley without Jack Grealish due to a virus. His absence presented Tyler Dibling, the club's most expensive summer signing, with the chance for just his second Premier League start since his move from Southampton and the 19-year-old produced an encouraging display.

Creativity was short in supply at both ends of the field though.

As the game started to get stretched in the second half, Beto, who was making his own first start since the 3-0 home defeat to Tottenham Hotspur over two months earlier, was denied as his audacious back-heel effort was turned around the post by Clarets goalkeeper Martin Dúbravka, who also did well to make a low save and deny the Guinea-Bissau international's replacement, Thierno Barry.

At the other end, Jacob Bruun Larsen should have done better with a shot that went over the bar while substitute Zian Flemming struck the foot of the post only for the flag to go up for offside.

Afterwards, David Moyes admitted that the contest had not been much of a spectacle, lamenting, 'I wouldn't have wanted to come and watch that myself.' He added, 'Missing Ili and missing Kiernan, we know we're losing creativity, and without Jack as well, that doesn't help, so it was always going to be a bit of a challenge. But I really hoped we would play much better than we did. That was probably as poor as we've played in some games. Our football wasn't good enough and lots of bits just weren't at the level I hoped they would be.'

For Tim Iroegbunam, the game marked his first consecutive 90 minutes since August 2024, and I asked him in the mixed zone about bouncing back from his struggles when being hooked against Newcastle a month earlier.

*Early sketches of Everton's new stadium, including ones on napkins, by architect Dan Meis*

*Bramley-Moore Dock on 25 February 2021, prior to its conversion to the site of the new stadium*

*A similar view of the completed Hill Dickinson Stadium on 19 April 2026*

*Dan Meis gestures to spectators ahead of Everton's first competitive game at Hill Dickinson Stadium, on 24 August 2025*

*Hill Dickinson Stadium looking south towards Liverpool city centre with views of the Royal Liver Building and both cathedrals*

*The author recording a podcast with New York Evertonians James Rogers, Stephen Neave and Michael Setterberg*

*New signing Thierno Barry goes for a stroll alongside Lake Michigan in Chicago with Iliman Ndiaye and Idrissa Gueye*

*The author recording a podcast with Atlanta Evertonians Christopher Harding, Bridget Bryson and her son Ben*

*Iliman Ndiaye scores the first goal in a competitive game at Hill Dickinson Stadium, against Brighton & Hove Albion*

*Jack Grealish celebrates scoring the first stoppage-time winner at Hill Dickinson Stadium, against Crystal Palace*

*The first major non-football event at Hill Dickinson Stadium as England face Australia in a rugby league international*

*Jordan Pickford tries to restrain Idrissa Gueye as he is sent off for slapping team-mate Michael Keane at Manchester United*

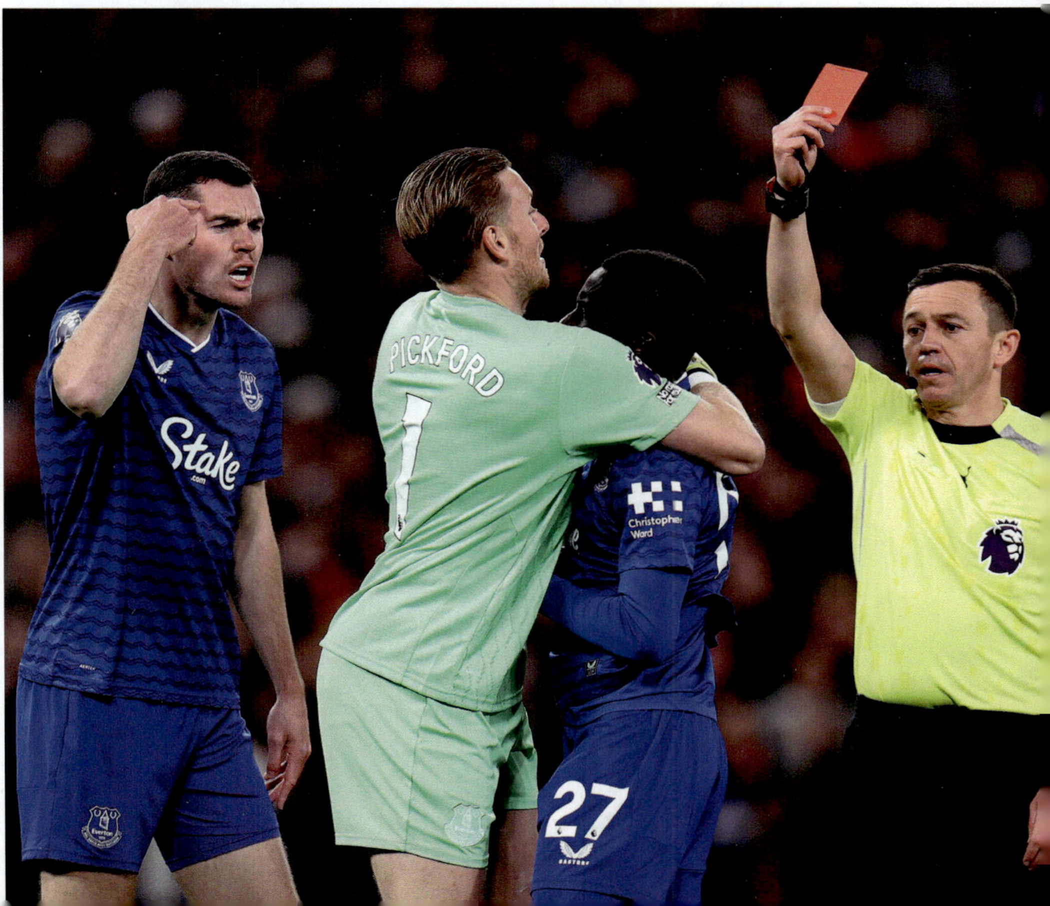

*Kiernan Dewsbury-Hall celebrates scoring the winner as ten-man Everton make history by triumphing at Old Trafford*

He said, 'I'd say the Newcastle game was definitely a bad day for me but obviously, you can have good games, you can have bad games. It's just about forgetting about it and just bouncing on and showing what you can do in the next game, and I happened to do that. I'm feeling good. I feel like I start to tire towards the end, so it's just about getting those fitness levels up so I can play really strong throughout the whole 90 minutes, but I think with more games that will come.'

*Line-up with player ratings:* Jordan Pickford 6; Jake O'Brien 7; Vitalii Mykolenko 6; James Tarkowski 6; Michael Keane 7; James Garner 7; Tim Iroegbunam 8; Tyler Dibling 7 (Nathan Patterson 89); Charly Alcaraz 6 (Merlin Röhl 69 6); Dwight McNeil 6; Beto 6 (Thierno Barry 69 6).

## Tuesday, 30 December 2025: Nottingham Forest 0 Everton 2, City Ground
## Attendance: 30,617 (3,048 Everton)

Everton were on cloud nine after this result as the figure matched their number of away wins under David Moyes in 2025.

This was a massive upsurge on the previous 12 months when the Blues triumphed just once on their travels, and that had come against an Ipswich Town side who had recorded back-to-back promotions before heading straight back down from the top flight.

Everton's nine away wins in 2025 – all in the Premier League – eclipsed their seven combined in the competition at Goodison Park and Hill Dickinson Stadium while matching the figure at both their previous and new home that year in all competitions.

The triumph at the City Ground, where the Blues hadn't been beaten since 16 September 1995, also ensured that they achieved a hat-trick of Premier League wins over the same opponent in a calendar year for only the third time with the previous couple of occasions both coming under Moyes against Manchester City in 2008 and 2010.

Of all the away-day victories, this was up among the most satisfying considering the circumstances in which it was achieved.

Everton were still unable to select any of their first-choice attacking midfield trio in the starting line-up – Jack Grealish would come on as a late substitute as he continued to shake off a virus – while Michael Keane, who had missed just the Bournemouth match all season, was injured, prompting Nathan Patterson to be handed his first start of the campaign.

Snapped up by Rafael Benítez for £12m just 12 days before the Spaniard was sacked, the arrival from Rangers was earmarked as the long-term successor for Séamus Coleman. However, whereas the man from Killybegs goes down as one of the great bargain buys with his fabled 60 grand fee, Patterson has seemingly not been fancied by the last three Blues bosses.

Whether it was Sean Dyche with Ben Godfrey or Jake O'Brien, under Moyes, Patterson found himself overlooked by team-mates who have been chosen out of position ahead of him while the club also tried to sign Kenny Tete from Fulham the previous summer before the Dutchman decided to accept improved terms at Craven Cottage.

Patterson's only previous start that season had been a hugely chastening experience playing for Everton's under-21s in their 5-1 EFL Trophy thrashing away to a League One Bradford City side managed by former Scotland international right-back Graham Alexander on 14 October.

Like Moyes, I was in the stands at Valley Parade – officially known as the University of Bradford Stadium these days for sponsorship reasons – reporting on the game for the *Liverpool Echo* and it was an excruciating watch.

Patterson, who was joined in Paul Tait's starting line-up by £20m man Dwight McNeil – who should have been running rings around third-tier opponents – and summer signing Adam Aznou, endured a nightmare as he diverted Stephen Humphrys' effort into his own net, almost put another one in, handled the ball on a rare foray forward and was shown a yellow card for good measure.

To add injury to insult as it were, the following week, Moyes revealed his fellow Glaswegian had picked up a plantar fascia tear in his foot in West Yorkshire and while he was sidelined with that, the club had decided to tidy up an issue with a hernia.

Despite his lack of previous outings though, Patterson, who had replaced Tyler Dibling in the 89th minute at Burnley three days earlier, hung in there, alongside deadline-day signing Merlin Röhl, who was making his first Premier League start full stop, coming in for another new injury victim, Charly Alcaraz, to begin the game behind restored striker Thierno Barry in the number ten role, and then replacing the Scot at right-back from the 72nd minute.

Although they were down to the bare bones, Everton produced a magnificent victory against adversity as they'd done on the last time they'd made a December trip to the City Ground two years earlier, starting the evening kick-off propping up the Premier League table following their initial ten-point deduction for a single PSR rule breach, only to triumph thanks to a spectacular strike from McNeil.

Against Dyche, the manager who had given him his professional breakthrough at Burnley and then been his gaffer again at Goodison Park, Rochdale-born McNeil this time turned provider when it came to opening the scoring – just as he had done for Abdoulaye Doucouré, moments after coming on in the Blues' previous visit on 12 April at a time when the hosts still had serious aspirations of qualifying for the Champions League.

With 19 minutes on the clock, McNeil, who had started on the left wing, popped up in the inside-right position to pick out a beautifully weighted through ball to James Garner, who fired a cool finish into the net.

While the rest of the away side were visibly jubilant, goalscorer Garner, who spent 18 months on loan at Nottingham Forest from Manchester United for the second half of 2020/21 and the whole of 2021/22 before sealing his switch back to his native Merseyside, consciously did not celebrate in front of the Trent End, who had applauded him before he took an earlier corner.

It was widely viewed as a respectful gesture from Garner, and the world has clearly moved on from when Mancunian Paul Power, who made 445 appearances for Manchester City, was similarly muted when netting his first goal for Everton against his previous employers at Maine Road on 29 November 1986, only to receive 'a rollicking' from manager Howard Kendall for his supposed lack of enthusiasm.

Nobody could accuse Garner of not being committed to the cause though as he ran the show in the East Midlands.

Although Forest would have 21 shots on the night, the Blues – with Jake O'Brien playing in his natural centre-back position alongside James Tarkowski – generally looked comfortable as they dug deep to keep them at arm's length.

The deserved away win was secured 11 minutes from the end as Barry doubled his Everton goal tally against the same opponents that he had broken his duck against earlier in the month.

Following a clever exchange of passes with Garner, the French striker, who revealed he'd been watching videos of the Blues' all-time leading scorer in the Premier League, Romelu Lukaku, ahead of the match, beat Brazilian keeper John Victor with a left-footed strike before – in Robin Hood's manor as well – delivering his bow and arrow celebration in front of the delirious away supporters.

Following the game, with his squad depleted, Moyes told Joe Thomas that it was 'more than likely' that Harrison Armstrong would be recalled early from his season-long loan at Preston

North End when the January transfer window opened, and the manager also hailed Garner's outstanding display: 'I think he's hugely developed as an individual. I think even when I came here, I still saw a bit of a boy and I think I now see someone who's turning into a really good leader as well, he is beginning to take a bit more responsibility and grow up and begin to start to act like a real midfield player.'

Captain Tarkowski concurred when I asked him about man of the match Garner, remarking, 'He can do absolutely everything – along with a few other players I think he's been a real standout performer. He's pretty much played every minute this season and you could see right until the very end he was sprinting around the pitch to win the ball back and finds the moment of quality to win us the game which is absolutely massive.'

***Line-up with player ratings:*** Jordan Pickford 7; Nathan Patterson 7 (Jack Grealish 72 7); Vitalii Mykolenko 7; James Tarkowski 8; Jake O'Brien 8; James Garner 9; Tim Iroegbunam 8; Tyler Dibling 7; Merlin Röhl 7; Dwight McNeil 7; Thierno Barry 8 (Beto 85).

12

# Previous plans – Peter Johnson bowled over

PETER JOHNSON dreamed big for Everton but ultimately most of his grand plans never came to fruition, including an ambitious vision to quit Goodison Park for a huge bowl of a new stadium.

By the mid-1990s, any post-Hillsborough clamour for Merseyside unity and a shared stadium had subsided and both the Blues and Reds were determined to go it alone, be it in ground redevelopment or moving to pastures new.

The Taylor Report, launched after the tragedy, called for all-seater stadiums which significantly reduced the respective capacities of Goodison Park and Anfield at the same time that attendances were on the rise again because of an increased interest in the game after the formation of the Premier League.

Liverpool would ultimately be able to redevelop by increasing their footprint on their existing site but with Goodison hemmed in on at least three sides, Everton looked to start afresh elsewhere.

The issue became a hot topic across the region and on 14 December 1996, the *Liverpool Echo* devoted a full page to letters on both sides of the debate. Gordon O'Rourke from Maghull wrote, 'At last, a forward-thinking, progressive board at Everton. A move to a new stadium is a must if we are to regain our place at the forefront of football.'

However, Edith Russell from Anfield implored, 'Goodison Park and Everton are my home and family. Leave it alone.'

John Thompson of Halewood warned, 'Goodison is outdated and, alone or in partnership, Everton have to move to a new stadium, or they too are in danger of becoming a great memory.'

Mr D. Connolly of Burscough was more wary and mocked the changes that Mr Johnson had already brought in, including experimenting with ditching *Z-Cars* for other run-out tunes and unveiling a new mascot called 'Dixie' who was a half man/half toffee. He declared, 'Mr Johnson should get real. This is not Middlesbrough, Sunderland or Derby County. This is EVERTON FC ... and unlike the aforementioned, it is steeped in history and its home is, and always should be, Goodison Park, Goodison Road, Liverpool 4.'

Six months later, when Everton hosted Chelsea in their final game of the season on 11 May 1997, fans voted on the issue having been presented with a glossy brochure which declared, 'It's your move – the choice is yours.'

A pen and ink illustration showed a large bowl-type 60,000-capacity stadium, bigger than any in the Premier League at the time, with ample parking on a spacious, open site.

Supporters were asked, 'Do you want to stay with poor facilities and obstructed views [illustrated by photographs of Goodison urinals and one of the Main Stand's chunky pillars] or enjoy an unhindered panorama of the ground?'

Johnson himself wrote to the fans in a grandiose letter in which he declared, 'When I became chairman of Everton Football Club, I made it be known that my ambition was to see this great club win the European Cup.'

Getting on to the matter at hand, he added, 'We have recently completed a feasibility study for the redevelopment of Goodison Park. Sadly, the study shows that this option is not viable. However, this means that we now have an opportunity to move to a purpose-built stadium just four miles away which boasts all the facilities that a club of Everton's status demands.'

The only thing was, it was never confirmed just where this location would be.

Kirkby Golf Course appeared to be the most likely option – an area that would prove hugely divisive a decade later – but other rumoured sites included Gillmoss and even the village of Cronton, which is closer to Widnes than Liverpool!

Some 30,000 brochures with voting slips on pre-paid cards were handed out to match-going fans and despite the lack of detail, 18,374 of respondents – approximately 84 per cent – said yes to leaving Goodison with 3,600 against.

A group called Goodison for Ever-ton raised concerns over Johnson's plans, hiring the architect responsible for the redevelopment of Twickenham, the home of English rugby union, to support their claims that Goodison could be transformed into a modern 50,000-capacity stadium on its existing site, but they needn't have worried because it remained a pipe dream.

Over a year on, as the Blues began the 1998/99 season, Johnson was still bullish about the project. In an interview with club magazine *The Evertonian*, he stated that the ground move plans were back on the agenda following the completion of a long-awaited feasibility study and its findings would be discussed by the board over the next couple of months before a final decision was made.

The Christmas hamper magnate claimed that the club had whittled down its search for suitable sites from ten to five and that all the remaining possibilities were within the city boundaries.

However, he had relinquished the chairmanship by the end of that calendar year after controversially selling star striker Duncan Ferguson to Newcastle United, according to manager Walter Smith, without his knowledge, and before 1999 was out he had sold his controlling stake in the club to Bill Kenwright.

# 13

# Villa thriller and a Scottish jig – January

EVERTON'S FIRST full calendar year playing at Hill Dickinson Stadium started with the arrival of a familiar face on 1 January.

As soon as the winter transfer window opened, homegrown hero Harrison Armstrong was recalled early from his season-long loan at Preston North End to help ease David Moyes's selection crisis.

The midfielder, who would turn 19 later in the month, had made 17 appearances, scoring one goal and providing one assist, to push Paul Heckingbottom's side to within a point of the Championship play-off places (without him they ended up in 14th).

**Sunday, 4 January 2026: Everton 2 Brentford 4, Hill Dickinson Stadium**
**Attendance: 52,004**

It's fair to say that 2026 did not start as Evertonians would have wanted in their new home as despite Beto and Thierno Barry both scoring in the same game for the first time, their efforts were overshadowed by the opposition's striker.

Many had kept saying that the Blues needed to spend big in order to acquire firepower that could be prolific at Premier

League level but while Brentford's hat-trick hero Igor Thiago was their record signing, at £30m he cost little more than the home pair who were acquired for around £27m apiece.

Making history by becoming the first player at Hill Dickinson Stadium to net a treble and take home the match ball, the Brazilian was enjoying a breakthrough season.

After starting out at Cruzeiro in his homeland, the Gama-born player's first port of call in European football came in Bulgaria with Ludogorets Razgrad. He then moved to Belgium to spend the 2023/24 season at Club Brugge before making his switch to England.

Thiago suffered an early setback when he picked up a meniscus injury on his debut in the Bees' 5-2 pre-season friendly win over AFC Wimbledon, and finally made his competitive bow as a 72nd-minute substitute on the club's final visit to Goodison Park, as Brentford earned a goalless draw on 23 November 2024 despite captain Christian Nørgaard being sent off after 41 minutes. It would be a frustrating campaign for him though as he only played more than 20 minutes once in his eight outings and failed to find the net.

Things would take off for Thiago in 2025/26 and he followed his hat-trick at Everton with a brace in the 3-0 home win over Sunderland in their next game three days later to take his tally to 16.

This ensured that before the first week of January was out he had set a new Premier League goalscoring record for a Brazilian in a season – overtaking the totals of Matheus Cunha (for Wolverhampton Wanderers in 2024/25), Gabriel Martinelli (for Arsenal in 2022/23) and Roberto Firmino (for Liverpool in 2017/18), who had each netted 15.

Although the Blues started brightly with a low shot by Dwight McNeil being turned around the post by Caoimhin Kelleher on four minutes, and James Tarkowski's goal-bound header from the resultant corner being cleared off the line by Thiago at the back post, having saved his side at one end to thwart the home captain the Brazilian would then punish him at the other.

Eleven minutes into the contest, Tarkowski gave the ball away cheaply when trying to pick out Tim Iroegbunam, and Brentford's Vitaly Janelt intercepted possession before lofting a cross towards Thiago, who slid in to score with a first-time finish from the edge of the six-yard box.

Everton needed a smart save by Jordan Pickford in first-half stoppage time to prevent the Brazilian from doubling his tally and given the lacklustre showing from his side in the first 45 minutes, David Moyes responded with a double switch at the interval, hooking McNeil and Tyler Dibling.

The change ensured the Blues played with two strikers after the break but while they both ended up netting, it's fair to say that the tactical alteration was not a success.

In the space of two calamitous minutes early in the second half, two further goals from the Londoners effectively ended the game as a contest.

Once again – despite all the height in their side – Everton failed to deal with a simple set-piece routine as captain Nathan Collins got between Tarkowski and Barry to head in Janelt's corner on 50 minutes.

Then, barely 60 seconds later, after Tim Iroegbunam's loose touch had sparked panic in the home ranks, Mikkel Damsgaard opened up the Blues' defence to pick out Kevin Schade, who took out Jake O'Brien with a clever spin and found the onrushing Thiago, who needed just two left-footed touches to knock the ball past Pickford without breaking his stride.

Six minutes after that, Everton pulled one back as Jack Grealish cut inside from the left and provided the first of his two assists that day with a right-footed cross that Beto headed in for his first goal since the 3-2 win at Wolverhampton Wanderers on 30 August.

There would be no rousing fightback though as, with the Blues pushing hard and committing bodies upfield, Brentford caught them with a devastating counter-attack on 88 minutes when Thiago picked up the ball just inside the hosts' half with only Pickford between himself and the goal.

While Pickford tried to narrow the angle as Tarkowski desperately attempted to rush back and help him, Thiago completed his hat-trick by calmly dinking the ball over the keeper's right shoulder.

Many had already left the stadium when Everton scored their second goal a minute into stoppage time as, popping up on the right, Grealish lofted a cross towards the back post for Barry to nod in.

Moyes admitted his alteration to go from 4-2-3-1 to 4-3-3 at the break did not go to plan. He said, 'We had to try and find another option at half-time and we felt that we would try and be as positive as we could. The game meant a lot to try to win it today, on the back of a good result in midweek. We didn't want to wait to 60 minutes or too late, so we tried and took the risk, but obviously it backfired.'

He wasn't happy with how his side played at the back though and added, 'We don't concede four goals too often, and I thought we conceded them in a really, really shabby manner today.'

Jake O'Brien, who had scored his first Everton goal to salvage a 1-1 draw in the sides' previous meeting at the Gtech Community Stadium in February 2025, concurred when I spoke to him. The Republic of Ireland international said, 'We gave away sloppy goals, didn't take our chances and let them into the game and they took their chances, so that's the difference. We've been down to the bare bones, but we can't use this as an excuse as we've got players coming in who are more than good enough and in the last two games they've shown they're good enough.'

*Line-up with player ratings:* Jordan Pickford 6; Jake O'Brien 6; Vitalii Mykolenko 5; James Tarkowski 4; Michael Keane 6; James Garner 7; Tim Iroegbunam 5 (Harrison Armstrong 77); Tyler Dibling 5 (Merlin Röhl 46 5); Dwight McNeil 5 (Beto 46, 7); Jack Grealish 7; Thierno Barry 7.

## Wednesday, 7 January 2026: Everton 1 Wolverhampton Wanderers 1, Hill Dickinson Stadium Attendance: 51,768

Somehow Everton saw themselves clinging on for a point at home to the Premier League's bottom club, having to play out nine minutes of stoppage time with just nine men after a chaotic double sending off late on, sparked by Michael Keane's dismissal.

This was for an act, which the author's old primary school headmistress used to do to celebrate young children's birthdays, deemed 'violent conduct'.

There is no way of denying that Keane, who went from hero to villain having fired the Blues ahead, tugged on Wolves striker Tolu Arokodare's hair when going up for a header.

However, was it really a 'violent' action that deserved a straight red card that came with a subsequent three-game suspension and was it deliberate? Everton certainly didn't think so and were furious when their appeal to get the ban overturned was rejected.

All appeared to be going well for the hosts when Keane fired them ahead on 17 minutes with his third goal of the season at Hill Dickinson Stadium.

Dwight McNeil's free kick was lofted towards James Tarkowski at the back post, but Wolves' attempted clearance only fell to Tim Iroegbunam on the edge of the area, whose shot into the ground fell to the feet of Keane, who fired it into the roof of the net with a predatory right-footed finish.

The Blues were unable to capitalise on their early dominance, a Keane header then striking the post, and with visiting boss Rob Edwards telling me in his post-match press conference that 'Everton were not as aggressive as I thought they'd have been', it came as no surprise when having gone up a gear in their play, the division's basement side levelled proceedings on 69 minutes.

Substitute Jørgen Strand Larsen, who had only entered the fray a couple of minutes earlier, picked up the ball inside the centre circle, turned and played a smart pass for Mateus Mané to run on to. The England under-18 prospect, who was born in Portugal but schooled at Rochdale's academy having moved to Manchester in 2016, calmly curled a right-footed shot from the edge of the area to beat Pickford.

Nobody could envisage what lay ahead in a bizarre end to the night though as the drama began in the 83rd minute.

At first, hardly anyone inside the ground, including referee Thomas Kirk, who was taking charge of just his second Premier League game, spotted anything untoward. However, eagle-eyed Chris Kavanagh, on VAR duty over 200 miles away at Stockley Park, flagged up Keane's action.

To say that the Greater Manchester official has 'previous' with Everton would be something of an understatement. As well as that penalty decision at Leeds in the first game of the season, what will be even more infuriating for the Blues when it comes to their quest for consistency is that Kavanagh was the on-duty video assistant referee assisting man in the middle Paul Tierney for the Rodri incident also discussed earlier.

Here are another four flashpoints when Kavanagh was the man in the middle:

*26 April 2025: Chelsea 1 Everton 0*

In Kavanagh's previous Blues game before the trip to Elland Road and with the score goalless at Stamford Bridge, home goalkeeper

Robert Sánchez wipes out Vitalii Mykolenko as the pair both go for a loose ball in the Chelsea area.

Kavanagh fails to award a penalty, but former refereeing chief Keith Hackett later says, 'The challenge by the goalkeeper is a clear reckless challenge and should have resulted in a penalty kick and yellow card. It amazes me that there is no intervention from VAR, who should have determined that the referee taking no action is a clear and obvious error. Poor officiating.'

*4 January 2024: Crystal Palace 0 Everton 0*

Playing in heavy rain on a wet Selhurst Park surface in an FA Cup third round tie, Dominic Calvert-Lewin is given his marching orders by Kavanagh for catching Nathaniel Clyne with a raised boot despite a free kick not being given in real time.

The overturned decision came on a night when Kavanagh was assisted by Craig Pawson as the main video assistant referee and Michael Salisbury as the support VAR, and despite them reaching their consensus after watching the incident back, the decision was then rescinded following an appeal by Everton.

*7 November 2021: Everton 0 Tottenham Hotspur 0*

Kavanagh's FA Cup assignment in south London saw him take charge of an Everton game for the first time in over two years. He spiced this stalemate up by awarding Everton a penalty when Richarlison went down under a challenge from Hugo Lloris, but then overturned his original decision following a review on the pitchside monitor, deeming that the visiting goalkeeper had got a fingertip on the ball. He also sent off Mason Holgate in stoppage time.

*1 March 2020: Everton 1 Manchester United 1*

Kavanagh showed another red card to Carlo Ancelotti after the final whistle when the Blues boss was furious with Calvert-

Lewin's last-minute winner against Manchester United being chalked off by VAR.

Gylfi Sigurðsson was deemed to be in an offside position, despite lying prostrate on the turf at the time.

***

Going back to the Wolves game, David Moyes offered no defence for Jack Grealish over the Blues' second sending off in stoppage time.

The on-loan star was dismissed due to two quickfire bookings for dissent, receiving his marching orders for sarcastically applauding the referee over a decision. This left the hosts on the back foot as Pickford saved them spectacularly in stoppage time, tipping a Hugo Bueno drive over the bar.

Moyes said, 'I didn't look for an apology. I just told him what I thought of him and that was it really. I didn't expect it. Probably the words I said to him were strong enough that he didn't need anything. He certainly let us all down with his sending off. We told him that after the game. And he was well told by the players inside the dressing room as well.

'But it can happen, you can get sent off. I thought he was stupid to applaud the referee, but we have actually seen other incidents [in which players mockingly applauded officials] which weren't sending offs or bookings or second yellow cards. So, there you go.'

The aftermath of the Keane incident brought a sharply contrasting response from Moyes though. Speaking a couple of days on in the embargo section of his pre-match press conference to preview the visit of Sunderland – when print journalists such as myself interview him after the live cameras have stopped rolling – he opened up about his disgust over the decision and subsequent rejection of Everton's appeal.

Moyes said, 'An experienced referee sent that young boy to the touchline monitor to make a decision on that. Well, let's be fair, most of the time you go to the screens, there's hardly ever an overturn [of the VAR official's recommendation]. What a position to put that young referee in. They should be ashamed of themselves, people at VAR, for what they've done.'

The Scot, who said he knew who the ex-players on the appeal panel were – which disappointed him further – insisted that Keane's action was not deliberate and indeed from a technical point of view, it 'nearly makes it impossible to be done'.

Moyes added, 'I don't think any of that was taken into consideration by the panel, or by the so-called experts who were saying that they were looking at it. I don't believe for a minute it was.'

*Line-up with player ratings:* Jordan Pickford 7; Jake O'Brien 6; Vitalii Mykolenko 6; James Tarkowski 5; Michael Keane 4; James Garner 7; Tim Iroegbunam 6; Harrison Armstrong 7 (Nathan Patterson 87); Dwight McNeil 6 (Merlin Röhl 90); Jack Grealish 4; Thierno Barry 5 (Beto 87).

## Saturday, 10 January 2026: Everton 1 Sunderland 1 (after extra time) 0-3 on penalties, Hill Dickinson Stadium
## Attendance: 51,588

There's always next time – Everton's record-breaking wait to end their trophy drought extended into a 32nd year as the Blues set a new unwanted first of failing to score a single penalty in a shoot-out.

After the damp squib that was the final FA Cup tie at Goodison Park – a tame 2-0 defeat to Bournemouth sandwiched between two fixtures that made the cut as a couple of late additions to *Spirit of the Blues,* the 4-0 romp against Leicester City and the 2-2 Merseyside derby draw, this was not how David Moyes's men would have wanted to start in the competition at Hill Dickinson Stadium.

However, with Iliman Ndiaye and Idrissa Gueye still on international duty with Senegal at the Africa Cup of Nations, the likes of Kiernan Dewsbury-Hall and Jarrad Branthwaite injured plus Michael Keane and Jack Grealish both suspended, the Blues were down to the bare bones.

Except they weren't even the Blues for this landmark occasion (well royal blue anyway), a decision that rankled with many supporters.

At 9am on matchday, just 195 minutes before the 12.15pm kick-off, Everton announced they'd be wearing a deep navy blue and pink 'fourth kit' for their historic first tie by the Mersey in world football's oldest competition.

On X, the account for the Everton Fan Advisory Board wrote, 'We've had lots ask if the FAB was consulted about the decision not to play in royal blue at home today. We were not. We think this decision, and the timing of launching a new range so soon after Christmas, are unacceptable. We will be raising both matters with the club.'

The Everton Fans Forum replied to that message with, 'To confirm the fans forum were also not consulted regarding the change of home strip in today's game vs Sunderland.'

Everton's deal with Castore curiously required them to produce four pieces of playing kit per season, and with Premier League rules restricting clubs to three the Blues chose to wear the fourth kit in the FA Cup, but their performance on the pitch also proved to be distinctly off-colour.

The game also represented a first for the Beesley family. Given my job covering Everton matches in a full-time professional capacity home and away, opportunities are few and far between to accompany my own children to games as I am usually working on them.

Therefore, when the Blues were handed a home draw, a chance presented itself for me to take my three daughters to their first game at Hill Dickinson Stadium.

While it was a new experience for them – only my youngest Jemima had actually stepped inside the ground before, on that sneak preview of the stadium tours – it was also a change for myself, with a day off from the press box.

From my first Everton game with my father and his work colleague 'Billy from Maghull', a 2-1 comeback win over Charlton Athletic on 10 February 1990, all my trips to Goodison Park for the subsequent 16 years were as a supporter before I started attending in a media capacity.

At the Blues' new home, it's the other way around and this was my inaugural opportunity to be there as a fan again, but along with all the other home spectators in another sell-out crowd there was precious little to cheer about.

A Sunderland outfit who just a couple of months earlier had looked game but technically limited when the sides met at the Stadium of Light were stroking the ball around like a Mackem Manchester City in the first half and were good value for their lead.

Half an hour into the contest, Everton were guilty of allowing the ball to bounce in their area from a long throw-in and Enzo Le Fée, a French midfielder snapped up from the Friedkin Group-owned Roma the previous January, fired Sunderland ahead with a curling shot.

Playing against his former club, Jordan Pickford was forced to make a couple of outstanding saves late in the first half to keep the hosts in the contest before the break, from a Nordi Mukiele volley and a long-range strike by Romaine Mundle.

The Blues improved in the second half, but it still took a dubious 89th-minute penalty to hand them a lifeline.

Substitute Adam Aznou, making his long-awaited debut following his summer switch from Bayern Munich, went down under a Trai Hume challenge and referee John Brooks pointed to the spot, but despite Sunderland's complaints an absence of VAR meant the decision stood.

James Garner, who was Everton's most accomplished outfield player on a difficult day, held his nerve with a low strike to Robin Roefs's left beyond the Dutchman's reach despite the keeper going the correct way.

However, after no further scoring in extra time, Roefs would prove to be the Black Cats' lucky charm in the subsequent shoot-out.

I was called upon to give a quick explanation of the rules to my kids, and unfortunately my caveat of 'both teams take five kicks each, unless one team misses them all and they lose 3-0' came to fruition.

Despite the Blues, who had also introduced Eli Campbell as a substitute for his debut in extra time, holding the dual advantage of going first and taking the kicks at their end in front of the huge bank of more than 14,000 Evertonians in the South Stand, they transpired to have all three of their efforts saved.

Garner led the way, but hit his shot towards the opposite corner to his earlier goal and was denied by Roefs. While he could be deemed to be unfortunate, the tame side-foot efforts of Thierno Barry and Beto were lamentable.

With England, Pickford has saved at least one penalty in every shoot-out he's been involved with, but there were no such heroics on this occasion as confidently taken strikes by Le Fée, Granit Xhaka and Luke O'Nien saw the Wearsiders through to the fourth round.

Afterwards, David Moyes lamented, 'I don't think you blame anybody when you lose a penalty shoot-out, it's something that can happen, the goalkeeper is there to make saves. Someone has to win a penalty shoot-out and someone has to lose it, but I do think there is a way to win it and a way to lose it. I didn't think the way we lost it today was the right way in the taking of it.'

***Line-up with player ratings (by Connor O'Neill):*** Jordan Pickford 7; Nathan Patterson 6 (Reece Welch 115); Vitalii Mykolenko 5 (Elijah Campbell 104 5); James Tarkowski 6; Jake O'Brien 6; James Garner 7; Merlin Röhl 4 (Adam Aznou 86 7); Tyler Dibling 4 (Thierno Barry 74 4); Harrison Armstrong 8; Dwight McNeil 5; Beto 4.

***

It was a backhanded compliment to Everton's most successful side of the mid-1980s that because they excelled through the perfect balance of their line-up, they were often dubbed 'the team with no stars', but in the dugout they boasted someone who bore an uncanny resemblance to one of television's most famous faces of the era.

Physio John Clinkard, who died aged 71 in the early hours of 16 January 2026 after a brave battle with cancer, was, to borrow another cultural reference from the time, the 'spitting image' of actor Tom Selleck, who played the title role in the American crime drama television series *Magnum, P.I.* with his height, rugged good looks and, of course, trademark moustache that was so in vogue back then.

He was such a convincing lookalike that when brewers Whitbread opened their Magnum Wine Bar at the Briars Hall Hotel in Lathom near Skelmersdale, Clinkard, complete with white tuxedo and bow tie, was hired to head the launch, adopting the role of the TV sleuth.

The likes of Neville Southall, Derek Mountfield, Alan Harper, Kevin Richardson, Neil Pointon, Paul Power, Ian Snodin and Paul Wilkinson all sported a 'tache at the Blues around this period, and even Kevin Ratcliffe and Howard Kendall adopted the look briefly, but nobody quite rocked the facial fuzz in the manner of Clinkard, who got to join the squad when they sang 'Here We Go' on *Wogan*.

Everton legend Peter Reid, who, like Clinkard, was at the club as they won two league championships, an FA Cup and the European Cup Winners' Cup, said, 'I am devastated to hear of Clinks' passing. What a man! All the players loved him and trusted him completely when he was with us. He was a brilliant character, and I'll always remember him with great affection. My thoughts are with Steph [John's wife] and all his family.'

### Sunday 18 January 2026: Aston Villa 0 Everton 1, Villa Park
### Attendance: 42,770 (3,979 Everton)

It's said that the darkest hour is just before dawn and following Everton's hat-trick of disappointments at Hill Dickinson Stadium, they pulled off arguably their best win of the season to take their total of away successes into double figures since David Moyes returned.

Aston Villa, who were bidding to go back up to second in the table, had won their previous 11 home matches, and the Blues had not won any of their previous 13 Premier League encounters against the West Midlands outfit since they were promoted in 2019, a sequence that had included nine defeats.

Joe Thomas and I were just grateful to have made it into Villa Park to witness this momentous occasion.

Having made our way past the Ozzy Osbourne tribute mural, an interesting juxtaposition next to the classic Holte End facade – the notoriously hell-raising 'Prince of Darkness' and heavy metal music pioneer who co-founded Black Sabbath died just 17 days after his Back to the Beginning farewell concert at Villa Park on 5 July 2025 – we were initially denied access to the ground.

It seemed as though our accreditation request was missing but after a fraught period of several minutes in which we feared we might have to take in the action on Sky Sports in a nearby hostelry, a series of frantic phone calls and emails being sent by the *Echo*'s head of sport Paul Wheelock ensured we were free to take our places with seats in the press box still thankfully available for us at this late stage.

Along with almost 4,000 travelling Evertonians, we were treated to another slick display on their travels from Moyes's men and what was Thierno Barry's most polished performance to date.

Merlin Röhl, who also produced what was his most promising display so far, almost put the visitors ahead after just 11 seconds when from a Barry knockdown he struck a shot against the foot of Emiliano Martínez's right-hand post to be denied what would have been the fastest goal of the season.

This was the 216th league meeting between the teams – the most in English domestic history – and although the victory extended Everton's record of 77 league wins against a single opponent, this latest success had been a long time in coming – almost a decade in fact – going back to a 3-1 triumph under Roberto Martínez on 1 March 2016.

The Blues had already had the ball in the Villa net in the first half through a Jake O'Brien header, only for the Irishman to be denied for the second time in the season by a team-mate, this time Harrison Armstrong, being offside when James Garner put the cross in.

A day shy of his 19th birthday, though, Armstrong was also one of the visitors' most polished performers with his smart passing.

Although Evann Guessand, who had come on as an 18th-minute substitute when home captain John McGinn was forced off early, struck the crossbar with a header late in the first half, Everton were good value for their winner in the 59th minute, keeping Unai Emery's side at arm's length.

A poor touch from centre-back Pau Torres enabled Dwight McNeil to curl in a shot that Martínez could only parry and Barry netted the only goal of the game with a delicate dinked shot over the keeper, displaying the kind of subtlety and confidence in his finishing lacking in his early months at the club.

Jordan Pickford showed his class with an impressive save to tip a Morgan Rogers effort over the bar to hold on for the three points, but this was another classic away success.

Afterwards, David Moyes described Barry's finish as 'exquisite', and a piece of 'brilliant improvisation'. On the 23-year-old's development since he signed, the Scot added, 'I think that to be a centre-forward in the Premier League is probably, well it is, it is the toughest job. If you look at the money we could be spending on some other centre-forwards, it doesn't always guarantee that it's going to work. So, we're the same, we've bought at a lower level, hoping that we can build him up.'

Speaking of works in progress, Röhl told Patrick Boyland of The Athletic and myself in the mixed zone, 'I'm on my own here, so it's maybe a little bit of a change that you're in a different country, trying to learn the language, trying to fit in, trying to understand the Scousers! But I'm doing everything to adapt, trying to get in some words that the Scousers are using.'

The strides he had made were displayed by his ability to use humour outside of his native tongue after we'd finished as he remarked 'sound interview' when walking off.

*Line-up with player ratings:* Jordan Pickford 8; Nathan Patterson 8; Vitalii Mykolenko 8; James Tarkowski 8; Jake O'Brien 8; James Garner 8; Merlin Röhl 8; Dwight McNeil 7; Harrison Armstrong 8; Jack Grealish 7; Thierno Barry 9 (Beto 83).

***

A few minutes after the full-time whistle sounded at Villa Park, 1,800 miles south of Birmingham in Rabat, Idrissa Gueye and Iliman Ndiaye, who had been away for seven matches, were both playing for Senegal in the Africa Cup of Nations Final against hosts Morocco.

That night, Hill Dickinson Stadium would be lit up green and gold to celebrate the Blues duo's triumph, but the path to getting their hands on the trophy was far from straightforward as their country's success was marred by controversy after they came back to win having earlier left the pitch in protest.

The game appeared to be heading for a stalemate but then sprang into life in stoppage time. First, on 92 minutes, Senegal thought they were ahead when Ismaïla Sarr nodded the ball in from close range after Abdoulaye Seck slammed a header of his own against the crossbar. However, referee Jean-Jacques Ndala judged that Seck had fouled Achraf Hakimi in the build-up, despite the replay suggesting that there was minimal contact on the Paris Saint-Germain defender.

Then, Morocco's Brahim Díaz tumbled to the turf following a tussle with El Hadji Malick Diouf from a corner in the fifth minute of stoppage time and while the man in the middle from DR Congo initially looked like he would allow play to continue, he was later persuaded to consult his monitor by VAR assistant Pierre Atcho of Gabon.

Ndala was subsequently surrounded by members of both teams' coaching staffs as well as their players, with pushes and shoves clearly visible throughout the process.

The Stade Prince Moulay Abdallah Stadium erupted when the referee pointed to the penalty spot, booking Diouf and Sarr on his way to the box. The awarding of the spot kick sparked intense protests from the Senegal players, but the madness was only just beginning.

In a shocking twist, Senegal head coach Pape Thiaw appeared to call his players off the pitch in response to the controversial call.

There was then a delay of over 15 minutes before the Senegalese players returned to the pitch but with the opportunity to hand his nation the AFCON title for the first time in 50 years, Real Madrid man Díaz dispatched a tame 'Panenka' penalty that proved a simple save for ex-Chelsea keeper Edouard Mendy, with Ndala immediately blowing for full time.

Senegal's tactics ultimately paid off, though, as four minutes into extra time Pape Gueye struck the winning goal for them as he fired in a stunning shot off the crossbar. However, their antics came under fire from FIFA president Gianni Infantino.

Although the Italian, who handed US President Donald Trump a newly created 'FIFA Peace Prize' at the previous month's draw for this summer's World Cup finals, congratulated the Lions of Teranga for their victory, he also issued the following warning in an Instagram post, 'Unfortunately, we also witnessed unacceptable scenes on the field and in the stands – we strongly condemn the behaviour of some "supporters" as well as some Senegalese players and technical staff members.

'It is unacceptable to leave the field of play in this manner, and equally, violence cannot be tolerated in our sport, it is simply not right. We must always respect the decisions taken by the match officials on and off the field of play. Teams must compete on the pitch and within the laws of the game, because anything less puts the very essence of football at risk.

'It is also the responsibility of teams and players to act responsibly and set the right example for fans in the stadiums and millions watching around the world. The ugly scenes witnessed today must be condemned and never repeated.'

Gueye and Ndiaye would both be given a hero's welcome by team-mates and staff alike when they returned to Finch Farm the following Friday, with David Moyes, quipping he'd shouted at them through the window of his office, 'What kept you getting back?'

The canteen at the club's Halewood base was decorated with a Senegal theme, including flags and balloons, plus images of Gueye and Ndiaye on television screens and posters, as shown in a video shared by Thierno Barry on Instagram which brutally starts with a close-up of Moroccan international Adam Aznou looking glum and shaking his head.

Although the 19-year-old was not part of the squad for the tournament, he has been capped three times with his French team-mate including a caption on the footage saying, 'Okay my friend?' complete with an emoji of the Moroccan flag.

Despite the party atmosphere, Aznou wasn't the only member of the Blues squad down in the dumps.

A mere 48 hours after he played the full 90 minutes of the impressive victory over Aston Villa, it was confirmed that Jack Grealish had suffered a major injury blow.

Speculation was rife about the prognosis but supporters feared the worst when the 30-year-old took to Instagram to display a post to his 8.4 million followers showing a blue broken heart emoji.

The full extent of the setback would not be confirmed for another eight days until Moyes's pre-match press conference to preview Everton's trip to Brighton, when he admitted that Grealish was probably going to need surgery for a stress fracture that was likely to keep him out for the remainder of the season.

The week also brought a much greater loss too as Everton mourned their legendary right-back Tommy Wright, who died aged 81 on 20 January 2026.

George Best, one of the most incredibly gifted creative football talents the British Isles has ever produced, is reputed to have declared that Wright was his most difficult opponent.

Wright, who was born in Norris Green on 21 October 1944, was a one-club man who won the FA Cup with Everton in 1966 and the league championship in 1970.

In his book, *Money Can't Buy Us Love: Everton in the 1960s*, Gavin Buckland says of Wright, 'Joining the club as an apprentice forward, the local-born player replaced the injured Alex Parker during the 1964/65 season, eventually making 374 appearances, all but three at full-back, a club record for the position that was only broken by Leighton Baines in 2017.

'Wright was very much an athletic modern full-back, accomplished both as a defender and an attacking threat, providing a stream of crosses for Joe Royle in particular.

'Wright, with Ray Wilson, formed possibly the club's most accomplished full-back pairing, as well as winning 11 caps for England from 1968–70 when competition for places in the national team was at its peak.

'Strong – but fair – in the tackle, the defender hardly missed a game until, like others, injuries started to strike after the 1970 title victory, and a knee problem ended his Everton career at the age of just 29 in 1973.'

On handing Wright his Everton Giant award in 2016, Joe Royle told him, 'I've got to say, a lot of people earn awards in football Tom, but this has never ever been more deserved mate. I've said before, you're still the best right-back that I was ever fortunate to play with. I can go further than that mate, I've been watching Everton a long time, and you're still the best I've seen in a blue shirt, with a lot of internationals around you, you're still the best pal.'

A modest Wright simply replied, 'Thank you very much – this award makes me very proud to be an Evertonian.'

Meanwhile, James Garner's long-running contract 'saga' finally came to an end on 23 January when it was announced that he'd signed a new deal.

When the Birkenhead-born player had returned to Merseyside in an initial £9m move from Manchester United on 1 September 2022, it was stated that he had penned a four-year agreement up until the summer of 2026.

However, as David Moyes had revealed earlier in the season, there was a clause that enabled Everton to extend by another year. It was understood that this was based on Garner playing quite a substantial number of games for the Blues in order to kick in though.

While given that he had become a regular under Moyes that wouldn't be an issue if he stayed fit – it could have only taken an untimely injury for him to have potentially ended up leaving on a free transfer if new terms had not been agreed.

Considering that Moyes had been championing his player for an England call-up for most of the campaign, finalising an improved package up until 2030 felt right for all parties.

Garner said, 'I've seen the progress we've made recently, now I want to be part of that progress and get us back to where the club deserves to be. I feel like I'm now a part of the club and I'm hoping to be a part of it for a long time. I've got family members who are all Evertonians, so I know exactly the passion and what it means to play for such a massive football club like this.'

For his part, Moyes added, 'Jimmy is a player who has developed hugely during his time at Everton. He's taking on more responsibility and we're now seeing a really important midfielder, with the versatility to play in other positions, as well as someone who is turning into a leader for us.'

## Monday, 26 January 2026: Everton 1 Leeds United 1, Hill Dickinson Stadium
## Attendance: 51,979

All the talk going into this match surrounded Leeds centre-forward Dominic Calvert-Lewin, who was returning to face his previous club for the first time.

But in the end the Yorkshireman drew a blank, while it was Thierno Barry, the player now tasked with leading the line for Everton, who grabbed his fourth goal in five starts.

There have been many figures at the Blues, whether players or managers alike, who have divided opinion among the fanbase, and Calvert-Lewin is right up there.

Like Iliman Ndiaye, who as a young Blade got his breakthrough at Hyde United, Calvert-Lewin was loaned out by Sheffield United to make his debut in senior football at a non-league club in Tameside, in his case Stalybridge Celtic.

Just 17 at the time, Calvert-Lewin would net six goals in five games for the Conference North side, but within 20 minutes of his debut he was smashed in the face by an elbow. He recalled, 'I had a big black eye and went to A&E that night. That was my first taste of it and they said to me, "Welcome to non-league football."'

By the time Calvert-Lewin was snapped up by the Blues he had still only played 11 League One matches for the Blades without scoring, but for a fee of just £1.5m on 31 August 2016 he proved to be one of the most astute signings by the club's first director of football, Steve Walsh.

The following summer, he scored the winning goal for England against Venezuela in the Under-20 World Cup Final in South Korea.

However, despite coming off the bench to also find the net in a Europa League qualifier in Slovakia against MFK Ružomberok in the previous match, Ronald Koeman infamously started the 2017/18 Premier League season by deploying Calvert-Lewin as a right wing-back for their 1-0 home win over Stoke City.

While many of Carlo Ancelotti's stellar successes as a coach have been put down to his ability to massage the egos of *galácticos*, rather than for tactical innovations, it was the legendary Italian who got the best out of Calvert-Lewin during his time in charge at Goodison Park.

Telling the player to stay within the six-yard box and focus on first-time finishes like his prolific former protege Filippo Inzaghi, Ancelotti got the Sheffield-born player to net 29 goals in 18 months, including a career-high 21 in the 2020/21 season, and he also scored on his international debut for England, a 3-0 win over Wales on 8 October 2020, under his watch.

However, after 'Don Carlo' had defected back to Real Madrid, Calvert-Lewin's scoring totals for his final four seasons on Merseyside were five, two, eight, and three, and that's just not good enough for someone wearing the coveted number nine shirt and being deployed as Everton's first-choice striker. With his contract expiring, the 28-year-old chose to leave as a free agent in the summer of 2025.

As I wrote at the time, Calvert-Lewin finished with an almost identical record to Duncan Ferguson, with both men playing 273 games and the Scot scoring one more goal (72). Both delivered big headed goals in front of the Gwladys Street against Liverpool, plus Manchester United for Ferguson and Crystal Palace for Calvert-Lewin, but each struggled with consistency and fitness, so will Everton history judge Dom as kindly as Dunc, I wonder?

Revived following his move back across the Pennines, despite Ancelotti-esque eyebrows being raised that he'd not landed a move to one of the several bigger clubs he'd been linked to, Calvert-Lewin had already netted nine goals for Leeds by the time he faced the Blues at Hill Dickinson Stadium.

With Everton severely below par, the visitors bossed the first half and their ten shots before the break was their highest tally in a Premier League away game since the opening 45 minutes at Newcastle on 17 September 2021; it was also the most any team had produced in a single half at Everton's new home.

Despite their dominance, Leeds only led 1-0 at the interval thanks to James Justin's first Premier League goal for them on 28 minutes, a left-footed finish at the back post after the hosts had failed to deal with a low right-wing cross from Anton Stach.

As away boss Daniel Farke would lament after the game, 'We had so many chances. Dominic probably had the best chance and should have scored with an opportunity to bury them.'

Moyes would ring the changes at half-time, making a double substitution and introducing a couple of previously hamstrung stars, Kiernan Dewsbury-Hall – who had missed the previous seven games – and Jarrad Branthwaite for what was his first competitive outing for eight months since the final game at Goodison in May 2025.

The pair both contributed to a revived display after the break and Branthwaite instantly brought a new dimension. Combining his colossal physical presence through his muscular 6ft 5in frame with an assuredness in possession, the Cumbrian proved he's a Rolls-Royce of a player with an ability to carry the ball out from the back and find team-mates further up the pitch in a manner that the other defenders at Everton – and indeed the entire division – are not capable of.

He ended the night with 100 per cent accuracy when it came to averaging the most successful passes into the final third over 90 minutes for a Premier League centre-back that week.

The equaliser came from an unlikely source though as Idrissa Gueye, who before kick-off posed for photographs with Iliman Ndiaye and fans representatives displaying a banner proclaiming 'Our kings of Africa' following their AFCON success, popped up on the right wing on 76 minutes.

He put in a low cross for Barry – who had earlier been denied by Leeds keeper Karl Darlow with an outside-of-the-foot effort – to this time crash into the roof of the net.

There was still time for Gueye to rattle the crossbar while an inviting opening fell to substitute Tyler Dibling, but he chose to cross when he probably should have shot.

However, having been so bad in the first half, with his team booed off, Moyes admitted he'd been forced to turn to his bench earlier than he'd have liked to.

He said, 'We were really poor in the first half, and it was very difficult to put your finger on why and how, because we were set up for the game and realised how big a game it was for ourselves. But in the second half we got more control, controlled them better than we had in the first half and in the end got a goal from it.

'My plan was not to use Jarrad as early or Kiernan, because Jarrad's probably not played for eight months and Kiernan could have probably played 45 minutes, but the idea was not to. So, it wasn't as if these boys on the bench could play, they couldn't, but I thought they made a big difference when they came on.'

*Line-up with player ratings:* Jordan Pickford 6; Nathan Patterson 6 (Tyler Dibling 71 6); Vitalii Mykolenko 5; James Tarkowski 6; Jake O'Brien 6; Idrissa Gueye 8; James Garner 6; Dwight McNeil 5 (Kiernan Dewsbury-Hall 46 7); Harrison Armstrong 6 (Jarrad Branthwaite 46 7); Iliman Ndiaye 7; Thierno Barry 7 (Beto 89).

## Saturday, 31 January 2026: Brighton & Hove Albion 1 Everton 1, Amex Stadium
## Attendance: 31,419 (3,000 Everton)

It was a moment of pure joy and although it would land David Moyes a one-match touchline ban, it was also a heartwarming scene that instantly became one of the defining images of Everton's 2025/26 season and secured a place on the cover of this book.

The Blues were seconds away from defeat at Brighton when birthday boy Beto, who was turning 28, fired them level to earn a share of the spoils with his 97th-minute equaliser.

While the substitute and his team-mates piled into the maniacal away end at the Amex Stadium where Evertonians on their longest away day of the campaign erupted in raucous fashion, Moyes enjoyed his own personal celebration.

The man who had been the youngest manager in the Premier League when he was first appointed at Goodison Park as a 38-year-old in 2002 was now the division's elder statesman and coming up against the latest baby of the bunch, Fabian Hürzeler, who is his junior by almost 30 years.

However, for a few glorious seconds at least, the decades melted away from Moyes's face as he took to the turf to treat us to an impromptu solo Scottish jig.

He was shown a yellow card for encroaching on to the playing surface by referee Chris Kavanagh, whose past record in Everton matches has already come under scrutiny in this chapter, and he hit out at the decision in his post-match press conference.

Moyes said, 'Who wants to see managers booked for celebrating? I don't think I'd have danced down if the goal was in the 55th minute, but it means they [the officials] have got nothing about them at all, no thoughts about what football means to the managers without absolutely just saying "no, you just can't step outside that line or I'm going to book you". Fucking sad, isn't it? Fucking sad. I'm still shaking my head.'

Asked if he'd repeat his actions in the future, Moyes replied, 'I bloody will do it again. Actually, I think if I'd been a bit more mobile, I might have done a knee slide. See, that would have only got me a yellow as well, so I might as well have gone the whole hog!'

Football management is the job that millions of us who follow the game think we can do, but in reality, even for people like myself, who for many years have spoken regularly to those who work in the Premier League, have no real understanding of when it comes to the magnitude of the task and the pressures these men are under.

It's even more the case now as we live in a world where, because technology brings us so many things straight away at the touch of a button, many fans naively expect similarly instant results with their football teams.

Like their players, they might be handsomely paid for reaching the top of their lucrative profession, but in a job where results will always be the barometer, and the only certainty is that you'll get the sack somewhere along the line, the demands of the position are incomprehensible for everyone other than the small, select band of brothers who have stepped into their shoes.

Moyes returned to Everton just 24 days after the Friedkin Group had completed their takeover of the club, but previous owner Farhad Moshiri churned through eight managers in as many years.

Only Sir Alex Ferguson at Manchester United and Arsène Wenger at Arsenal have now taken charge of more Premier League games than Moyes, who moved above Howard Kendall in 2025/26 when it came to total matches in charge of Everton, and if he remains in place he is due to overhaul Harry Catterick in top spot during the 2026/27 season.

While he elusively still hasn't won silverware with the Blues, he is by far their most consistent boss of the Premier League era, having steered them to nine top-eight finishes in his first spell in charge, including a peak of fourth in 2004/05.

With Joe Royle delivering the club's last major trophy, the FA Cup in 1995, but only lasting one full season in charge, and Roberto Martínez enjoying Everton's highest Premier League points haul in his first year – 72 – but then flattering to deceive with what was arguably a stronger squad than even Moyes possessed, you could even make a convincing case to say that the Scot is the only man to have managed the Blues effectively over a prolonged period in modern times.

Yet he was still getting pelters from the armchair 'experts' for his team selection in this game on the Sussex coast.

For the first time in the season, Moyes had all four of his centre-backs available to him, and with Vitalii Mykolenko pulling out injured on the eve of the match, he started with the full quartet as Jake O'Brien played in the right-back role where he'd been for prolonged periods since the manager's arrival, while Jarrad Branthwaite made his first start of the campaign at left-back in place of the Ukraine international.

Once again, Everton found themselves on the back foot in the first half, but they kept Brighton at arm's length and had enjoyed the better of the chances after the break, two of the best falling to Kiernan Dewsbury-Hall on his first start since returning from injury, before the hosts took the lead against the run of play on 73 minutes.

Yasin Ayari played a low right-wing cross into the visitors' penalty area, and the defence was caught cold by Charalampos Kostoulas's dummy that enabled Pascal Groß to nip between James Tarkowski and Jake O'Brien to smartly sweep the ball past Jordan Pickford.

Defeat would have been cruel on the Blues though and they kept on plugging away, right until the end before securing their deserved last-gasp equaliser.

With whistles ringing out from many of the home fans, substitute Charly Alcaraz found James Garner on the right wing who took a touch before lofting a cross into the penalty area. Brighton captain Lewis Dunk's headed interception only fell to the feet of O'Brien – who had swapped to left-back following Nathan Patterson's 89th-minute introduction – and although Bart Verbruggen parried his shot, Beto was on hand to slam in the rebound with a left-footed finish from inside the six-yard box.

In opposition boss Hürzeler's native Germany they have a phrase for a defence of four centre-backs – *Viererketter aus Innenverteidigern* – a big term for a big set of players, so I was in search of some key figures in the mixed zone after the game.

I'd seen varying reports of what James Tarkowski's official height was with some sources saying he was 6ft 1in. However, given that's my height and he seemed taller than me when I've looked him in the eye in many an interview, I plucked up the courage to ask him about such vital statistics.

The captain insisted he's '6ft 3in with big studs on', but finding himself in the unusual position of being the shortest member of the backline, he admitted it was something of a new experience for him: 'I think Keano is probably a bit taller than me, he's got a long neck. The other two are giants, aren't they? It must be the first time in history that two full-backs have been taller than the two centre-backs!

'Myko went down injured, so we had to adjust. Four centre-halves went across the back four, but Jarrad and Jake are more than capable of playing high.'

When it came to late hero Beto, the Mancunian added, 'He is open for feedback, open for a bit of criticism. He just works his hardest to improve and get better, so it's great for him to get a moment like that.'

*Line-up with player ratings:* Jordan Pickford 7; Jake O'Brien 7; Jarrad Branthwaite 7 (Nathan Patterson 89 7); James Tarkowski 7; Michael Keane 7; Idrissa Gueye 6 (Tim Iroegbunam 80 6); James Garner 7; Harrison Armstrong 7 (Tyler Dibling 80 6); Kiernan Dewsbury-Hall 7 (Charly Alcaraz 80 7); Iliman Ndiaye 6; Thierno Barry 6 (Beto 89 8).

14

# Cottage pied plus Toon raiders – February

WITH JACK Grealish sidelined, Everton finally went back into the transfer market as for the second consecutive winter window their only acquisition came on deadline day in the shape of a loan move.

For most of January and as recently as his pre-match press conference for the trip to Brighton, David Moyes was telling reporters that while Everton were on the lookout for new signings, 'I would say it's probably less likely than likely.'

Grealish's crushing injury blow added impetus to their search though and little over 24 hours later when speaking at the Amex Stadium after his side's last-gasp draw, the 62-year-old revealed he was hopeful as the club explored a move for Chelsea's Tyrique George.

Like the Blues' previous signing from Stamford Bridge, Kiernan Dewsbury-Hall, who had arrived for £25m the previous August, George had been used regularly by Enzo Maresca in the triumphant UEFA Conference League campaign in 2024/25, if not so much in the Premier League.

Brought up in Selsdon, south London, he'd been at Chelsea since under-eight level with half of his appearances in the previous season coming in European matches, although he remained on the bench for the 4-1 win over Real Betis in the final, unlike Dewsbury-Hall, who came on as an 80th-minute substitute and provided the assist for Jadon Sancho to net the team's third goal three minutes later.

George was also in the matchday squad but unused when Chelsea defeated Champions League winners Paris Saint-Germain 3-0 in the FIFA Club World Cup Final, and footage showed him passing the opportunity to shake US President Donald Trump's hand after he'd received his medal from FIFA chief Gianni Infantino.

Turning 20 a mere two days after his switch to Merseyside, George was first included in Chelsea's senior matchday squad for their 6-0 mauling of Sean Dyche's Everton on 15 April 2024 and his loan move included an option for a permanent transfer in the summer.

On joining, the player said, 'I'm really excited to be here and to enjoy this massive club, I just can't wait to get started. The fans here are exceptional, I know Evertonians are really passionate. They like hard work – and that's what I'm going to show, I want to be exciting and I want to impress them.

'The gaffer – David Moyes – was another reason I wanted to join. He's an amazing manager who has coached so many players, like Wayne Rooney, and players like that.'

One player who was supposed to be moving in the opposite direction between Liverpool and London on transfer deadline day of the winter window was Dwight McNeil, whose proposed loan to Crystal Palace with an obligation to buy for £20m collapsed at the 11th hour.

McNeil's partner Megan Sharpley took to social media to question the integrity of the football industry soon afterwards. Writing on Instagram, she said, 'Tonight, and the last 48 hours, have broken my heart to see how the football world you love so much can be so cruel to you. To have something promised to you,

you have been dragged along an emotional rollercoaster, and to be toyed with until the final minute.

'To have four-and-a-half years of your life promised to you, travelling, medicals, agreements made ... promises made. To have prepared to move your entire life, our lives 100s of miles away in the space of a few hours.

'For it to be torn away from you at the last second, with absolutely no explanation. Going from everything to radio silence, no phone call, no communication and be left, broken-hearted with nothing but confusion, has hurt more than I can say.'

Speaking in his pre-match press conference to preview Everton's game at Fulham, their first subsequent fixture, Moyes revealed that McNeil had been to see him a couple of times since but insisted 'there's no problem at all' when it came to his own relationship with the player.

Moyes chose not to elaborate on the reasons for the deal not going through but remarked, 'I can tell you 100 per cent it was nothing to do with Everton Football Club, that's for sure.'

One topic he did open up on was the situation facing his most expensive signing of the summer, Tyler Dibling, when asked how he would feel if he was the £35m purchase from Southampton, seeing the Blues snap up another attacking wide player less than two weeks older than him in George when he was struggling for minutes on the pitch.

Moyes replied, 'I'd be thinking I'd better get my finger out and show the manager what I was really all about. The one thing Tyler has got on his side is that he is young and he is quite a quiet boy who might take more time to settle in. *Might.* But he needs to show when he gets the opportunities.

'I think there are just little glimpses of him just beginning to get angry, which I am enjoying, just beginning to be someone who might have to get angry in order to show what he wants to do.'

## Saturday, 7 February 2026: Fulham 1 Everton 2, Craven Cottage

## Attendance: 27,155 (2,701 Everton)

'Cottage Pied' was the simple two-word response from Everton's account on X following this game after what seemed like a bizarre and unnecessary use of the headline 'Toffees Crumble' by their Fulham counterparts in an advertisement to sell tickets for the game the previous month.

It was a strange statement to make from London's oldest club, who have never won a major trophy in their 147-year existence, especially given that Everton also came from behind to beat them 3-1 in the corresponding fixture the season before.

The Blues in contrast need no such promotions, though, given that they're selling out their 52,769-capacity Hill Dickinson Stadium every week, a venue where they also strolled to a 2-0 success against Marco Silva's side in their most recent prior meeting the previous November.

Unlike the misguided members of Fulham's marketing department, the staff we meet at Craven Cottage are some of the friendliest on the Premier League circuit.

Everything is all very nice in this well-heeled corner of the capital, perhaps *too* nice. Maybe that's one of the reasons they've never lifted major silverware?

Unlike Everton on the banks of the Mersey, the football almost seems secondary in many ways in this quaint spot by the Thames.

Certainly, that appears to be the case with many of the patrons in the club's new Riverside Stand, who like Fulham's players were distinctly sluggish in the second half with thousands of spectators returning to their seats from the corporate hospitality at a leisurely pace long after the action on the pitch had resumed.

Someone who was there for the duration, watching with intent at the top of the stand though was David Moyes, who was serving a one-match touchline ban following his on-field encroachment at Brighton a week earlier.

With Séamus Coleman alongside him, Moyes had to make do with a bird's-eye view of proceedings. He admitted he'd have preferred to have been closer to the action, but when assessing the luxurious surroundings, quipped, 'It even has a pool on the roof. I had a wee swim when I was up there!'

The tide was certainly against his team in the first half.

With Jarrad Branthwaite having played 135 minutes in the space of six days following his return from an eight-month lay-off after undergoing an operation to cure a hamstring injury, Moyes restored the fit-again Vitalii Mykolenko at left-back.

Fulham took the lead on 18 minutes when the Ukraine international unfortunately put the ball into his own net.

Loose touches from former Blue Alex Iwobi and Michael Keane in the area saw the ball fall to Ryan Sessegnon, who put a chance on a plate for Raúl Jiménez at the back post. The Mexican's shot was kept out by a smart reaction save by Jordan Pickford, but the rebound ricocheted off Mykolenko's body and into the goal.

The Cottagers almost doubled their lead from their next attack less than two minutes later only for Samuel Chukwueze's shot to be turned around the post by Pickford's fingertips.

After that, Emile Smith Rowe rattled the Everton crossbar with a curling shot from the edge of the area, an act that was repeated from distance by Chukwueze just before the interval.

Fulham would be punished for their profligacy though, leaving Marco Silva to lament, 'We should have scored four more goals and killed the game and decided it in the first half ... you have to be clinical at the level we are playing.'

Indeed, at the midway point of the second half, Moyes sent down instructions to make a double substitution that helped change the momentum of the game and achieve a feat that Silva never managed during his 18 months in charge at Goodison Park – coming from behind to win in the Premier League.

With 75 minutes on the clock, Mykolenko redeemed himself for his earlier error as he marauded forward, shrugging off a challenge from Fulham captain Joachim Andersen, and picked out Kiernan Dewsbury-Hall with a low delivery that the midfielder swept into the net through a first-time left-footed finish without breaking his stride.

The comeback was complete with seven minutes remaining as Dewsbury-Hall curled in an inswinging left-footed corner from the right wing and with Jake O'Brien standing in front of him, home keeper Bernd Leno made a hash of dealing with the delivery and punched the ball into his own net.

This proved to be a tale of two keepers with Pickford's heroics in sharp contrast to Leno's gaffe.

Like with the 'Toffees Crumble' jibe, pride comes before a fall and there's a word in the Fulham keeper's native German tongue, *Schadenfreude*, which is apt given that when he was once asked where Pickford ranked among his top ten goalkeepers, he thought it was funny to say 20th.

Afterwards, I asked Dewsbury-Hall about what his plan was with the match-winning corner and it turned out that Everton were the beneficiaries of his late change of heart.

He said, 'I was going to go short because they only had one man out and it was me and Ili [Ndiaye], so, I thought, "We've got a chance here to create something." I don't know why, but at the last minute I just saw it and I thought, "Let me stick it on the keeper." We know they can be vulnerable from set pieces and luckily it went in.'

*Line-up with player ratings:* Jordan Pickford 8; Jake O'Brien 7; Vitalii Mykolenko 6 (Jarrad Branthwaite 85); James Tarkowski 6; Michael Keane 7; Idrissa Gueye 6; James Garner 7; Harrison Armstrong 6

(Tyrique George 68 7); Kiernan Dewsbury-Hall 8 (Tim Iroegbunam 94); Iliman Ndiaye 6; Thierno Barry 6 (Beto 68 7).

***

The day before Everton hosted Bournemouth, Jack Grealish posted a fitness update following an operation on his left foot after picking up a stress fracture.

Sharing an image of him sat in a hospital bed giving a double 'thumbs up' gesture while his foot was up in plaster with the toes peeping out, the 30-year-old remarked, 'Didn't want the season to end like this but that's football, gutted. Surgery done and now all focus on getting back fit. I know for sure I will come back fitter, stronger and better than before.'

## Tuesday, 10 February 2026: Everton 1 Bournemouth 2, Hill Dickinson Stadium Attendance: 50,196

Talk about being given a taste of your own medicine.

Just four days after Everton had capitalised on Fulham's profligacy at Craven Cottage, Bournemouth did exactly the same to them to secure what for a long time seemed like an unlikely comeback victory.

For the first time at Hill Dickinson Stadium, there were significant gaps of empty seats in the stands as Bournemouth did not take their full allocation for what was a 530-mile round trip on a Tuesday night.

While the Cherries might not have a sizeable fanbase, and not one willing to travel in numbers when there was an inconvenient kick-off time, with the Blues supposedly going into their new home with around 30,000 people on their season ticket waiting list, the block of spaces was not a great look.

But it was the gaps in the home defence throughout what proved to be a spectacular eight-minute capitulation in the second half, conceding twice and then having a man sent off, that left David Moyes fuming though.

A brace of misses from Thierno Barry would end up costing Everton dearly as the hosts failed to capitalise on being in the ascendancy.

With half an hour gone and the game being played in slippery conditions because of the rain, James Garner tested Đorđe Petrović from distance with a 30-yard free kick. Bournemouth's Serbia international goalkeeper duly spilled the shot but despite reacting sharply to the rebound, Barry fired wide with a first-time left-footed shot.

Moyes's men found a breakthrough on 42 minutes when Jarrad Branthwaite won the ball from teenage Brazilian winger Rayan on the edge of the visitors' area and his raw opponent needlessly chopped him down for a penalty which Iliman Ndiaye expertly converted, low to Petrović's right, beyond the keeper's reach.

That should have been the cue for Everton to go on and win the game as they then piled on the pressure early in the second half.

Kiernan Dewsbury-Hall saw a shot headed over the bar by James Hill just moments after Barry had been denied by a block from the same player after being fed by Ndiaye, who had intercepted a slack pass out by Petrović.

In truth, it had been a poor delivery by Ndiaye but that wasn't the case the next time the Blues surged forward when the Senegal international delivered an inviting chance on a plate for Barry with a low delivery to feet only for Álex Jiménez to get his body in the way; in truth, a Premier League calibre striker should have given him no chance.

The next ten minutes saw Bournemouth rally strongly though and Moyes had already spotted the danger so had substitutes Beto and Harrison Armstrong primed when the visitors equalised just after the hour.

Finding himself in a defensive position, Ndiaye probably wasn't expecting Cherries left-back Adrien Truffert to cut inside and deliver a cross on his right foot but that's what he did, finding Rayan, who scored emphatically with a back-post header.

Despite Rayan's tender years, and that earlier rash challenge to concede the spot kick, it looked like men against boys as he devoured Vitalii Mykolenko in the aerial duel to level proceedings.

Almost six months younger than Tyler Dibling, who operates in a similar position, the Rio de Janeiro-born prospect, snapped up from hometown club Vasco da Gama for £24.7m the previous month as a replacement for Antoine Semenyo who joined Manchester City for £65m, became only the third teenager to have a goal contribution in his first three Premier League matches.

Having provided an assist on his debut against Wolverhampton Wanderers and then a goal against Aston Villa, Rayan joined an exclusive club also containing Robbie Keane in 1999 plus Anthony Martial in 2015 and would finish the season being called up for Carlo Ancelotti's Brazil World Cup squad.

Just three minutes later Bournemouth were ahead through another header as Alex Scott floated a free kick from deep into the Everton area which Hill headed sideways into the path of Amine Adli, who nodded them in front.

The dramatic collapse was complete five minutes after that as Eli Junior Kroupie opened up the home defence with a through ball to Adli, who was taken out by Jake O'Brien. Referee Andy Madley deemed the Republic of Ireland international to have committed a professional foul and he was shown a straight red card.

Despite their numerical disadvantage, the Blues had another chance to go level late on when Branthwaite headed over from Garner's free kick and it was another home defeat.

Bournemouth manager Andoni Iraola, who would replace Arne Slot at Liverpool at the end of the season, admitted that his side probably didn't deserve to win and remarked, 'I'm happy with the result. To be honest, I don't think this has been our best performance, but football is like this. We were playing very well until the red card. I think it has probably simplified Everton's game. We haven't played well, 11 against ten.'

But while the Basque boss was able to be magnanimous, his opposite number Moyes was barely able to conceal his frustration in what was a generally monosyllabic three-minute post-match press conference.

Refusing to point the finger of blame, he insisted, 'The players are doing a great job here, we just didn't have quite enough tonight.'

In the build-up to Bournemouth's second goal, Enes Ünal missed the ball but was clearly offside and attempting to play it, a set of circumstances with Armstrong that had led to Everton having O'Brien's goal disallowed at Aston Villa the previous month.

Asked whether he had any issue with that call, Moyes simply said, 'Referees are making their decisions, so we have to go with what they say.'

On O'Brien's challenge on Adli, Moyes was asked how it compared to Marc Guéhi's pull on Mohamed Salah when Manchester City faced Liverpool two days earlier, a decision that, to the anger of Slot, did not lead to the defender being sent off. He responded, 'No opinion on it, no opinion on referees any more.'

***Line-up with player ratings:*** Jordan Pickford 6; Jake O'Brien 4; Vitalii Mykolenko 4 (Michael Keane 92); James Tarkowski 5; Jarrad Branthwaite 6; Idrissa Gueye 5; James Garner 7; Iliman Ndiaye 7; Kiernan Dewsbury-Hall 6; Tyrique George 5 (Harrison Armstrong 62 5); Thierno Barry 4 (Beto 62 5).

***

At least Moyes wasn't at as low an ebb as Sean Dyche after Everton's away game with Bournemouth 13 months earlier which proved to be his last in charge as Blues boss.

Later that week though, the man who held the reins at Burnley for almost a decade was getting sacked again after just 114 days in charge at Nottingham Forest.

Following a goalless draw at home to Wolverhampton Wanderers that left the East Midlands outfit three points above the relegation places with 12 games remaining, Forest announced at 12.31am on 12 February – three hours after the final whistle – that Dyche had been 'relieved' of his duties.

Curiously, trigger-happy owner Evangelos Marinakis then turned to Vítor Pereira, sacked by Wolves on 2 November a mere 45 days after signing a new three-year deal at Molineux, with his winless side rock bottom of the Premier League table having taken two points from their first ten matches, to be Forest's fourth 'permanent' manager of the season.

The Portuguese coach, who was dismissed by Forest on 30 June, remains infamous at Everton having conducted a toe-curling interview on Sky Sports News which made for 'car crash television' as he tried to make his case to land the Goodison Park hot seat in January 2022.

His televised telephone conversation lasted for over 20 minutes and you could tell that Sky were trying to milk this golden opportunity of getting a Premier League managerial candidate on the blower for all it was worth (Frank Lampard would ultimately replace Rafael Benítez).

The circus plummeted to new depths when a phone was heard ringing in the background and Pereira was asked if it was Everton, to which he replied, 'No!'

For his part, Dyche broke his silence on his Forest dismissal the following month when speaking to renowned football journalist Henry Winter on podcast *The Football Boardroom*.

Hinting that 'keyboard warriors' contributed to his exit and the record during his tenure would have placed the team 12th in the Premier League, he said, 'People come out with these stories about how "we're this club". You go, "No, you're not. You've had one good season in 30-odd."'

In the same interview, Dyche spoke about Everton's 1-0 win over Bournemouth on 28 May 2023, when with their Premier League status on the line for the third time going into the final day of the season they avoided what would have been a first relegation in 72 years by a single Abdoulaye Doucouré goal despite posting the lowest equivalent points total in their history.

Recalling the build-up to the crucial fixture, he said it was, 'A turgid week that, you know. We were down to brass tacks, we had injuries everywhere, we had players – who will remain nameless – who didn't want to play, almost.'

Crucially, that word *almost* seems to be doing a lot of heavy lifting, but then so were the Blues' loyal but long-suffering supporters that day.

Dyche added, 'I've never heard a louder stadium than that ever in my career and I've been in football all my life. The noise of that moment [Doucouré's goal] was incredible, and the final whistle, they're two things I'll never take away from my career and that's those two moments at Everton. It was unbelievable. The power, the sheer volume, it was almost shaking you, you know what I mean? I can feel it now.'

## Monday, 23 February 2026: Everton 0 Manchester United 1, Hill Dickinson Stadium
## Attendance: 52,326

With Manchester United having ambitious plans to replace Old Trafford – which has long had the largest capacity of any club ground in England – with a 100,000-capacity stadium that would be the biggest in the United Kingdom, this visit to the Mersey brought Everton's new home in front of lots of interested eyes from down the East Lancs Road.

Like Goodison Park several decades earlier, the so-called 'Theatre of Dreams' is now counting the cost of going first and once being streets ahead of its rivals but then standing still for too long and allowing others to overtake them.

United's dominance in the early years of the Premier League era saw them develop Old Trafford into an impressive fortress, but a generation on and compared to 21st-century newbuilds, it's now looking badly dated.

The infamous waterfall feature from the leaky roof that plays up each time there's a frequent Mancunian shower has proven to be a repeated embarrassment for one of the world's richest clubs – at least Accrington Stanley could plead poverty when my laptop was destroyed at their ground in pre-season.

Missing out on being a host venue for the 2028 European Championship – a tournament in which Hill Dickinson Stadium will stage five matches – to Manchester City's Etihad Stadium must also have been a wake-up call.

However, at the time of writing it remains to be seen whether the bold vision for a £2bn, 370-acre regeneration project comes to fruition, although the club revealed on 8 July the planned location of their proposed future home, just 350 metres north west of Old Trafford.

After all, it appears to be in stark contrast to the parsimonious manner Sir Jim Ratcliffe has been widely criticised for when it comes to running the club on a daily basis, with hundreds of staff having been made redundant.

Plenty of their own fans have branded United a 'circus' under the current regime, and detractors of the unusual designs that the Red Devils have drawn up claim it looks like a big top.

One interested visitor, witnessing the ground for the first time, who gave Hill Dickinson Stadium his seal of approval was the *Daily Mail*'s chief sports writer Oliver Holt, whose attendance at the fixture enabled him to rejoin the coveted '92 club' of having been to every Premier League and Football League venue and revise his rankings.

Edgeley Park – the ground that lost its pub quiz teaser status as being the closest to the Mersey through the building of Hill Dickinson Stadium – remains unabashedly at number one for the Stockport County fan.

However, the Blues' new home comes in at number three on Holt's list (behind another of Everton's former grounds that will remain unnamed here) with Goodison Park having previously been placed ninth.

The journalist started his career at the *Liverpool Echo* and had previously remarked that he loved Goodison because of its 'fierce, fierce intensity' and claimed it was 'the most authentic stadium and passionate crowd in the top flight'.

He said of Hill Dickinson Stadium, 'I loved everything about it, from its setting on the banks of the Mersey, at the heart of the city's dock culture, which is such a critical component of Liverpool's heritage, to its vertiginous stands and its community feel. It still feels like Everton. It doesn't feel as if the club has been deracinated by its move, as West Ham has been by the change to the London Stadium.

'Everton now has a stadium that is one of the city's great landmarks, the first thing visitors to the city see when they sail in on the cruise ships that visit Liverpool from all over the world. Even more than the Tottenham Hotspur Stadium, Everton's ground is a standard-bearer for the new generation of English stadiums.'

On the pitch, there was no home win to mark the occasion though as despite the Blues' 1-0 triumph in the reverse fixture at Old Trafford, with Ruben Amorim having been replaced by Michael Carrick, United, who extended their unbeaten run in the Premier League to ten matches, were now a very different animal.

With Jake O'Brien – who is a natural centre-back anyway but has played predominantly at right-back for David Moyes – suspended and Vitalii Mykolenko having struggled against Bournemouth, Everton named a starting line-up without any natural full-backs.

James Garner filled in at right-back while centre-half Jarrad Branthwaite switched to left-back as he'd done for the 1-1 draw at Brighton less than a month earlier, when Moyes deployed four central defenders.

There was drama in the opening seconds when United captain Bruno Fernandes knocked the ball back to his keeper Senne Lammens from the kick-off but while the Belgian's subsequent clearance was closed down by Thierno Barry, who could have scored one of the quickest goals in Premier League history, the ball ricocheted closer to the corner flag than the net.

A frantic start then saw a shot by Amad Diallo hacked off the goal line by Blues captain James Tarkowski, but for long periods this contest became a war of attrition.

Everton went even closer in the first minute of the second half as Harrison Armstrong should have scored his first goal for the club but when picked out by Kiernan Dewsbury-Hall on the left side of the area, the teenager's tame effort was too close to Lammens.

Ultimately, it was through trying to win the game that the Blues were beaten as they were caught out on the counter-attack by United in devastating fashion on 71 minutes.

Harry Maguire headed out Idrissa Gueye's right-wing cross and a cushioned touch from substitute Benjamin Šeško to Luke Shaw displayed the level of quality that would catch Moyes's men out. Shaw in turn found Matheus Cunha, whose pinpoint diagonal ball upfield ripped open Everton's defence.

Michael Keane was left one-on-one with Bryan Mbeumo and with nobody else back for the hosts as Tarkowski was outpaced by Šeško, the Slovenian international netted the only goal of the game with a decisive sweeping finish from 12 yards; the three attacking protagonists had been acquired the previous summer for a combined outlay of over £200m.

There was still time for Keane to test Lammens with a thunderous left-footed strike from outside the area that was tipped over the bar while, when in a similar position to his goal, Šeško this time took too many touches and Jordan Pickford was able to block his effort.

Speaking in his post-match press conference, Moyes referred to United's transfer outlay proving decisive, 'I thought we were probably, certainly in the second half, the more likely team to score. But we couldn't get the goal. It's the quality ... the quality which costs big money.'

Although winning plaudits for his display, Lammens described Everton's corner routines of putting as many players as they could around him and floating the ball into the middle of his box as 'over the top'.

In turn, Garner admitted, 'We were just trying to get in and around the goalkeeper and cause as much chaos as possible.'

*Line-up with player ratings:* Jordan Pickford 6; James Garner 7; Jarrad Branthwaite 6; James Tarkowski 7; Michael Keane 5; Idrissa Gueye 5; Tim Iroegbunam 7 (Beto 79 6); Iliman Ndiaye 5; Kiernan Dewsbury-Hall 6; Harrison Armstrong 6 (Tyrique George 72 6); Thierno Barry 6 (Beto 62 5).

## Saturday, 28 February 2026: Newcastle United 2 Everton 3, St James' Park
## Attendance: 52,247 (Everton 3,214)

Following the home game against Manchester United, Kop idol Jamie Carragher declared on Sky Sports, 'The stadium Everton have got is fantastic. The one thing that is missing from there is a statue for Neville Southall.'

After this match, I quipped in my analysis for the *Liverpool Echo* that they should build a statue for Jordan Pickford at St James' Park!

On a serious note, the Southall statue debate has been a cause that I – along with others – have been championing for several years now.

When Everton were building their new stadium, there was a discussion over what would happen to the existing statues at Goodison Park, and whether some additional ones should be erected at their future home.

Regardless of Goodison's fate – it has been spared the bulldozers for now having been kept on as the home of Everton Women – there was a feeling among some that the monuments to Dixie Dean and the 'Holy Trinity' of Colin Harvey, Howard Kendall and Alan Ball should stay where they are, by the location of many of their great deeds.

But what about those who also graced Goodison but were not honoured before the Blues' departure? Perhaps Everton should build a statue at Hill Dickinson Stadium for the club's record appearance-maker? Perhaps they should build one for the player who won the most trophies for the club? Perhaps they should build one for a player who was widely regarded as being the best in the world in his position at the peak of his powers?

All three of those feats should be enough to qualify you for such an honour by the banks of the Mersey but ultimately only one statue would be needed for them because they were all achieved by Southall.

In addition, over four decades on from becoming the last of four goalkeepers to be voted Football Writers' Association Footballer of the Year in 1985, Southall is now the anomaly in terms of being given a permanent tribute to his achievements.

Bert Trautmann of Manchester City (1956) has a statue at the Etihad Stadium; Gordon Banks of Stoke City (1972) has one at the bet365 Stadium and Pat Jennings of Tottenham Hotspur (1973) has one on Kildare Street in his home city of Newry.

In my eyes, Pickford is Everton's best goalkeeper since Southall and despite a hugely impressive team performance against Newcastle United, they required his brilliance in the dying seconds to deny their hosts a third equaliser of the afternoon.

Following their much-maligned corners against Manchester United, the Blues mixed it up from early on here and took the lead in the 19th minute when James Garner's delivery from the left was met by Jarrad Branthwaite at the near post and he nodded in for what was his first goal in 22 months since his shot in the 2-0 win over Liverpool proved too hot to handle for Alisson.

Newcastle netted the first of their two deflected equalisers on 32 minutes as, when picked out by Sandro Tonali just outside the area, Jacob Ramsey's strike went in via Branthwaite with the defender's touch wrong-footing Pickford.

Just 105 seconds later, the Blues were back in front as Dwight McNeil – recalled on the right wing for his first appearance since his move to Crystal Palace collapsed – played a neat exchange of passes with Beto and Nick Pope could only spill his shot.

Like with his last-gasp equaliser at Brighton, Beto – himself making his first start since the goalless draw at Burnley on 27 December – was sharpest to the rebound and with the Newcastle keeper still flailing around on the turf, he slammed the ball into the unguarded net from inside the six-yard box.

The Guinea-Bissau international, whose physicality had the home defence on the back foot from the start, should have put the game to bed midway through the second half though.

After outmuscling Malick Thiaw by the touchline – with Newcastle claiming the ball went out of play – he cut inside and found himself one-on-one with the keeper but instead of placing his shot in the corner of the goal, he smashed it against the crossbar.

Beto had already made way for Thierno Barry when with eight minutes remaining, another deflection got Newcastle level for a second time as Joelinton's cross was met by a shot from substitute Jacob Murphy that was hit into the ground and, in a crowded penalty area, bounced in off Idrissa Gueye.

Thankfully for Everton, this time they only had to wait for just 74 seconds before they got their noses in front again with what proved to be the match-winner.

Iliman Ndiaye robbed possession from former homegrown Blues hero Anthony Gordon then fed Kiernan Dewsbury-Hall, who drove forward and squared to Barry at the back post where the Frenchman threw his body at the ball – well, it looked like he went down due to a shove from Lewis Hall – and it went into the net off his backside.

It was the right cheek to be precise as Joe Thomas, Gavin Buckland and I all answered correctly when asked by Ian Croll in his end-of-season quiz which I triumphed in to make up for my near-miss in Atlanta.

There was still one more piece of drama to come as a headed clearance from substitute Michael Keane was met plum on the volley by Tonali, who let fly with a thunderous shot only for Pickford to deny him – and leave the Toon Army gasping in disbelief – as he tipped the effort on to the crossbar with a stop that earned him the Coca-Cola Save of the Season award in the Premier League, a prize he'd previously received for 2021/22, when denying Chelsea's César Azpilicueta.

David Moyes described it as a 'brilliant display' from his players but on Pickford's save, he remarked, 'Tonali couldn't have hit that any better or any sweeter if he'd tried again, it was technically brilliant, his volley. But I have to say, the save was out of this world. To get your hand to that with the speed of the ball and get it on to the bar.'

Meanwhile, Beto was entertaining and refreshingly honest as always when I spoke to him in the mixed zone.

When I asked him about getting on the scoresheet, he said, 'This is the best finish ever. This is the best goal ever, as I always say to the keepers on the training ground.'

However, in terms of playing to the whistle, he acknowledged he should have put Everton 3-1 up before Newcastle's second equaliser.

Beto said, 'It was my bad. If the ball was out, I don't care. But I can't miss this one, it's important for me, so I need to get better at this. Thierno came on and he did what he needed to do. We help each other out and we talk a lot in training.'

*Line-up with player ratings:* Jordan Pickford 8; Jake O'Brien 7; Vitalii Mykolenko 7; James Tarkowski 8; Jarrad Branthwaite 8; Idrissa Gueye 8; James Garner 8; Dwight McNeil 7 (Harrison Armstrong 81); Kiernan Dewsbury-Hall 8 (Michael Keane 89); Iliman Ndiaye 7; Beto 8 (Thierno Barry 74 8).

# 15

# Toasting victory over Chelsea – March

**Tuesday, 3 March 2026: Everton 2 Burnley 0, Hill Dickinson Stadium**
**Attendance: 51,959**

There had been various reasons why Everton had failed to taste victory by the Mersey waterfront for almost three months, but they just had to return to winning ways here – and thankfully they did.

With home matches against Chelsea, Liverpool and Manchester City on the horizon, the pressure would have just mounted for David Moyes's men had they not triumphed, so there was relief all round as the Blues stopped the rot.

During their winless run, Everton had been unfortunate against Premier League leaders Arsenal, with officials retrospectively admitting they should have been given a penalty. They were ragged against Brentford, self-destructive against Wolves, down to the bare bones and fatigued against Sunderland in the FA Cup, slow starters against Leeds United, profligate against Bournemouth, and undone by one moment of expensively assembled quality against Manchester United.

Throughout this same period, there had been four away victories at Nottingham Forest, Aston Villa, Fulham and Newcastle, plus the feel-good factor of the last-gasp equaliser at

Brighton, which produced one of the images of the season when Moyes embarked on his celebratory dance.

While the die-hard supporters who, like my *Liverpool Echo* colleague Joe Thomas and myself travel the length and breadth of the country to watch all of Everton's matches, were getting the fully rounded picture, the vast majority of the fanbase – like at any club – who only get to see the home games were getting increasingly frustrated.

Although this disappointment was understandable, there was far less logic among some of the theories that certain Blues started to conjure up as reasons for their team's lack of home successes.

Some started to point the finger at Hill Dickinson Stadium itself, which really was clutching at straws.

Moyes commented on how visitors were enjoying their days out at the venue, making an occasion of their first trip and luxuriating among the improved facilities, but any suggestions that Everton would have won the same games had they been played at Goodison Park seemed overly sentimental, desperate and just plain wrong.

The power of Goodison had been demonstrated on many occasions in the past but the truth is that the Blues won just five league matches there in their historic final season – the joint-lowest total in their history, along with 1957/58.

It was up to the players on the pitch to put things right and while they had to be patient, Everton ultimately did that with the minimum of fuss against opponents who were heading straight back down into the Championship.

The breakthrough came on 32 minutes as James Garner curled in a free kick from the right which was met by the head of James Tarkowski, who nodded in his first goal of the season.

While an increasing number of players choose not to celebrate strikes against previous employers – as we'd witnessed with

Garner at Nottingham Forest when netting just before the turn of the calendar year – the captain had no such qualms.

Tarkowski replicated the 'cupped ear' gesture he'd produced when last finding the net, in rather more tumultuous circumstances, thundering in his volley in that final Merseyside derby at Goodison Park.

A Jarrad Branthwaite header was then clawed away by Martin Dúbravka in first-half stoppage time, while in the second half Idrissa Gueye waited too long before passing to Iliman Ndiaye, who found the back of the net only to have his effort ruled out because he was in an offside position.

However, the decisive second goal to settle the nerves arrived on the hour, and Dwight McNeil, who produced his best performance of the season – like Tarkowski, playing against his former club – played a pivotal role in the move.

Fed by Jake O'Brien, McNeil, deployed as an inverted right-winger, played a one-two with Beto before picking out Ndiaye on the left.

Kiernan Dewsbury-Hall pointed to the Senegal international where he wanted the ball in front of him, before the midfielder dinked a left-footed finish over the keeper and into the net from the edge of the six-yard box.

With the three points secured, McNeil's redemption story following his collapsed move to Crystal Palace on deadline day of the winter window was marked by the standing ovation he received from the home supporters when he was substituted in the 86th minute.

Afterwards, Moyes said of him, 'His control and his pass for the second goal to get out and then pass to Ili, he did really well and I'm really pleased for Dwight because he's probably had a tough time.'

Tarkowski, who also played alongside McNeil at Turf Moor, concurred and said, 'His training levels have been through the roof and that's why he's in the team. I thought he was terrific at the weekend, and he stepped up another level tonight.'

I asked the skipper about his goal celebration and he replied, 'I don't know why really. I got a bit giddy and it was the first thing that came into my head. I thought I'd repeat it because I don't score many and I'd better enjoy them while I can.'

Someone who was left witnessing others celebrating goals against Liverpool was Dewsbury-Hall.

Asked in a TNT Sports interview by presenter Jules Breach what Moyes was doing to help the 27-year-old achieve his best goalscoring season in the Premier League, having just hit six for the campaign, the midfielder was just about to answer when cheers could be heard from the stands in what appeared to be an empty ground.

However, with Liverpool's game at Molineux having kicked off 45 minutes later than Everton's fixture, Blues supporters still enjoying the hospitality around Hill Dickinson Stadium were celebrating André's stoppage-time winner for bottom club Wolverhampton Wanderers.

To be fair to Dewsbury-Hall, he got several sentences into his answer before being unable to ignore the noise any longer and asking, 'Has somebody scored?'

When it was pointed out what had happened, co-presenter Joleon Lescott, who joined Everton from Wolves in 2006, remarked, 'That will get a big cheer around here,' while Dewsbury-Hall replied, 'That's even better!'

*Line-up with player ratings:* Jordan Pickford 7; Jake O'Brien 6; Vitalii Mykolenko 6; James Tarkowski 8; Jarrad Branthwaite 8 (Michael Keane 83); Idrissa Gueye 7 (Tim Iroegbunam 86); James Garner 7; Dwight McNeil 8 (Tyrique George 86); Kiernan Dewsbury-Hall 8; Iliman Ndiaye 7 (Tyler Dibling 93); Beto 6 (Thierno Barry 83).

## Saturday, 14 March 2026: Arsenal 2 Everton 0, Emirates Stadium
## Attendance: 60,176 (3,003 Everton)

While there were some jitters – especially the following month when they lost 2-1 at Manchester City – for all of us inside the Emirates Stadium for the game, this felt like the day that Arsenal won the title.

Such is a goalkeeper's lot, Jordan Pickford produced another clutch of smart saves, frustrating the Premier League leaders until the 89th minute but still ended up being the fall guy.

In a drought second only to their 'capital punishment' across London at Stamford Bridge, Everton haven't won away to the Gunners – in front of fans at least – for over 30 years since second-half strikes by Graham Stuart and Andrei Kanchelskis cancelled out Ian Wright's opener and gave Joe Royle's side a 2-1 comeback win on 20 January 1996 (like at Anfield, they triumphed there behind closed doors in 2021 due to coronavirus restrictions).

David Moyes's men were up against it here and while they acquitted themselves well in testing circumstances, it was yet another glorious failure for the Blues.

With an 11-day gap since their previous fixture, Everton, who had explored a potential trip to the United Arab Emirates before conflict in the region prompted them to go to Portugal instead, had spent time away from their Finch Farm base to take part in some warm-weather training.

Just as when the Blues had flown to the USA for the Premier League Summer Series in pre-season, Jarrad Branthwaite did not travel, and this put the rumour mill into overdrive with claims the club's most valuable player could be facing another two-month spell on the sidelines.

Those close to the defender insisted the 23-year-old, who had undergone a medical procedure for a hamstring problem back in October and spent eight months out before returning to action in late January, had not suffered a new injury but conceded that his minutes might have to be managed.

David Moyes said as much himself in his pre-match press conference, but without being quizzed on specific members of his squad, when asked about team news, 'There's nothing really new, no, no. We're hoping everyone is fine and Jarrad, we think, will be OK, so, we'll go into the game and hopefully we're all fine.'

Yet when the line-ups were announced 75 minutes before kick-off, not only was Branthwaite absent from the squad, but fellow centre-back James Tarkowski was missing too.

Tarkowski made 109 consecutive starts in the Premier League for Everton before suffering a hamstring injury against Manchester City on 19 April the previous year.

However, following surgery, he returned to the side in the Premier League Summer Series and was ever-present in all competitions until he missed the trip to Arsenal.

The enforced double switch at the heart of defence saw Jake O'Brien paired with Michael Keane, with the former's move to his natural position ensuring James Garner was also displaced from midfield to right-back.

The Blues had to be on their toes against the fabled/infamous (delete as appropriate) set pieces of Mikel Arteta's side.

Yet with Pickford already having kept out a Noni Madueke drive from a Declan Rice corner, the England number one was spotted mouthing 'oh ref' when the assistant's flag went up for offside after he had got down spectacularly to his right to keep out a close-range header from his international team-mate Bukayo Saka.

Everton went toe-to-toe with their high-flying hosts though and Dwight McNeil was twice denied a first goal of the season in quick succession, first by a Riccardo Calafiori block and then when his rasping effort struck David Raya's right-hand post.

Either side of the break, Kiernan Dewsbury-Hall and Beto were thwarted by saves from Raya, but while they were facing increasingly regular waves of pressure from Arsenal, the Blues had looked good value for what would have been a hard-earned point until the breakthrough finally arrived a minute from the end of normal time.

Pickford flapped at a left-footed right-wing cross from Arsenal substitute Max Dowman and the loose ball struck Piero Hincapié and fell to the feet of Viktor Gyökeres, who had also come off the bench but found himself in the enviable position of being able to fire into an empty net from two yards.

The outpouring of relief around the ground from the home supporters seemed to cascade through the stands of the Emirates Stadium but for all his brilliance, it has to go down as a blunder for a custodian of Pickford's calibre.

He wasn't done there though as he made things worse with what is one of my true pet hates in football – goalkeepers coming up for corners when chasing a game.

I'm old enough to remember a time when it hardly ever happened.

Before the backpass rule was introduced in 1992 many keepers were surprisingly bad at controlling a football with their feet considering they spent their lives working alongside numerous colleagues who excelled in such a field.

Anyway, because of this, even as the 1990s progressed, most of them knew their place and wouldn't get ideas above their station, such as venturing into the opposition half.

Those who did were exotic novelties like eccentric South American pair René Higuita, who wowed Wembley with his 'scorpion kick' but had earlier come a cropper against Roger Milla in the 1990 World Cup when attempting to be a 'sweeper keeper', and José Luis Chilavert, a dead-ball expert who succeeded with a string of free kicks and penalties.

Closer to home, Daniel Amokachi failed to make the most of a breakaway chance at the end of the 1995 FA Cup Final when Manchester United's Peter Schmeichel, who had netted several times for previous club Brøndby, ambled upfield in search of a last-gasp equaliser.

The Dane would duly net for the Red Devils against Rotor Volgograd the following season and become the first keeper to score in the Premier League, for Aston Villa in a 3-2 defeat to Everton at Goodison Park in 2001.

However, the 'culprit' in my eyes for creating this monster is Jimmy Glass, the on-loan Carlisle United keeper whose stoppage-time winner against Plymouth Argyle ensured they avoided relegation from the Football League.

It was a gloriously absurd moment of delight for Cumbrian fans, but it spurned legions of hapless copycat antics.

In fairness, if you've got the technique of Liverpool's Alisson to actually head a ball in from a corner then fair enough, but most keepers coming up at the death just get in the way and prevent a more able team-mate from making contact with the ball.

We know that Pickford can strike a penalty – he's done so successfully for England – and his old school teacher told me how he was a tough-tackling, goalscoring midfielder in his youth, but I'd still include him in this category.

What he did at the Emirates too was the worst of both worlds as he went forward, but then didn't commit, instead hovering around on the edge of the opposition area and leaving his defenders exposed on the counter-attack.

Dowman had the speed of thought – and foot – to get past desperate attempts from Vitalii Mykolenko and Dewsbury-Hall to stop him, and like Gyökeres he was able to put the ball into an empty net, his moment coming seven minutes into stoppage time.

In doing so, at just 16 years and 17 days of age, the Chelmsford protege became the Premier League's youngest-ever goalscorer, breaking a record that had been set before he was born – by an Everton player.

James Vaughan was 16 years and 270 days old when Moyes brought him off the bench to seal the Blues' 4-0 win over Crystal Palace on 10 April 2005, on the same day that Arteta also scored his first goal for the club.

Vaughan, who at the age of 37 was magnanimous in passing over the baton, told Sky Sports, 'My little boy loves going to the Everton games and we'd never been to an away fixture, so I'd promised I'd take him to one. To be in the stadium, with my son watching, I think he was a little bit disappointed, but for me, I couldn't think of a better player to break it.'

Afterwards, Moyes admitted, 'I'm gutted. We've done such a good job from all periods in the game and just missed out. No disappointment regarding performance or how the players went about it or their effort, nothing like that, we just missed out in the last few minutes.

'I said to the players at half-time, "This is OK, but if we're really going to get people talking about us and putting us as headliners, then we're going to have to win and we're going to have to find a way of at least coming away from here with something." In the end, we weren't able to do that.'

In the mixed zone, O'Brien revealed to me that he'd found out the previous day that it would be himself and Keane at centre-back.

When it came to the mistake for Arsenal's opening goal, the Republic of Ireland international said, 'Jordan has come in and apologised but he has kept us in a lot of games. We'll put it behind us and it's not something he does very often, but also he's made some really good saves, so I'm not sure anyone can say anything because he's been amazing for us.

'We're disappointed as we defended well through the match but in games like this it's small margins that have seen us lose. We defended well until the final moments and just got caught out at the end while for the second goal, we were just chasing the game, searching for an equaliser.'

***Line-up with player ratings:*** Jordan Pickford 5; James Garner 7; Vitalii Mykolenko 6; Jake O'Brien 7; Michael Keane 7; Idrissa Gueye 6 (Tyrique George 94); Tim Iroegbunam 7 (Merlin Röhl 86); Dwight McNeil 7 (Harrison Armstrong 86); Kiernan Dewsbury-Hall 7; Iliman Ndiaye 7; Beto 6 (Thierno Barry 69 6).

***

Never mind '60 years of hurt' – imagine saying that England's win over West Germany in the 1966 World Cup Final no longer counts as modern technology has proven that the ball did not entirely cross the line for Geoff Hurst's second goal or because spectators were on the pitch for his hat-trick effort in the dying seconds.

It seems a bizarre concept to reverse the result of a major tournament in retrospect, but that's just what happened with Everton pair Idrissa Gueye and Iliman Ndiaye's triumph with Senegal over Morocco in the Africa Cup of Nations Final with a ruling on 17 March 2026.

Two months on from the game, the Confederation of African Football overturned the result of the final following Senegal's controversial walk-off before the fixture was played to its conclusion.

Their statement said Senegal had been 'declared to have forfeited the final match' with the 'result of the match being recorded as 3-0 in favour' of Morocco.

In turn, the Senegalese Football Federation said it would appeal against CAF's decision at the Court of Arbitration for Sport, calling it 'an unfair, unprecedented and unacceptable decision which brings discredit to African football'.

At the time of publication, the matter still remains unresolved.

## Saturday, 21 March 2026: Everton 3 Chelsea 0, Hill Dickinson Stadium Attendance: 52,547

As well as being their biggest victory, both in terms of the scoreline and the magnitude of the opposition, this was the watershed moment that Evertonians had been waiting for from the start at Hill Dickinson Stadium when it came to their new ground feeling like home.

With their winter woes and the near three-month winless streak on their own turf behind them, the Blues and their supporters basked in the sunshine on a day that warmed their hearts as this was an occasion that ticked many boxes.

Spring was in the air with the temperatures rising and after five consecutive Premier League home games being played during the week, Everton supporters were able to take their time going to the match and soaking up the atmosphere.

This also included, thanks to The 1878s, a raucous coach welcome, complete with the now de rigueur blue pyrotechnics, which attracted a significant and passionate crowd even if the bus journey with supporters watching was little more than crossing Regent Road from the Titanic Hotel to the outer perimeter of the stadium's footprint.

Indeed, it was a journey that former Blues striker Yakubu – who would later be captured on the big screens sat next to Tim Cahill as the former team-mates pointed at each other like the Spiderman meme – made on foot, waving at his adoring public.

Another fiery ingredient added to the mix in the week building up to this match was the revelation that Chelsea had been handed a Premier League record fine of £10.75m and a suspended transfer ban for making secret payments to unregistered agents and third parties over transfers between 2011 and 2018.

However, unlike Everton's unprecedented brace of points deductions in 2023/24 for single breaches of PSR rules in back-to-back years, they would not be punished on the pitch. In an interview with BBC Radio Merseyside's Giulia Bould, football finance expert Kieran Maguire, who is a senior teacher in Accounting and Finance at the University of Liverpool Management School, said, 'There does appear to be an inconsistency and if I was an Everton fan I suspect I'd be fairly angry about this.

'We're now in an era and an environment when smart accountants and smart lawyers are becoming just as useful to a football club as a fantastic goalkeeper or somebody that can knock it in from 30 yards and as an accountant who is rubbish at football, I really don't think that's a good thing to have.'

Thankfully for the Blues, while Chelsea have spent a fortune on their side both past and present, it was David Moyes's men who dominated on the pitch here and were sharper from the off.

Everton had been bossing proceedings from the start and deservedly took the lead on 33 minutes when James Garner drove forwards and threaded a perfectly weighted through ball for Beto to chase and delicately scoop over the advancing Robert Sánchez, having earlier almost embarrassed the Chelsea keeper when closing him down in possession.

Recovering from his error at the Emirates Stadium the previous weekend, Pickford was back on form to become only the fifth goalie to keep a century of clean sheets for Everton after Neville Southall (269), Gordon West (155), Tim Howard (133) and Ted Sagar (120).

He twice denied Chelsea captain Enzo Fernández shortly after his side went ahead, showing a powerful wrist to tip his stinging effort over the bar in a penalty box melee and then tipping his curling shot around the post in the second half before the hosts grabbed their second goal.

Seconds after the latter though, with 62 minutes on the clock, the Blues took control as Idrissa Gueye showed the greater desire to get between Fernández and Marc Cucurella to win a loose ball inside his own half before the 36-year-old marauded over 50 yards up the pitch and picked out Beto.

Twelve yards from goal, the striker spun and hit his shot straight at Sánchez but his effort proved too hot to handle for the Spaniard, who fumbled it over the line.

The rout was completed on 76 minutes with what incredibly was Iliman Ndiaye's first goal for Everton from open play since his wonder strike at Sunderland on 3 November and his first at Hill Dickinson Stadium since the inaugural competitive match on 24 August.

A long punt upfield by Pickford was flicked on by a Beto header which Ndiaye brought down by the edge of the area before cutting inside past Moisés Caicedo and firing his shot into the roof of the net to wrap up Everton's best day so far by the banks of the Mersey.

A strange but memorable image from the match was the photo showing home supporter Matty Byrne celebrating while holding a boxed toaster in one hand and a packet of crumpets in the other.

Fresh from speaking to Kieran Maguire about Chelsea's finances, Giulia Bould was on the case again as the Blues fan, dubbed online as 'Toaster man', told her, 'I was going to a wedding that night. I didn't want to leave it in the boozer, so I decided just to walk in with it.'

Every time Everton scored, the toaster was tossed into the air and surrounding supporters wanted to join in.

Matty added, 'Someone asked me to just throw it to him, so I threw it. The next thing it was halfway round the stadium. It came back to me though!'

Perhaps the only thing more bizarre was Chelsea's under-fire head coach Liam Rosenior, who had now lost four games in a row, insisting his side were beaten by a 'moment of switching off' as he claimed, 'We controlled their possession and they didn't expect it, they ended up kicking the ball back to us a lot of the time and then we gained control of the game.'

David Moyes was in no doubt about his own team's dominance though and, responding to a reporter's question about Rosenior's remarks, he said, 'Our goalkeeper made a couple of wonderful saves at 1-0, which could have changed the game. I think it would be hard to say that we didn't deserve to win that game tonight if you were trying to allude to that at all, which I don't think you were, as you would be off your head if you were.'

***Line-up with player ratings:*** Jordan Pickford 9; Jake O'Brien 7; Vitalii Mykolenko 7; James Tarkowski 8; Michael Keane 7; Idrissa Gueye 8; James Garner 8; Dwight McNeil 6 (Jarrad Branthwaite 77); Kiernan Dewsbury-Hall 7 (Tim Iroegbunam 89); Iliman Ndiaye 8 (Merlin Röhl 89); Beto 9 (Thierno Barry 81).

***

Four days after Everton's landmark victory over Chelsea at Hill Dickinson Stadium, the Blues recalled what is widely regarded as Goodison Park's greatest night, the 3-1 win over Bayern Munich in the European Cup Winners' Cup semi-final second leg on 24 April 1985.

I was among those invited to 'The Night That Made History' at Everton's new waterfront home as members of the 1985 squad – everyone apart from Andy Gray and Gary Stevens were present – were joined by the likes of Howard Kendall's widow Lily, club doctor Ian Irving and iconic kit man Jimmy Martin, who used to drive the team bus in those days, plus commentator Martin Tyler, to receive a limited-edition timepiece called 'The Goodison 3.1' from Mike France, the CEO and co-founder of manufacturer Christopher Ward.

I managed to obtain some exclusive interviews with the legends, including Paul Bracewell who told me, 'We've been celebrating our great European night, let's look forward to the next one!'

There were some poignant words from former Wales captain Kevin Ratcliffe, who was also Everton's most-successful skipper.

Two days before James Garner was named player of the match on his England debut, the 1-1 draw with Marcelo Bielsa's Uruguay at Wembley, Ratcliffe said, 'I think if James was playing for a London club, then he'd have been in the squad a few months ago. I believe he's been so under the radar for England which is a shame because I thought he was outstanding last year and outstanding this year.'

On the final day of March, there were a couple of major events at Hill Dickinson Stadium – the release of the club's annual accounts and the venue's first international football match.

The former saw Everton record a loss of £8.6m for the 2024/25 financial year, a period that included the first six months of ownership by the Friedkin Group (TFG).

As Joe Thomas reported in the *Liverpool Echo*, 'The headline figure was a significant drop on the £53.2m losses of the previous 12 months though the accounts showed that number would have slightly increased had it not been for the sale of Everton Women within TFG owner Dan Friedkin's empire for a fee of £49.2m.

'The overall picture presented by the accounts is one of progress however, with documents showcasing the initial work of TFG to restructure the club's debts and move Everton to a position of stability after years of turmoil under former owner Farhad Moshiri.

'Moshiri's final years were characterised by chaos on and off the pitch as the club lurched between relegation battles while the businessman sought to sell a club that, at times, used the support of prospective buyers to pay the bills.

'Huge interest payments on debts owed to a host of lenders impeded the ability of the club to find a firm financial footing, one of several problems that continued in the wake of unprecedented points deductions for two breaches of Premier League spending regulations.

'The new accounts bear the hallmarks of the final stages of that period of uncertainty. They also detail the work carried out by TFG to lay the groundwork for the progress that is currently visible.

'One of the US outfit's first acts was to pay off those lenders and refinance the club's debt, consolidating it with the renowned JP Morgan Chase, with whom the club has entered a £350m, 30-year, stadium financing package.

'The £450.7m of shareholder loans essentially owed to Moshiri, which had the potential to cause regulatory problems if not appropriately dealt with, were converted into equity as part of the takeover deal.

'Another move intended to have an immediate impact on the club's finances was the sale of Everton Women, and with it their home of Goodison Park, to Roundhouse Capital Holdings, the wider group run and controlled by Friedkin.

'Within the regulations that transaction – for almost £50m – significantly reduced Everton's losses and would have helped the club towards compliance with PSR – the financial rules the club twice breached under Moshiri.

'The internal sale of the women's team for such purposes is a move previously adopted by Chelsea and Aston Villa.'

Moving to on-the-pitch matters, later that day Everton hosted their first international in more than 30 years as Ivory Coast faced Scotland in a pre-World Cup friendly for two teams who had qualified for that summer's tournament in North America.

As well as five games at the 1966 World Cup, Goodison Park hosted ten internationals in the British Home Championship between 1895 and 1973 plus three England friendlies, including their first home defeat to opponents from outside the UK when Ireland beat them 2-0 in 1949.

However, reflecting the diminishing status of the Grand Old Lady in recent decades, her last full international had been on 6 June 1995, when world champions Brazil defeated Japan 3-0 in an Umbro Cup game in front of a crowd of 29,237.

That figure was eclipsed at Hill Dickinson Stadium with an attendance of 33,034 including David Moyes plus a brace of Caledonian footballing knights from a couple of Everton's north-west rivals, Sir Alex Ferguson and Sir Kenny Dalglish.

Scotland had also featured in Goodison Park's first international on 6 April 1895 when they stayed at Compton Hotel on Church Street – which for many subsequent years served as the flagship store in the city for Marks & Spencer – while hosts England were based at the Alexandra Hotel on Dale Street.

Back then, the Three Lions extended their unbeaten run to 18 matches with a comprehensive 3-0 victory.

Legendary Derby County forward Steve Bloomer, the man who would later coin Everton's 'School of Science' nickname, opened the scoring on 25 minutes and he was set up by the Blues' 5ft 4in centre-half Johnny Holt, the 'Little Devil'.

A Neilly Gibson own goal ten minutes later doubled England's lead before the rout was completed a minute before the interval by Aston Villa's Steve Smith, netting on his only international appearance.

Fast forward to 2026 and Everton's catering department tried to make their guests feel at home with a special matchday menu that included battered Mars bar with whisky custard, haggis and bacon pizza, Stornoway black pudding-loaded jacket potatoes, and Ivorian beef stew.

Looking forward to the fixture, Moyes told the club's supporters, 'No doubt that night will see Liverpool full of lots of kilted men, and I hope you make them all welcome.'

The city did indeed witness many such fans but their efforts in the stands were unable to prevent another defeat for Scotland as Villarreal's former Arsenal winger Nicolas Pépé struck the only goal, a dozen minutes into the contest, firing in from point-blank range after Elye Wahi's initial shot had struck the foot of the post.

Everton's Nathan Patterson – who had started just one Premier League game at Hill Dickinson Stadium – came on for his 24th cap as a 63rd-minute substitute in what was his first international appearance since 9 June the previous year but there was no way back for Steve Clarke's side.

16

# Previous plans – other 21st-century attempts

PERHAPS IN some kind of parallel universe, Everton have already been playing by the banks of the Mersey for almost two decades, while in another they've decamped from the city of Liverpool altogether and are plying their trade out in Kirkby, such are the vagaries of the Blues' previous attempts throughout the 21st century to relocate from Goodison Park before they finally turned their dreams into reality with the long-awaited construction of Hill Dickinson Stadium at Bramley-Moore Dock.

At the time, the failure to land a move to a waterfront site in the shape of King's Dock was seen as the wasted opportunity of a lifetime by many Evertonians who feared their club would never again be handed the chance to build on such a prime piece of real estate.

The Blues submitted their ambitious plans for King's Dock in October 2000 at a time when they were just one of seven bidders to acquire the land.

Like predecessor Peter Johnson, Bill Kenwright consulted the fans in November 2000 with 15,049 voting in favour of moving to King's Dock and 2,349 wanting to redevelop Goodison.

Everton were expected to face stiff opposition from what was described as six other world-class proposals, but they were granted 'preferred bidder' status in June 2001 by Liverpool Vision, the first urban regeneration company founded in the United Kingdom, set up in 1999 and tasked with leading the physical transformation of the city into the new millennium.

Their finished project was supposed to be one of the most advanced structures of its kind in the world at the time, a 55,000-capacity football stadium with a retractable roof and pitch that could be rolled off on wheels, also doubling as an entertainment venue holding between 5,500 and 24,000.

There was set to be a housing and leisure complex featuring apartments, a cinema, family entertainment centre, health clinic, fitness club, hotel, bar, restaurants, shops and offices.

Kenwright said at the time, 'The King's Dock is a great opportunity for Everton and one we cannot afford to miss. It is a chance for everyone at the club, from the ball boys to the office staff, from the players to the board and the supporters, to move forward together with one common goal.'

However, Everton were forced to abandon their plans in April 2003 after failing to raise enough cash – reportedly around £30m – towards their share of the £155m project and instead the site would become the location of the 11,000-capacity indoor Echo Arena (now the M&S Bank Arena).

For many years, this was cited as the major stumbling block, but it is now understood that Kenwright pulled the plug on Everton's previous attempt to relocate to the waterfront because the club would not have owned their stadium at King's Dock.

However, as detailed in a *Liverpool Echo* news article I wrote on 4 May 2024, an interview given by Paul Gregg, a former business partner and friend of Kenwright, who he worked with on several major theatre projects before investing millions in True Blue Holdings Ltd when the late Everton chairman purchased Peter Johnson's majority shareholding in the club, provided a fresh interpretation of events.

Speaking to talkSPORT, Gregg said, 'The thing I regret the most is losing, no Evertonian wants to lose and we lost the stadium. I think the stadium is something that would have saved Everton and put them into the right position to compete and it would have been 20 years ago.'

Asked why the stadium did not happen, the then 82-year-old said, 'Because Bill [Kenwright] said no. We spent two and a half years with the Liverpool council and with the development trust – the government had put half a billion [pounds] into Liverpool for redevelopment and we'd sort of persuaded the council that they should build a multi-purpose stadium that had a roof on it so you could close it with the weather, you could play Madonna tonight and Arsenal tomorrow.

'It was even better [than the Tottenham Hotspur Stadium being multi-purpose] because it was effectively a closed stadium whenever we wanted it to be. We could have played concerts all year round and still played football.

'He said he wanted to own the club. We had a meeting with Bill and his advisor at the time and the advisor said, "You should get on with letting them borrow another £30m to pay Everton's share of the stadium."

'Bill said at the lunch on the Tuesday, he'd support it but then on the Thursday he told the AGM he wasn't going to take secondary funding, which was news to me at the AGM, I was like "aargh", I wanted to kill him to be honest.

'The good news was that I rang David Henshaw who was the chief executive of Liverpool City Council and I said, "David, you're not going to believe this but he's turned down the funding, he didn't want to do it, he's saying no to it."

'David said, "Don't worry, we really need it, we want it for the [2008 European] City of Culture, we want to get on with it, we'll put the money in, you just lease it off us."

'So, I rang Bill and said, "Look, the council are prepared to fund it completely and the deal is 125 years, ten per cent." He didn't want to though and I said, "Why don't you want to take it? It's right in the middle of Liverpool, everyone going into the city centre whether they're Everton, Liverpool or anybody, is going to see that stadium, it's going to be a fantastic flagship."

'I said, "The concert artists, when they've finished their show, when they take an encore and take to the stage with an Everton scarf and bobble hat, our publicity brand will just rise beyond anything else in the Premier League."'

At the time Everton insiders questioned why Mr Gregg had brought the issue up then rather than when Kenwright, who died on 23 October the previous year, was still alive but conceded that the financial contribution to the project was beyond the club's means.

While they concurred that Everton not owning the proposed stadium was a big concern, they also questioned whether the council could have footed the bill themselves anyway as Gregg claimed.

I understand that Kenwright wanted to own the stadium, a point he was steadfast upon, and was unwilling to accept offers to securitise it and while the project would have been challenging for Liverpool City Council, those involved at the time believe they could have still delivered it and were happy to take the proposal forward with the help of grant money.

Sir David Henshaw, who was chief executive of Liverpool City Council from 1998 to 2005, and now serves as chair of National Museums Liverpool, Wirral University Teaching Hospital NHS Foundation Trust and Natural Resources Wales, told the *Liverpool Echo*, 'It was an opportunity and Everton could have had a new stadium earlier, assuming everything went through properly in terms of planning application and grant funding. However, what is being produced now looks extraordinary so that's great to see and hopefully the team can make it work.'

With the Blues struggling to go it alone, it would be the neighbouring borough of Knowsley that then tempted club chiefs to move them outside the municipal boundaries of their home city.

In 2006, the *Liverpool Daily Post* revealed that Knowsley had offered Everton three prime development sites to build a new stadium.

Liverpool City Council responded by putting up two sites of its own but by now Everton had brought supermarket giants Tesco – headed by Terry Leahy, their Belle Vale-born chief executive and lifelong Evertonian – on board for a joint venture dubbed 'Destination Kirkby'.

Everton's new home would have been part of a retail park complex with the stadium itself – holding 50,000 but with an option to expand to 60,000, yet looking somewhat utilitarian compared to earlier proposals – costing the club £78m to build with Tesco providing £52m of 'value'.

In many ways though, the look of the proposed stadium seemed to be the least of Everton's troubles in what was always a much more divisive project than their previous relocation attempts.

Some 36,662 Blues fans voted on the issue in August 2007 but this time less than half of them gave the club the thumbs-up. While 15,230 said they were in favour of the move, 10,468 were against and a further 10,901 abstained.

The club's then chief executive Keith Wyness described the move as 'the deal of the century' but his remarks prompted the leader of Liverpool City Council, Warren Bradley, to respond that it would be 'a glorified cow shed built in a small town outside Liverpool'.

For Everton, relocating outside of Liverpool was a public relations own goal and an opposition movement called Keep Everton In Our City was formed.

Retailer Bestway suggested an alternative site off Scotland Road in the 'Loop' junction off the Kingsway (Wallasey) Tunnel, but Reds fans were already licking their lips in anticipation and would taunt their neighbours in Merseyside derby matches with the chant 'Fuck off to Kirkby – the city's all ours'.

'Called in' for an inquiry by the government in August 2008, plans were finally quashed in November the following year when communities secretary John Denham decided the £400m project would breach shopping policies which discourage supermarket chains from sucking business away from town and city centres.

Having had their fingers burned over Kirkby, Everton's next relocation efforts were closer to home as the city council helped them identify a site at Walton Hall Park.

Although the club subsequently built a 2,000-capacity ground for their women's team there – before they in turn moved to Goodison Park for the 2025/26 season – significant protests from local residents fought the proposals of building a large stadium at the park and the plans never made much progress.

## 17

# Leaving it late – April

THE PENULTIMATE month of 2025/26 began with Everton continuing the restructuring of their youth system by appointing Dean Rastrick as academy director after an extensive recruitment process led by technical director Nick Cox.

The 50-year-old, who would take up his duties on 1 June having arrived following a second spell at Norwich City as head of football development, previously spent 13 years at Tottenham Hotspur. There, he oversaw significant academy success with the club producing many talented young players who have subsequently enjoyed careers in the Premier League, European football and the wider professional game, including Troy Parrott, Noni Madueke, Harry Winks, Marcus Edwards, Nabil Bentaleb, Japhet Tanganga, Oliver Skipp and Kyle Walker-Peters.

Following his appointment, Rastrick said, 'I feel privileged to be joining this incredible club and academy at what is an extremely exciting period in its history. Everton is renowned for its track record of developing young talent and, with the help and support of everyone at Finch Farm, I'm relishing the challenge of building on the strong foundations that are already in place.'

On the same day, it was also announced that Neil Dewsnip was returning to Everton to provide support across the men's, women's and academy football departments on a consultancy basis. The Whiston-born 64-year-old previously spent 17 years in significant leadership roles in Everton's academy, coaching future England internationals Wayne Rooney, Ross Barkley, Leon Osman and Jack Rodwell.

A day before they returned to action, Everton revealed their season ticket prices for 2026/27. The club said that following an evaluation of feedback and supporter preferences during the first campaign at Hill Dickinson Stadium, pricing zones had been simplified, with five tiered pricing categories across the North, East, South and West Stands offering supporters a range of options and views.

However, the Everton Fan Advisory Board released a statement which said, 'While a small number of supporters will see no increase, many loyal match-going fans now face rises of up to almost ten per cent, close to three times the current rate of inflation.

'For regular match-going supporters, these increases add to an already challenging financial environment and will have a real impact on overall affordability.'

## Saturday, 11 April 2026: Brentford 2 Everton 2, Gtech Community Stadium
## Attendance: 17,220 (1,722 Everton)

On the day of the year that the world's eyes are on Liverpool for the city's largest annual sporting spectacle, the Grand National, 220 miles south-east of Aintree Brentford fell at the finish line to be denied victory against Everton in their European qualification showdown.

Jubilant Blues who had travelled to this corner of the capital, next to Kew Bridge by the banks of the Thames, celebrated Kiernan Dewsbury-Hall's 91st-minute equaliser wildly as for the second time that afternoon David Moyes's men had come from behind to ensure they remained level on points with the Bees in the table.

However, little did they know at the time, their other two games in April would also see stoppage-time goals, both for the opposition to inflict damaging defeats, with a third conceded in added-on time for Manchester City's equaliser in their first match of May.

Following their emphatic 3-0 win over Chelsea, the Blues had been out of action for three weeks due to the final international break of the season being followed by the quarter-finals of the FA Cup, a competition in which they'd fallen at the first hurdle.

They didn't start well in west London on this occasion either, and having discussed who my fancies were for the big race with Joe Thomas, who, as always for domestic fixtures, was sat alongside me in the press box, I was still putting away my Grand National betting slips when Jordan Pickford conceded a penalty less than 90 seconds into the contest.

I'm not a regular gambler and along with many others, the Grand National is my only flutter of the year. After a clutch of each-way wagers, I still managed to finish the day 25p down despite backing eventual favourite I Am Maximus, who romped home to become the first horse since the legendary three-time winner Red Rum to triumph more than once in the race.

My focus quickly returned to what was unfolding in front of our eyes though as Brentford's Kevin Schade tried to take the ball around Pickford but was clipped by the keeper with referee Farai Hallam, taking charge of just his third Premier League game, pointing to the spot.

Pickford guessed the correct way and dived to his right, but the penalty from Igor Thiago, who stuttered in his run-up, was beyond his reach to give Brentford a third-minute lead.

Despite going behind early, the Blues got themselves back into the contest and home keeper Caoimhin Kelleher, a former understudy to Alisson at Liverpool, made a smart double save to palm away Idrissa Gueye's left-footed effort from the edge of the area and then Beto's rebound – the latter was flagged offside – midway through the first half.

Everton were not to be denied on 26 minutes though as Jake O'Brien got to the byline on the right wing and outmuscled Keane Lewis-Potter (there was a VAR check on his challenge, but he was just too strong for the left-back) before dragging the ball back to Gueye, who lofted a cross to Beto, the striker doing well to smartly angle his neck backwards and head into the net.

Pickford then redeemed himself somewhat for his earlier misdemeanour as he made an acrobatic fingertip save to turn a right-footed drive by Mathias Jensen around the post.

In the second half, he looked to turn provider down the other end of the pitch as his long kick upfield on 73 minutes fell to the feet of Dewsbury-Hall, but the midfielder couldn't get the ball to drop kindly for him after initially looking like he'd have a one-on-one chance with Kelleher.

That miss appeared costly just three minutes later as Brentford right-back Michael Kayode escaped the attentions of Tyrique George, who had just come on as a substitute, cut inside and let fly from the edge of the area with his effort being deflected into the net off Thiago. The Brazilian's touch ensured the shot wrong-footed Pickford for what was his fifth goal against the Blues of the season.

Defeat would have been cruel on the visitors though and Dewsbury-Hall was not to be denied second time around.

With heavy rain falling around the ground, to add to the combination of sunshine and swirling winds that made for rather unusual playing conditions, Vitalii Mykolenko fired in a left-wing cross that couldn't find the head of Thierno Barry but dropped to the feet of Iliman Ndiaye at the back post.

Ndiaye played the ball back to O'Brien, whose shot was blocked by Kayode, but the rebound fell to Dewsbury-Hall on his stronger left foot and he slammed home from an angle on the edge of the six-yard box to secure a share of the spoils.

Afterwards, I asked Pickford about the late equaliser, and he admitted he'd have liked to have seen his team-mate score sooner. The England number one said, 'I'm disappointed he missed one earlier because I'd have got an assist on FPL [Fantasy Premier League]. He's scored some big goals in big moments and has been a great signing with the quality he has on the ball but also the work he does off the ball, goes unseen.'

Dashing back from the mixed zone to the media room, I was also able to ask Brentford's rookie boss Keith Andrews about what it was like going head-to-head with David Moyes, the most experienced manager in the Premier League.

The Dubliner, who had penned a new deal with the Bees in February, extending his contract until 2032 following his bright start after succeeding Thomas Frank, told me, 'It's a brilliant challenge, every week. I'm also a huge traditionalist and I have huge respect for managers like David who have achieved so much in the game over such a long period. I think what he has achieved now both times at Everton has been pretty special. I think the way he conducts himself is just class, just very, very classy.'

*Line-up with player ratings:* Jordan Pickford 7; Jake O'Brien 7; Vitalii Mykolenko 6; James Tarkowski 7; Jarrad Branthwaite 7; Idrissa Gueye 8 (Tim Iroegbunam 74 6); James Garner 7; Dwight McNeil 6 (Tyrique George 74 6); Kiernan Dewsbury-Hall 8; Iliman Ndiaye 7; Beto 8 (Thierno Barry 74 6).

***

Having had that earlier taster stadium tour back in September, in between the matches against Brentford and Liverpool I was given the full experience while accompanying a dear friend of mine who was visiting 'the old country' having lived in North America for almost five decades.

This was no casual day-tripper though but rather Everton superfan Dr David France, the man who has surely done more for the Blues than anyone who has ever lived without being employed by the club.

The first person to receive the Citizen of Honour title from Liverpool's Freedom of the City panel for services to football since Bill Shankly, the Widnes-born former oil and gas executive has travelled over two million miles attending Everton matches as well as spearheading several incredible initiatives.

These include the Everton Collection (originally the David France Collection), a vast compendium of football memorabilia, consisting of more than 10,000 items related to the birth and development of Everton Football Club.

It took Dr France over 25 years to assemble it and despite receiving numerous offers from private investors, his dream was to make the collection available to what he called the 'Everton Family' and he transferred his world-class archives to an independent charitable trust, at a heavily discounted price.

He also established Gwladys Street's Hall of Fame, the Everton Former Players' Foundation – a pioneering model to care for retired professional footballers that has since been copied by many leading clubs – and the EFC Heritage Society.

Having known me since I was a fresh-faced cub reporter in my early 20s, David still likes to refer to me as a 'youngster', when I am in fact now longer in the tooth than Joe Royle when he steered Everton to the FA Cup in 1995.

By his own admission, he is now an 'old man', and despite having some serious health issues in the months prior to making this round trip of over 10,000 miles from his home in Arizona, against the advice of his devoted wife Elizabeth – who he tells me was the other good thing to come out of Farnworth along with Alan Ball – and his physician, he quips that he has told the latter to keep him going at least until he reaches the age of 80 or when Everton win the EFL Cup.

While he is over for business rather than taking in any football action this time around (he did return to watch the final home game of the season the following month when I got to show him the view of Hill Dickinson Stadium from the opposite bank of the Mersey), it was a joy and a privilege to be asked to accompany him on what was essentially his first proper look around the Blues' new riverside home courtesy of entertaining tour guide Kenny Rice and his staff.

There were even opportunities for us to pose for a couple of photographs, firstly on the other side of the raised managers' interview chair in the media theatre where David Moyes and visiting bosses usually look down upon myself and my journalistic colleagues, and then the replica of Goodison Park's Littlewoods Stores clock located in the stadium store.

## Sunday, 19 April 2026: Everton 1 Liverpool 2, Hill Dickinson Stadium
## Attendance: 52,585

This historic day brought us a new venue and a new era for Merseyside derbies but ultimately what has become normal service was resumed as Everton lost in heartbreaking circumstances again.

It's always illuminating to hear what others think of the flashpoints in a Merseyside derby and the historic first one at Hill Dickinson Stadium was of course no different.

After Everton and Liverpool faced each other in the league for the first time in over 11 years on 22 September 1962, Leslie Edwards wrote in the *Liverpool Echo* of the day's contentious decisions, 'Just as 73,000 saw all these incidents so there must be 73,000 different versions of what happened and why. They will mostly be coloured according to the redness or blueness of the people who hold them.'

Quite. So, a day later, it was interesting to be in earshot of a couple of neutral fans who support other clubs when it came to digesting Liverpool's 100th-minute 2-1 win.

Even they felt there was an air of inevitability to the game's dramatic final act but they both concurred that if there is a God then he wouldn't keep allowing Everton to lose Merseyside derbies in such a fashion.

This once evenly matched fixture has, on the whole, become ridiculously lopsided in recent times. It took Liverpool 87 years to move ahead in terms of victories, following a 3-1 triumph at Anfield on 7 November 1981, but the Reds have now romped ahead with 34 more successes than their neighbours and of course the Blues are just expected to grin and bear it.

Everton have always stood shoulder-to-shoulder with Liverpool when it comes to honouring the Hillsborough dead.

On the 37th anniversary of the disaster – just four days before this fixture – the Blues unveiled a permanent tribute at Hill Dickinson Stadium to the 97 victims as they welcomed representatives of the Hillsborough families and Liverpool Football Club to pay their respects.

On matchdays, the rivalry between the clubs remains as intense as ever though, even if they're no longer merely separated by Stanley Park.

There was the seemingly obligatory raid on Card Factory by travelling Kopites with the inflatable birthday balloons depicting '31' visible in the away section as a reminder of the club-record-breaking number of years that Everton have now endured without lifting a major trophy.

At the other end of the ground though, thanks to the efforts of The 1878s – who, following the success of the coach welcome ahead of Chelsea, staged an even bigger one before this game –

there was a new giant tifo for the South Stand, which had already caused a stir with supporters of both clubs following an online leak, such is the inability of some people to hold their own water.

After debuting with a namesake slogan of this book's title with the 'On the banks of the Royal Blue Mersey' display ahead of Arsenal on 20 December, this time the work was named 'The Originals'.

It included a sign that read 'We built this city', a reference to Everton constructing the ground at Anfield ahead of Liverpool FC existing, before moving on to Goodison Park and then Hill Dickinson Stadium.

The inclusion of the Beatles proved somewhat controversial given that Paul McCartney was the only one of the Fab Four to have any genuine True Blue credentials, having watched Harry Catterick's side in the 1968 FA Cup Final at Wembley.

These days Macca diplomatically claims to have a foot in both camps, quipping that he's got special dispensation from the Pope to cheer for Everton as well as Liverpool, but what is perhaps even flakier in terms of historical accuracy is the image showing the group wearing a long blue and white scarf given that the original was seemingly red and white.

What can't be disputed though on the graphic is the Liver Bird motif on the medal that was handed out to Everton players for winning their first league championship while still at Anfield in 1891, the year before their neighbours were formed.

Overall, it was a reminder – ahead of a fixture beamed out to a global audience – that while Liverpool's decades of success have brought them a huge worldwide fanbase of patrons eager to share in the reflected glory of latching on to a dominant football team, within the Reds' home city itself, there is another club, that has been competing at the top level almost continuously since the professional game began, who are followed just as passionately.

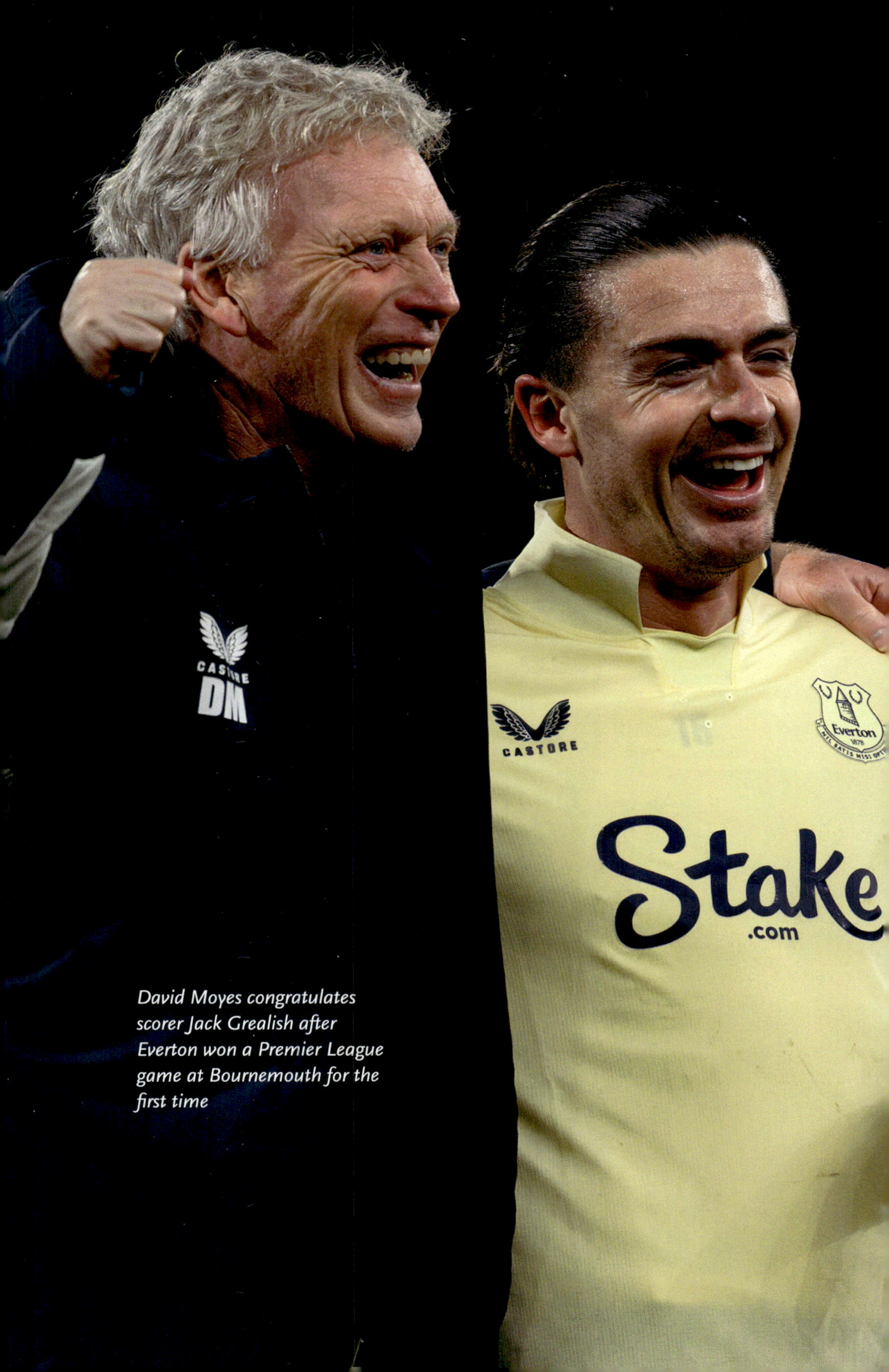


*David Moyes congratulates scorer Jack Grealish after Everton won a Premier League game at Bournemouth for the first time*

*Supporters are jubilant as Thierno Barry breaks his scoring duck at home to Nottingham Forest*

*Player of the season James Garner ran the show away to Nottingham Forest but was muted in his celebrations after scoring*

*There was no holding back from David Moyes when he ran on to the pitch to celebrate Beto's last-gasp equaliser at Brighton*

*The away end at Craven Cottage goes berserk as Everton come from behind to win at Fulham for the second straight year*

*Jordan Pickford after making his Premier League save of the season to deny Newcastle United's Sandro Tonali*

*James Tarkowski celebrates after scoring against former club Burnley, his first goal since Goodison's final Merseyside derby*

*Beto scores against Chelsea to put Everton on their way to their best – and final – win of the season*

*Scotland fans outside Hill Dickinson Stadium before the ground's first football international against Ivory Coast*

*The author with Dr David France in the Media Theatre while on the Hill Dickinson Stadium tour*

*Fans and team-mates alike celebrate as Jake O'Brien put Everton ahead against Manchester City but they couldn't hold on to win*

*Departing club captain Séamus Coleman with his family following his final home game for Everton, against Sunderland*

On the pitch at least, Liverpool's supporters have not suffered for a long time given that since they were last promoted in 1962 their team has never finished lower than eighth, a period that has seen them win their six European Cups plus numerous additional honours at home and abroad.

Throughout that same period, every other club other than Arsenal and Everton – who have had to endure a hat-trick of final-day escapes in the Premier League era – has been relegated at least once. That's a pretty cushy number.

When Everton secured their last derby win, 2-0 on 24 April 2024, it was their first at Goodison Park for some 13 and a half years. They haven't triumphed in front of fans at Anfield this century with their loyal but long-suffering supporters still waiting to party like it's 1999 again.

Among all of that, we've had Jürgen Klopp, the same manager who declared that the derby was like a 'World Cup Final for Everton' – when previewing a Liverpool game against Manchester United (I was in the room when he said it) – run into the centre circle to celebrate a stoppage-time winner and also snap at a child when a ball boy made a quip about the quote after a goalless draw at Goodison.

Unlike the passionate German, his successor Arne Slot was generally much more cool, calm and collected. Curiously, despite delivering the club's first title success in front of fans for 35 years, his more mellow approach seemed to have prompted plenty of Kopites to call for his head in 2025/26 after a downturn in results and he was duly sacked less than a week after the Premier League season finished.

However, the one time that the Dutchman did boil over was after the 2-2 draw at the Blues in his debut season and unfortunately he was far from alone given he was one of four recipients of a post-match red card with others also overstepping the mark among ugly scenes.

Liverpool didn't even lose the game as despite what Slot moaned about to Michael Oliver at the time, the result was never going to derail their title tilt.

Yet, when speaking in his pre-match press conference for this trip to Hill Dickinson Stadium, Slot insisted it was the referee rather than the atmosphere that got to him.

That's strange, because despite a lengthy VAR check, there was nothing wrong with James Tarkowski's late equaliser.

We're told the Stockley Park investigation took so long because not only was the goal being checked for offside, it was also being examined for a Beto challenge on Ibrahima Konaté in the build-up.

That in itself is rich irony given how when the tables were turned, the Frenchman escaped a second yellow card for a blatant pull on the striker in the Anfield derby of the previous season.

But despite this fixture having infamously produced the most sendings off in Premier League history, the strange phenomenon of Liverpool players avoiding bookings continued by the waterfront: the Reds committed 12 fouls to the Blues' eight, yet somehow none of their players were cautioned.

Possibly the most inexplicable call of them all surrounded the match-winner himself, and it wasn't just Evertonians with their supposed blue-tinted glasses who thought so.

Even esteemed journalist Henry Winter, someone without a dog in the fight, told his 1.1 million followers on X, 'How on earth did Virgil van Dijk not get booked for that challenge on Gueye? An angry Jordan Pickford booked for dissent.'

Never mind decades of refereeing injustices from the likes of Clive Thomas, Graham Poll and Mark Clattenburg, or Alan Robinson, who twice denied Everton what looked like clear-cut penalties against Liverpool in Wembley cup finals in the 1980s – there doesn't have to be a huge, smoking-gun moment when it comes to the men in the middle giving the Blues a raw deal.

It was cruel to chalk off Iliman Ndiaye's 27th-minute goal, but VAR showed that Jake O'Brien was indeed offside in the build-up, so instead this was a case of 'death by a thousand cuts' in terms of Chris Kavanagh's general approach to proceedings.

For Liverpool, it was a fourth game in a row that this particular official had not booked any of their side.

'Ref Cam' footage also showed him appearing to take a distinctly different approach with the two sets of players.

Reds pair Van Dijk and Salah were referred to by pally abbreviations of their first names, 'Virg' and 'Mo', yet when the visiting captain ploughed through the back of Gueye, he stated that it was 'Pickford' (not Jord mind you), who was to be shown a yellow card.

Those wearing the armband are afforded some scope to speak to the man in the middle though, yet when Tarkowski dared offer his thoughts from a blue perspective, Kavanagh sarcastically chastised him by remarking, 'Are you going to take the whistle when you retire you, or what?'

For Everton, just add this latest disappointment to the string of Kavanagh controversies already discussed earlier.

The Blues had started on the front foot with a Beto header forcing a smart save from derby debutant Giorgi Mamardashvili in the Liverpool goal.

When Kiernan Dewsbury-Hall was pushed to the turf by Curtis Jones in a challenge that the home player and his manager thought should have resulted in a penalty, with replays showing the only Scouser on the pitch also caught his opponent with his leg, Kavanagh and Paul Howard on VAR were unmoved.

Then, one-on-one, Beto somehow hit a shot closer to the corner flag than the goal but less than two minutes after Ndiaye had been denied a historic hat-trick – having netted the last goal at Goodison Park and first at Hill Dickinson Stadium – the Blues suffered a double whammy.

Instead of being 1-0 up in a contest they had bossed thus far, they were suddenly 1-0 down.

A loose ball by Dwight McNeil when facing his own goal went straight to Liverpool's Cody Gakpo who found Mohamed Salah with a diagonal pass and the Egyptian international, playing his final Merseyside derby after a nine-year stint at Anfield, scored with an emphatic first-time left-footed finish, hardly needing to break his stride.

After appearing shell-shocked having gone behind, Everton were on the ropes somewhat for the remainder of the first half but regrouped after the interval and drew level with 54 minutes gone.

Vitalii Mykolenko played a searching ball upfield that Dewsbury-Hall brought down and put into the danger area with a low delivery where it was met by Beto to poke home.

Mamardashvili was then forced off due to an accidental collision with the Blues' number nine when he was scoring and with regular number one Alisson already sidelined because of a hamstring injury, Freddie Woodman came on for his debut.

Although the 29-year-old was no rookie given that he had played over 200 matches in the Championship, it's fair to say that he had never before played in a fixture of this magnitude, and in that respect Everton were guilty of not testing him enough from that point onwards.

This was also a phenomenon that had echoes of a previous derby disappointment for David Moyes, as when facing an earlier out-of-sorts Liverpool side in the 2012 FA Cup semi-final – it must be noted that in 2026, the Reds were still favourites with every bookmaker – the Blues suffered another 2-1 defeat, having given their opponents' third-choice keeper Brad Jones an easy ride at Wembley.

The current crop's cause was not helped by Beto going off with concussion – a golf ball-esque swelling had developed on his cheek and was impairing his vision – with replacement Thierno Barry coming under fire for a lacklustre display.

Everton then lost Jarrad Branthwaite when he was stretchered off in the 87th minute with tears in his eyes, suffering from a new hamstring problem that would prematurely end his season after just ten appearances.

The Blues could have dearly done with the aerial dominance of the pair as the contest entered its 100th minute and Liverpool delivered the sucker punch.

Dominik Szoboszlai's left-wing corner was met by the head of Van Dijk, who left home captain Tarkowski in his wake to nod the ball into the net and that was that.

Afterwards, I went down to the mixed zone where McNeil held his hand up for Liverpool's first goal and admitted, 'I've watched it back about ten times already.' He believed that Branthwaite's injury had 'massively' affected Everton's team and said, 'Everyone is just gutted for him.'

Moyes was asked if he thought Dewsbury-Hall had been fouled by Jones for the penalty shout and he replied, 'I do, yeah. Why would he go down if he's not?'

In terms of the overall result, the manager added, 'We didn't deserve the outcome we got. Football is cruel sometimes and we have to bounce back and go again when adversity goes against you.'

*Line-up with player ratings:* Jordan Pickford 6; Jake O'Brien 6; Vitalii Mykolenko 6; James Tarkowski 6; Jarrad Branthwaite 7 (Michael Keane 87 6); Idrissa Gueye 6; James Garner 7; Dwight McNeil 6 (Tyrique George 80 6); Kiernan Dewsbury-Hall 7; Iliman Ndiaye 7; Beto 7 (Thierno Barry 73 5).

***

On St George's Day, just shy of 48 hours before they kicked off at West Ham, Everton announced a new deal for one of their England internationals.

It had been five and a half years since centre-back Michael Keane won the last of his dozen caps for the Three Lions, but throughout 2025/26 he had re-established himself as an important member of the squad, especially with Jarrad Branthwaite's injury struggles and Jake O'Brien primarily being deployed at right-back.

The previous summer, Everton had let Keane briefly lapse into free agency before tying him down for a further 12 months but following a solid campaign personally in which he'd already played 30 times, his spell with the club was extended into a tenth season.

Having penned his extension, the 33-year-old said, 'The club means a lot. It's one of those things that's easy to say, but it has become part of me. It's who I am, and it feels like family to me – the people around the club, the fans, the players, the staff. So, it's really special to me and I couldn't really imagine my life without Everton.

'Last summer, I didn't know what was going to happen. I didn't know where I was going to end up. I'm guessing people were doubting me and sometimes those doubts can creep in, but I've always had that belief in myself, and to prove that again this season, that I am good enough, that I can do it, has been really pleasing.'

## Saturday, 25 April 2026: West Ham United 2 Everton 1, London Stadium
## Attendance: 62,454 (2,800 Everton)

It's often said that 'lightning doesn't strike twice' but for the first time in their history, Everton lost consecutive matches to stoppage-time goals from the opposition.

Having steered West Ham to their first major trophy in 43 years, lifting the UEFA Europa Conference League in 2023, David Moyes made his first return as a visiting manager to London Stadium on what was a triple landmark occasion.

It was also his 63rd birthday and 750th game as a Premier League manager – a feat only previously achieved by Sir Alex Ferguson of Manchester United and Arsène Wenger of Arsenal – but he was in no mood for a party after a second straight capitulation in the dying seconds.

Such is the weird and not-so-wonderful world of referees when it comes to Everton matches though, it was a flashpoint that occurred before two of the afternoon's three goals had even been scored that remained on everyone's lips after this contest.

In truth it was a staggering call and unlike the partisan lines of Mersey allegiances during the derby the previous weekend, nobody seemed to be in any doubt that it should have resulted in a penalty for Moyes's men – apart from those making the decision themselves.

With Beto forced to miss his first game of the season after suffering his concussion against Liverpool, Thierno Barry spearheaded the visitors' attack and was in the opposition area when Hammers midfielder Mateus Fernandes, who was grappling with the Frenchman, reached out for the ball and handled it.

Referee Stuart Attwell failed to spot the offence on the pitch while Michael Salisbury on VAR duty didn't recommend that it should be given either.

When asked if he thought it was a penalty, Nuno Espírito Santo replied, 'I was scared,' which is about as big an admission as you're going to get from an opposition boss.

Speaking to Gary Lineker on his *The Rest Is Football* podcast, after the former Everton striker remarked, 'That's a penalty, isn't it?', the Premier League's all-time leading goalscorer Alan Shearer replied, 'It's a ridiculous decision not to give that as a handball.'

The following week, I reached out to former referees' chief Keith Hackett, who took charge of Everton's 1-0 win over Liverpool at Wembley in the 1984 Charity Shield before replacing Philip Don as the general manager of the Professional Game Match Officials Board, for an interview in the *Liverpool Echo.*

He told me, 'This is a clear example of a simple decision not given, it's deplorable. If we look at VAR, seven years in, it isn't working. What is the outcome for [Michael] Salisbury? These days I'm just an ordinary spectator, but I have bags of experience, and I don't think he's good enough for the Premier League. I don't think there's a level of accountability that operates or a drive to improve things in the Premier League now. I just don't see it.'

In the aftermath of the fixture, it emerged that Everton chief executive Angus Kinnear was to speak to Professional Game Match Officials Ltd to raise concerns about the consistency of officiating in the Premier League.

However, when speaking in his pre-match press conference for the Manchester City home game the following Friday, Moyes was asked if he had heard anything back and replied, 'Yes, but it's always rubbish what you get back. You never get anything good back.'

Speaking of rubbish, the first half in London was something of a non-event but the contest soon livened up after the break.

Having been untested in the first 50 minutes, Jordan Pickford was rushed into action to deny Taty Castellanos from close range. That challenge also went to VAR with certain angles suggesting that the keeper might have been fortunate to avoid conceding a penalty in two consecutive trips to the capital after giving one away at Brentford a fortnight earlier.

It quickly became a moot point though as Tomáš Souček headed West Ham in front from the resultant corner delivered by Jarrod Bowen.

Tellingly, both men had been brought to the club by Moyes in January 2020 and had gone on to become a couple of his best players with the scorer having claimed his former manager had tried to take him to Hill Dickinson Stadium in the final days of the summer transfer window the previous August.

Despite not getting their penalty, Everton, who had produced a flat display for long periods, finished the game strongly – Barry also had a headed effort cleared off the line by Souček – and they were good value for their equaliser on 88 minutes.

Vitalii Mykolenko's left-wing cross was nodded down by James Tarkowski at the back post and Dewsbury-Hall lashed the ball into the net on the half-volley.

As the midfielder would later admit, that should have been the cue for the visitors to go on and tee up a late comeback win against their nervy hosts, but they switched off again as West Ham struck on 92 minutes.

El Hadji Malick Diouf pumped a speculative diagonal ball into the Blues' area which Mykolenko and Keane made a hash of, enabling Bowen to head it back into the centre, and old nemesis Callum Wilson, who had been introduced as a substitute 11 minutes earlier, coolly side-footed into the net for his ninth career goal against Everton.

When I was down in the mixed zone following the final whistle, Dewsbury-Hall pulled no punches about how the visitors had let themselves down, 'The two goals are awful to concede, so there's no excuse and accountability needs to be taken. We're men, we need to do that. We've put ourselves in a position to at least get a point from the game, to be the team to go on and take the three points. But a lapse of judgement two minutes later has killed us, and that's not enough if you want to do something this year.'

***Line-up with player ratings:*** Jordan Pickford 5; Jake O'Brien 6 (Tim Iroegbunam 65 6); Vitalii Mykolenko 5; James Tarkowski 6; Michael Keane 6; Idrissa Gueye 6 (Charly Alcaraz 87); James Garner 6; Dwight McNeil 6 (Tyrique George 65 7); Kiernan Dewsbury-Hall 7; Iliman Ndiaye 6; Thierno Barry 5.

18

# Sting in the tail – May

**Monday, 4 May 2026: Everton 3 Manchester City 3, Hill Dickinson Stadium**
**Attendance: 52,257**

This was one of the best games of the Premier League season and a rollercoaster ride for the neutrals but despite all the pulsating twists and turns, the thrilling draw ultimately left both teams dissatisfied.

The Blues came within seconds of what would have been their first win over Manchester City since Pep Guardiola's debut season in England; the all-conquering Catalan coach would depart later that month after a decade in charge having secured a domestic cup double to take his Etihad Stadium trophy haul to six titles, three FA Cups, five League Cups, one Champions League, one UEFA Super Cup and one FIFA Club World Cup.

But while David Moyes's side relinquished what would have been a hugely morale-boosting victory with almost the last kick of the game, the point also proved scant consolation for the visitors.

City had struck first and if they'd won then they'd have been just three points behind leaders Arsenal in the title race with four matches to play and a game in hand.

Instead the two points dropped handed the destiny of the Premier League trophy back into the Gunners' hands, Mikel Arteta's men holding on for Arsenal to be crowned champions for the first time since Arsène Wenger's 'Invincibles' of 2003/04.

Without wanting to sound like a broken record – there's a metaphor for the teenagers – or being accused of sour grapes, once again Everton were left ruing a contentious penalty decision that the game's authorities subsequently admitted should have been given, which was of scant consolation to beleaguered Blues, watching their team's season unravel in spectacular fashion before their eyes.

For much of the first half, it looked like it would just be another stroll in the park for City against Everton as the visitors had the home side pegged back for prolonged periods.

After Jordan Pickford had parried an effort from Rayan Cherki though, the Blues did threaten with a couple of opportunities on the break.

A Kiernan Dewsbury-Hall shot from outside the area was deflected wide by Abdukodir Khusanov while the Uzbekistan international defender also got a crucial block on a Beto shot from a rebound after Gianluigi Donnarumma palmed away a low cross by Merlin Röhl – restored to the starting line-up for the first time since the win at Aston Villa on 18 January as a right-winger – intended for the striker.

The breakthrough for City arrived a couple of minutes before the interval as Tim Iroegbunam gave the ball away cheaply to Nico González just outside his area and with typically slick close passing, Guardiola's side patiently waited for their chance with Cherki picking out Jérémy Doku who cleverly used the advancing James Garner as a shield to expertly curl his left-footed shot into the top corner of Pickford's goal.

In a game in which Everton chances were few and far between, Iliman Ndiaye – usually such an assured finisher when one-on-one – knew he needed to be more clinical when getting between Matheus Nunes and Marc Guéhi to chase a long ball over the top but then tamely side-footed his effort straight at Donnarumma.

The Blues' dramatic revival came courtesy of a self-inflicted blow from City on 68 minutes as the usually assured Guéhi played a backpass straight into the path of substitute Thierno Barry, who coolly slotted past Donnarumma with a low left-footed finish.

Guéhi then partially redeemed himself by making a last-ditch interception to deflect an Ndiaye shot wide for a corner but from the resultant set piece, the roof felt like it had come off Hill Dickinson Stadium as Jake O'Brien, who had previously had a brace of headed goals disallowed earlier in the season for team-mates being offside, met Garner's delivery at the near post to nod Everton in front on 73 minutes.

City appeared shell-shocked at this stage and Ndiaye squandered yet another big chance, cutting inside past Khusanov but again dispatching a shot down Donnarumma's throat.

The Blues extended their lead on 81 minutes as Röhl chased an O'Brien throw-in up the right flank and after a lung-busting run, shrugging off Mateo Kovačić, his diagonal pass deflected off Khusanov to Barry for a tap-in.

Home supporters were delirious but in a moment in which they needed to keep focused, Everton's players were guilty of switching off.

Within four passes from the resultant kick-off, Kovačić played a measured through ball to Erling Haaland, who produced his old party piece of hardly having a kick all game and then finding the net, dribbling between James Tarkowski and Michael Keane before dinking the ball over the advancing Pickford.

Whatever happened from now on, Evertonians knew it was not going to be an easy ride to the final whistle.

They should have been given a chance to restore their two-goal cushion though when David Silva wrestled Röhl to the ground as the home side took another corner.

In an incident unseen by referee Michael Oliver, VAR Paul Howard decided the holding had taken place before the corner was taken, so he could not intervene.

Moyes, who made his way on to the pitch after the final whistle to confront the officials about the incident, blasted in his post-match press conference, 'I've seen it, I've had a look. If that doesn't get given as a penalty then it's an absolute free-for-all from now on. I might have to start coaching my defenders how to defend differently completely. It looks like now you're able to sort of grapple and wrestle on the ground if you want.'

Retrospectively, all five members of the Premier League's Key Match Incidents panel unanimously agreed with the Glaswegian and stated, 'There is a clear, sustained holding offence which continues as the corner is taken and the ball comes into play.'

That was scant consolation to the Blues though as, unlike celebrity fan Noel Gallagher, who had made his way out of Hill Dickinson Stadium after Everton's third goal went in – don't look back in anger at missing the late drama – City's players kept going right until the very end.

A Phil Foden corner was laid off by Guéhi to Doku who – with substitutes Nathan Patterson, who slipped, and Charly Alcaraz, who turned away from the shot – unable to close him down, showed he is just as deadly with his right foot, curling in from outside the area.

Assessing his return to the side in a new role, Röhl said, 'I'm here living my dream, playing for a great club, playing in the best league in the world and inside me, there's no need to only play in one position.'

Personally, I was on away manager duties for the post-match quotes that night, so with Guardiola having described Goodison Park as 'so cool and so British' in his pre-match press conference, I asked him about his thoughts on what proved to be his only visit with Manchester City to Hill Dickinson Stadium.

He told me, 'It's beautiful, congratulations. They are rich. It [the atmosphere compared to Goodison] was quite similar, they were proper. Proper English football, an English game. Proper, really, really good. A "men game" ... definitely.'

*Line-up with player ratings:* Jordan Pickford 6; Jake O'Brien 8; Vitalii Mykolenko 6; James Tarkowski 6; Michael Keane 6; Tim Iroegbunam 8 (Harrison Armstrong 96); James Garner 7; Merlin Röhl 8 (Nathan Patterson 92); Kiernan Dewsbury-Hall 7 (Charly Alcaraz 92); Iliman Ndiaye 6; Beto 6 (Thierno Barry 64 9).

## Sunday, 10 May 2026: Crystal Palace 2 Everton 2, Selhurst Park
## Attendance: 24,958 (2,680 Everton)

After extending their sequence of conceding result-altering stoppage-time goals to three matches, Everton knew that when it came to their European hopes, their trip to south London realistically looked like a must-win.

Although there was no late collapse in the dying seconds this time around, the Blues were still left feeling deflated as twice they took the lead against the Eagles only to be pegged back on both occasions.

The omens looked good going into the game: David Moyes had won all four of his previous matches against Crystal Palace as Everton manager, the Blues had triumphed in the most recent three head-to-heads, had not lost in the last ten meetings and had been beaten just once in 22 Premier League encounters.

While that unbeaten record continued though, the share of the spoils left Everton's aspirations of competing in continental competition hanging by a thread.

Despite Thierno Barry's brace off the bench against Manchester City six days earlier, Beto retained his place up front in an unchanged starting line-up and the visitors enjoyed a dream start just five minutes into the contest when James Tarkowski fired them ahead.

Kiernan Dewsbury-Hall's inswinging left-footed corner from the right wing was flicked on at the near post by Jaydee Canvot under pressure from Michael Keane and the ball fell to Tarkowski at the back post, the 33-year-old skipper coolly side-footing into the net with the assuredness of a prolific striker rather than a centre-back.

The Blues – sporting their pastel-yellow away shirts – squandered the chance to double their advantage just moments after Jordan Pickford had blocked a shot from Maxence Lacroix as Iliman Ndiaye carried the ball upfield and fed Dewsbury-Hall, but after cutting inside the midfielder slipped as his right-footed effort was kicked away by home keeper Dean Henderson.

Ndiaye's fellow Senegal international winger Ismaïla Sarr restored parity on 34 minutes with what was his 20th goal of the season – and a soft one for Everton to concede as Keane could only hack his clearance from Sarr's original scuffed right-footed shot straight back into his path and the Palace man made no mistake with the rebound, finishing emphatically with his left.

Ndiaye's deflected header from a corner was cleared off the line by Sarr just before the interval but then a couple of minutes into the second half, the Blues were back in front.

A pass by Jørgen Strand Larsen was blocked by Tarkowski and his interception became an inspired through ball for Beto to chase on to. Everton's number nine used his strength to shrug off the attentions of Lacroix, turned inside the defender and then fired the ball into the net through Henderson's legs.

James Garner then had a free kick tipped over the bar by Henderson and with 77 minutes played, the visitors made it all too easy for Palace to level again: rookie right-winger Röhl was unable to cut out Tyrick Mitchell's low left-wing cross and substitute striker Jean-Philippe Mateta, who later that month would grab the only goal of the game against Rayo Vallecano in the UEFA Conference League Final in Leipzig, was left unmarked in the Blues' area to get between Tarkowski, Keane and Tim Iroegbunam to sweep the ball into the roof of the net.

Everton still had another opportunity to snatch victory at the death but after being picked out by substitute Tyrique George, Ndiaye's finishing suffered a Manchester City hangover and instead of giving Henderson the eyes and casually slotting the ball to the keeper's side like we'd seen on several occasions in the past, he fired his effort over the bar.

Speaking in his post-match press conference, Palace boss Oliver Glasner made a damning claim about Everton's fitness after his own side had been involved in their Conference League semi-final second leg against Shakhtar Donetsk less than 72 hours earlier, 'In the end, it felt like Everton had played like three days ago because we looked fresher and that's credit to the players.'

When asked by my colleague Joe Thomas about seeing out games, Moyes said, 'Good sides have to do the business at this time of the season, this is the business end of the season. If you really want to be in it then you've got to get wins and that's why we see the big teams there. We have got to learn to deal with the pressure of winning the games and how we can do it.'

Meanwhile, Beto was telling me and Patrick Boyland of The Athletic in the mixed zone that he felt 'tough love' on the training ground from Moyes was helping him to produce the best football of his career.

Always personable, candid and insightful, he said, 'This is the best period of form because I'm better than I was last season. Last season, I was confident and everything but now, even if I'm not 100 per cent fit, I can read the game more and I can analyse the game more. I'm cleverer in my play, I understand my body more and I understand the Premier League better and how it works.

This isn't just physically, because mentally I have improved from last season.'

*Line-up with player ratings:* Jordan Pickford 6; Jake O'Brien 6; Vitalii Mykolenko 6; James Tarkowski 7; Michael Keane 5; Tim Iroegbunam 6; James Garner 7; Merlin Röhl 6 (Tyrique George 80); Kiernan Dewsbury-Hall 6 (Charly Alcaraz 93); Iliman Ndiaye 5; Beto 7 (Thierno Barry 70 5).

***

If this were Hollywood, there would be a fairy-tale ending on the way and Everton would win their last two matches and qualify for Europe for the first time in nine years.

There would probably be more of you reading this if that were the case. But if you've got this far then you, like me, already know that doesn't happen and unfortunately this is real life where beleaguered Blues have become used to being let down repeatedly by their team and the tale doesn't end on a high.

So, before moving on here, as you gird your loins for the chastening finale, I feel it's time for a bit of light relief.

Joe Thomas and I have been on the road together covering Everton matches for the *Echo* for over four years now.

He first joined our team with a baptism of fire in another harrowing fixture, Burnley's 3-2 comeback victory at Turf Moor on 6 April 2022, the night when Sean Dyche revealed he had told his Clarets players in the dressing room at half-time that Frank Lampard's men 'don't know how to win'.

During this time, we have had to do a lot of travelling together.

When holding an event for *Spirit of the Blues* at Waterstones' Liverpool One store, Joe, along with several other friends and colleagues, kindly attended to offer his support and I told one of the staff that if I wasn't with my wife Chloe, I was usually with him; his face creased up when the bookseller quipped he was in some ways the 'other Mrs Beesley'.

During our lengthy travels, Joe and I invariably end up with a few tales to tell, but while there had been several incidents in previous seasons, I must admit that 2025/26 – other than the opening-day shenanigans at Leeds – had been pretty event-free, up until this point that is.

That hadn't always been the case. In previous years, Joe had found himself in at least a couple of dining debacles.

Given the high prices/low quality at most service stations, we tend to only use them for toilet stops and swapping the driver and – unless we're heading north and can pop in at the enchanting exception to the rule that is Tebay – we prefer to find one of the many hidden gems that are the country pubs located in close proximity to motorway junctions.

It was while eating at one such establishment in the South Downs on the way back from a game at Brighton that Joe was left feeling particularly violated when a fellow customer helped themselves to a portion of his meal.

Already smarting from me sticking a finger in his curry sauce at the Amex Stadium earlier in the day when he'd invited me to taste it (we do have to share a steering wheel), a couple staying in a nearby Airbnb took it upon themselves to join us.

The gentleman, who was celebrating his birthday, was a Crystal Palace fan and on finding out we'd been to the match he engaged us in conversation about Everton's upcoming move to the new stadium and his own team's rivalry with the Seagulls.

His good lady, who already seemed somewhat merry, had declared that my colleague reminded her of someone off *Coronation Street* but my suggestions of Percy Sugden and Fred Elliott didn't ring any bells. Nevertheless, she extended the welcome to food sharing as she reached across the table to grab a generous handful of Joe's chips!

At least on this occasion, there was no critique of his menu choice.

Just a few weeks later, we stopped off at a Warwickshire village inn that was halfway to Bournemouth on Good Friday to see Everton lose to a stoppage-time own goal by Séamus Coleman, ensuring their winless run in the Premier League extended beyond Christmas to Easter.

Joe was about to tuck into his fish and chips and felt the ire of an Italian waitress when asking for tomato ketchup to accompany the dish as she raised her arms theatrically and declared 'mamma mia', seemingly disgusted by his demand.

In his defence, Joe was pretty much the innocent victim in both of these incidents but his habit of talking to people everywhere he goes can also get him into trouble. He might argue that this sociable trait is part of what makes him a great journalist but sometimes you have to adopt a filter.

Once, on a train journey back from London, a couple of ruffians came into our carriage somewhere in the Midlands. You could just tell immediately they were trouble as one of them had what was left of his T-shirt hanging off. Yet somehow, our Joseph ended up in a dialogue and, concealing his identity when they started quizzing him, he told them he was a schoolteacher from Wirral.

I really couldn't be bothered getting caught up in such nonsense, so I pretended to be asleep before opening my eyes after they disembarked at Crewe, I think. Joe still hasn't forgiven me for that one, but he needs to learn.

Of course, I'd have waded in if it had turned nasty, but I've been doing this job a lot longer than him and after another long day, I wasn't in the mood for small talk with idiots.

Joe can stand up for himself though, even against known hardcases, and it was such boldness that sparked his seemingly unlikely friendship with Troy Deeney.

They were debating Jordan Pickford ahead of Everton's 2-0 win over Ipswich Town at Portman Road on 19 October 2024 and rather than go along with what the big man was saying, Joe told the burly striker turned pundit, 'No, I disagree with you.'

Such boldness seemed to earn him a degree of respect from Deeney and over the rest of the season they would often chew the fat whenever he was attending Blues games; the pair were even photographed together the following year at a media awards function, although it will be intriguing to see if their bond survives the former Watford player's latest World Cup pop at Pickford and the chastening response from Everton's socials.

But if this was one of the finest hours for 'Chatty Man' he seemingly found himself in over his head post-Crystal Palace.

Getting on to the tube at Victoria station, a young woman, who it turned out was from Hong Kong and spoke very little English, made a beeline for Joe. Maybe he's got one of those honest faces like someone who you might trust to do your grandmother's shopping, but he does seem to attract these situations.

The woman wanted to get to Euston – which was where we were also heading to get back to Lime Street station in Liverpool – and in a conversation reminiscent of *Race Across the World* with heavy use of a translator app on a phone and plenty of 'thumbs up' gestures from Joe, all seemed well.

By the time we had got to Euston and were heading up the escalators to the main national rail station, the *Echo*'s chivalrous Sir Galahad was carrying her suitcases, but when we got upstairs he was met with something of a bombshell.

It turned out she wanted to get the train from Euston to Birmingham and given her communication limitations, Joe was asked to make the call to the person she was supposed to be going to see and speak on her behalf.

Dutifully he held the phone and a Brummie voice answered but it certainly wasn't genial Jack Grealish on the other end. The angry man told Joe that he didn't have time to see her and to tell her not to bother coming!

I still had work to do with my Beto quotes to write up ahead of that evening's impending deadline, so I informed him I was off to reopen my laptop via a quick pit stop to grab some food.

Joe told me he warned her she should only make the journey if she felt safe, but she still insisted on going. What a mess. Let's hope she's OK wherever she is.

## Sunday, 17 May 2026: Everton 1 Sunderland 3, Hill Dickinson Stadium
## Attendance: 52,590

Speaking of messes, this is exactly how Everton DIDN'T want to finish their historic first season at their new magnificent riverside home or wave goodbye to modern-day icon Séamus Coleman.

The Blues' European hopes were dangling by a thread at this point, but the visit of Sunderland provided them with the opportunity to at least bow out on a high in front of their own supporters after the huge disappointments against Liverpool and Manchester City on returning to action following the post-Chelsea break.

There was no such respite though as both teams struggled for quality in what was the worst game I'd witnessed all season.

Yet, while Evertonians were left raging afterwards, the Black Cats began the day 12th and leapfrogged them in the table before embarking on a late surge for continental competition themselves, finishing the job on the final day with a 2-1 win over Chelsea that ensured they ended up in seventh and with a place in the Europa League.

It was a day of great emotion on and off the pitch and there were also tributes to the late Bradley Lowery, on what would have been his 15th birthday, as well as to lifelong Everton supporter Michael Jones, killed in an accident during the construction of the club's new stadium, who would have turned 29 the day before this game.

Bradley was the little Sunderland fan who touched the hearts of many in football and struck up a special bond with the Blues during his cancer treatment before his death aged just six in 2017.

He became a symbol of hope and inspiration through the courage he showed in his fight against stage four high-risk neuroblastoma, a rare and aggressive form of childhood cancer, and appeared as Sunderland's mascot against Everton at the Stadium of Light in September 2016.

Following that fixture, Everton chairman Bill Kenwright made a £200,000 donation to support Bradley's treatment and the connection was further strengthened when Bradley returned for the reverse fixture at Goodison Park in January 2017, where he was carried on to the pitch in his Sunderland kit by Blues striker Romelu Lukaku.

Everton and Sunderland supporters came together to mark the occasion with a banner in his honour, stretching from the upper tier of the north-west corner of Hill Dickinson Stadium down into the lower section housing visiting fans with a period of applause in the 15th minute, followed by a similar gesture for Michael in the 29th minute.

Other than a rash challenge in the centre circle from Tim Iroegbunam on Reinildo Mandava that earned the Blues midfielder a yellow card, there had been precious little on-field incident in the first half before the hosts struck first blood a couple of minutes before half-time.

Vitalii Mykolenko got forward from left-back and found Kiernan Dewsbury-Hall, whose cross ricocheted off Michael Keane to Merlin Röhl on the opposite flank. Röhl drove back to the edge of the area, cutting inside on his left foot, and his shot was deflected off Sunderland captain Granit Xhaka and into the net for what was the first goal by a German player for Everton.

That should have been the platform for David Moyes's men to go on and win the game but yet another second-half collapse was on the way.

On 59 minutes, a loose touch by Jake O'Brien inadvertently went straight to the feet of Enzo Le Fée, who threaded the ball through to Brian Brobbey with the Sunderland number nine shrugging off the attentions of James Tarkowski before slamming past Jordan Pickford.

The turnaround was complete on 81 minutes with a goal inspired by the Wearsiders' homegrown hero Chris Rigg, who had been on the Blues' radar the previous summer.

Fed by Xhaka, the 18-year-old drove up the right wing and took Mykolenko out with a pass to Habib Diarra, who in turn picked out Wilson Isidor. He laid the ball off back to Rigg who switched it to Le Fée to put the visitors ahead with a left-footed finish that beat Pickford, who displayed an uncharacteristic weak wrist when trying to keep out the effort against his former club.

O'Brien was then denied a headed equaliser as his effort was saved by Robin Roefs's shoulder in front of the same South Stand where the Dutch keeper had saved all three penalties in the FA Cup shoot-out exit in January, and with the 6ft 6in defender making way for his fellow Republic of Ireland international soon afterwards, it was time for the club captain to take centre stage.

Forty-eight hours before this game, Coleman had announced that he was calling time on his Everton career after over 17 years of service. The 37-year-old, who serial winner Frank Lampard had declared as 'the best man I've met in my life' during his time as Blues boss, had delivered a farewell message that included the line 'I want to thank the fans for their unbelievable support'.

He added, 'You've helped me in more ways than you could imagine. I've always tried my best to put Everton Football Club first and you all mean the world to me. I live in the city – I see you all daily – and I've taken your love of the football club back into the dressing room to explain to the lads how much Everton means to the people.

'I also thank my managers, team-mates and all the staff at Everton. They've seen me happy, sad, angry, emotional, but the greater cause has always been Everton Football Club. Thank you for making me a better captain and team-mate. It's an incredible football club with incredible people.'

With two minutes left, Coleman was brought on for a final home outing in royal blue that took him to 434 appearances, knocking Leon Osman and Dixie Dean – another former Sligo Rovers player – out of the top ten, the pair both having recorded 433 appearances.

However, rather than a glorious goodbye for the stalwart from Killybegs in County Donegal, there was instead still enough time for Sunderland to deliver the *coup de grâce*: in the 91st minute Keane and Coleman allowed Diarra's low right-wing cross to go across the face of goal and into the path of Isidor to fire a third goal for the visitors into the net.

Following a considerable wait, Coleman and the rest of the Everton squad then embarked on what was an understandably downbeat lap of appreciation around all four sides of the ground. Given the capitulation, that left the Blues with a losing record for the season and facing up to finishing in the bottom half after challenging for Europe for so long, it was a truly sorry sight.

Many fans had already left by the time Coleman and company, with the players joined by their families, applauded those hardy supporters who had remained in their seats.

It was the fifth game in a row Everton had been unable to hold on to a positive result, with the final two goals meaning they had conceded a league-leading 11 goals in the final 15 minutes since 28 February.

Moyes, facing a major backlash from significant elements of the fanbase for the first time following the defeat, was asked what that might be down to and replied, 'I don't think there's any one reason for it. I think that today's was a pure mistake. I think the other games, and let's be fair, we're just off the back of two or three of the worst decisions for us, which have made our results look far worse than they are.

'We've actually, in truth, played pretty well. Maybe not so much today, but in the other games we've played pretty well wherever we've been. We've lost out on a couple of penalty kick decisions, which would have got us points.

'So if the points had gone in our favour in any one of those other games, we would be disappointed about today, but we would still be thinking that we've done OK. So I do think it's not really like us.

'We've lost three goals here against Man City, we lost three here today and we're playing Sunderland, who are not a side who score many goals. We should be better.'

*Line-up with player ratings:* Jordan Pickford 4; Jake O'Brien 4 (Séamus Coleman 88); Vitalii Mykolenko 5; James Tarkowski 6; Michael Keane 5; Tim Iroegbunam 5 (Tyrique George 73 6); James Garner 6; Merlin Röhl 7 (Dwight McNeil 88); Kiernan Dewsbury-Hall 5 (Charly Alcaraz 93); Iliman Ndiaye 4; Beto 5 (Thierno Barry 73 5).

## Sunday, 24 May 2026: Tottenham Hotspur 1 Everton 0, Tottenham Hotspur Stadium
## Attendance: 61,876 (3,038 Everton)

Played just four days before the third anniversary of Everton's last 'Great Escape' from relegation on the final day of a Premier League season, in truth Tottenham's own near miss with the drop was far less frantic than any of the Blues' such scenarios.

Inexplicably going short with a first-minute corner rather than pumping the ball into the home side's box and testing their nerves early on, David Moyes's men were second best all afternoon and found themselves pinned back for prolonged periods.

Indeed, with Spurs knowing a victory would guarantee their safety, there was not even a discernible change in mood within the stadium when news started filtering through midway into the second half that six miles across London, rivals West Ham United were winning their own survival showdown against Leeds.

Despite not having won a Premier League home game that calendar year and triumphing on their own turf just twice all season going into this fixture, also having sacked Thomas Frank – only appointed the previous summer – and interim boss Igor Tudor, who lasted just seven matches, Roberto De Zerbi's side, or their supporters, were never made to sweat as Everton barely laid a glove on them.

Thirty-four years on from the formation of the Premier League, the Blues and Tottenham are two of just six ever-present clubs along with Arsenal, Chelsea, Liverpool and Manchester United.

The rest of the quartet have all been champions with a combined haul of 24 titles (Arsenal four, Chelsea five, Liverpool two, Manchester United 13) between them and up until this point, only Everton, in 1994, 1998 and 2023, had gone into the final game of a season with their top-flight status on the line.

Mercifully, the Blues were at Goodison Park each time and by hook or by crook, they always pulled through.

First, there was the 3-2 comeback win over Wimbledon when they didn't even know whether they were safe when the final whistle blew, but despite the *Liverpool Echo* running the headline 'Never again... please' after that nerve-shredding afternoon, Everton found themselves in a similar position just four years later.

Second time around, Howard Kendall's side took a seventh-minute lead against Coventry City through Gareth Farrelly but after Nick Barmby's 84th-minute penalty was saved by Magnus Hedman, there was an anxious finish with Dion Dublin heading the visitors level a minute from the end.

Rather than saving themselves, the Blues were reliant on Chelsea – who had a European final against Stuttgart just three days later – to defeat Bolton Wanderers 2-0 at Stamford Bridge and keep them up on goal difference.

Then, in 2023, Sean Dyche's men at least knew that their destiny was in their own hands as a win over Bournemouth would be enough.

However, with the score still goalless at half-time and Leicester City beating Moyes's West Ham at the King Power Stadium – the Foxes would remain ahead for the rest of the day, triumphing 2-1 – Everton were heading down at the break. In the end, Abdoulaye Doucouré's goal on 57 minutes was enough for survival.

As I arrived at Tottenham Hotspur Stadium before kick-off, the scenes on Tottenham High Road were reminiscent of those on Walton's County Road 1,093 days earlier when Evertonians gathered in the street to prepare for battle.

There was a difference though inside the ground. While there was no doubting that the atmosphere was loud at times as almost 60,000 followers of the Lilywhites did their utmost to roar their side over the line, it was not hostile in the way Goodison had been when the Blues were fighting for survival.

Perhaps Spurs' patrons couldn't quite believe their expensively assembled squad had found themselves in such a predicament? Whatever the reason, this was a more sanitised environment and Everton only had themselves to blame for not cranking up the pressure.

The Blues were already creaking just six minutes into the contest when Michael Keane and Jordan Pickford collided while both going for the same cross and from the resultant scramble, Conor Gallagher fired a shot just wide.

Spurs grabbed the goal they needed on 43 minutes as Mathys Tel curled in a corner from the left wing which João Palhinha headed against the post and with Merlin Röhl leaving him unmarked for both that initial effort and then the rebound, the Portuguese midfielder poked the ball into the net with his left foot at the second time of asking, Thierno Barry unable to hack it off the goal line in time.

On what was a sweltering day in the capital with the match being played in temperatures of over 30°C, Everton's challenge wilted and it was only substitute Tyrique George who came close to getting them back into the contest in search of an equaliser that itself would not be enough to thwart Spurs' survival effort.

The on-loan Chelsea youngster tried to square the ball to Beto, who had also come off the bench, in the 87th minute when he probably should have had a go himself, and then in the ninth minute of stoppage time the Blues finally had their first shot on target as George cut inside with a curling right-footed effort that home keeper Antonín Kinský tipped over the bar, and Tottenham held on.

In the end, despite West Ham hoping for a helping hand from their old boss, the Irons' 3-0 win over Leeds was in vain but it instead did Everton a favour.

The result spared the Blues from the ignominy of being leapfrogged by the Yorkshire side, who themselves had been looking over their shoulders for much of the season, and potentially finishing in a lower position than the previous year as they ultimately had to settle for a repeat of 13th, where they had been 12 months earlier.

Asked by Joe Thomas how he felt about the way the campaign had drawn to an end, Moyes said, 'I'm disappointed in the last six or seven weeks. For probably three quarters of the season we've been very good. In the last six or seven weeks we have been really disappointed, but not always.'

Meanwhile, I was over in the mixed zone where I got to see a high-ranking Spurs delegation including chief executive Vinai Venkatesham heading into the home dressing room.

I then got to say my own goodbye to Séamus Coleman, thanking him for all that he had done for Everton as I shook his hand and wished him all the best for the future.

In between, I spoke to James Garner, who on the Thursday night had been named both Everton's player of the year and players' player of the year. He told me, 'I'm disappointed. We've not won in seven, so that's even more disappointing – to finish the season off without a win in seven is very disappointing.

'Personally I've had a half decent season but it's not just me, there's a team as well and there are 11 different people on the pitch and subs that can come on so I'll help in whatever way I can but ultimately I need my team-mates there to help me to pick up points.

'It's definitely been a progressive season, a better season than we've had over the last four or five years. Six or seven games ago, we were talking about maybe having a European run. I think if the games had gone differently and a couple of games we were even leading but we've lost points, so it could have been a lot different season if we'd picked up points over these last seven games.'

*Line-up with player ratings:* Jordan Pickford 5; Jake O'Brien 4 (Harrison Armstrong 62 6); Vitalii Mykolenko 5; James Tarkowski 6; Michael Keane 5; Tim Iroegbunam 5 (Séamus Coleman 84); James Garner 5; Merlin Röhl 4 (Tyrique George 62 7); Kiernan Dewsbury-Hall 5 (Charly Alcaraz 84); Iliman Ndiaye 5; Thierno Barry 5 (Beto 84).

19

# Player ratings and statistics for 2025/26

Games are starts plus substitute appearances.

Ratings based on competitive matches only as awarded in the *Liverpool Echo*.

| *Name* | *Games* | *Goals* | *Assists* | *Minutes* | *Average rating* |
|---|---|---|---|---|---|
| Jarrad Branthwaite | 10 (7+3) | 1 | 1 | 681 | 7 |
| Adam Aznou | 1 (0+1) | 0 | 1 | 34 | 7 |
| James Garner | 41 | 3 | 7 | 3714 | 6.93 |
| Jack Grealish | 22 (19+3) | 2 | 6 | 1723 | 6.82 |
| Kiernan Dewsbury-Hall | 32 (30+2) | 8 | 6 | 2683 | 6.8 |
| Nathan Patterson | 8 (4+4) | 0 | 0 | 356 | 6.8 |
| Harrison Armstrong | 15 (8+7) | 0 | 2 | 738 | 6.7 |
| Iliman Ndiaye | 34 (32+2) | 6 | 3 | 2833 | 6.53 |
| Jordan Pickford | 39 | 0 | 0 | 3540 | 6.51 |
| Michael Keane | 35 (31+4) | 3 | 1 | 2770 | 6.47 |
| James Tarkowski | 37 | 2 | 3 | 3630 | 6.35 |
| Idrissa Gueye | 25 | 2 | 3 | 2102 | 6.28 |
| Jake O'Brien | 40 (37+3) | 1 | 1 | 3337 | 6.26 |
| Tyrique George | 11 (1+10) | 0 | 0 | 210 | 6.25 |
| Tim Iroegbunam | 31 (18+13) | 0 | 3 | 1588 | 6.12 |
| Beto | 40 (18+22) | 10 | 1 | 1759 | 6.1 |
| Merlin Röhl | 17 (7+10) | 1 | 0 | 764 | 6.08 |
| Dwight McNeil | 25 (17+8) | 0 | 1 | 1426 | 6.05 |

| | | | | | |
|---|---|---|---|---|---|
| Thierno Barry | 41 (23+18) | 8 | 0 | 2066 | 6.03 |
| Charly Alcaraz | 22 (8+14) | 1 | 1 | 808 | 6 |
| Séamus Coleman | 7 (3+4) | 0 | 0 | 188 | 6 |
| Mark Travers | 2 | 0 | 0 | 180 | 6 |
| Vitalii Mykolenko | 36 (35+1) | 0 | 1 | 3164 | 5.75 |
| Tyler Dibling | 17 (6+11) | 0 | 0 | 513 | 5.56 |
| Elijah Campbell | 1 (0+1) | 0 | 0 | 16 | 5 |
| Reece Welch | 1 (0+1) | 0 | 0 | 4 | n/a |

## 20

# It grew from the dock

HILL DICKINSON Stadium is Dan Meis's vision but as the stadium prepared for its first competitive Everton match, the American architect was also the last man standing.

There are a series of photographs taken on 14 October 2016 of an Everton delegation examining the site at the disused Bramley-Moore Dock, the same day that the party also looked at an alternative location, Stonebridge Cross in Croxteth.

To the best of my knowledge, nobody bothered to take a picture of the Stonebridge Cross element of the day, and it doesn't seem to have left much of an impression with those who were present either.

Standing behind a fleet of silver Mercedes-Benz vehicles and a coach from Ellisons, who supply Everton with their team bus, and watching their step among a stack of wooden pallets and rusty metal pipes, the high-profile contingent included Meis.

Among those joining him were Farhad Moshiri, who had obtained his majority shareholding in Everton earlier that year; club chairman Bill Kenwright; the then mayor of Liverpool and lifelong Evertonian Joe Anderson; Everton chief executive Robert Elstone; deputy chief executive Denise Barrett-Baxendale, who would succeed Elstone the following summer when he took up a similar title with rugby league's Super League; and Alexander Ryazantsev, the club's chief financial and commercial officer.

Although Moshiri would turn up to watch Everton's inaugural first-team game against Roma at what became Hill Dickinson Stadium, other than Meis, nobody else would be actively involved in the project at its moment of completion.

When Everton broke ground on their new stadium project in 2021, Kenwright proclaimed, 'We're leaving something beautiful for something astonishing. May we have well over a hundred years of happiness here too – I think we will – and I think I'll be here for all of them!'

He might now be there in spirit, but the Blues' long-serving chairman, who passed away aged 78 on 23 October 2023, never got a chance to watch a match on the banks of the Mersey.

The others, at various junctures, all moved on to pastures new. Even Meis found himself embroiled in a temporary parting of the ways, revealing in June 2020 that he was 'not currently engaged' in the project and that it was one of the 'greatest disappointments' of his career.

Everton had chosen to use a different firm, Pattern, for the delivery phase, but he was back on board in October 2021, having been handed the title of stadium concept design guardian.

Thirty years on from the opening of his first major UK design project, the Manchester Arena, Meis was almost like a proud father-to-be counting down the days to the birth when I spoke with him in Manhattan while reporting on Everton's participation in the Premier League Summer Series.

Originally hailing from Colorado, he divides his time between bases on the American East and West Coasts.

Before we start our formal interview, I enquire about how his family are coping after their Pacific Palisades home was feared lost in the huge wildfires that had ripped through the suburbs of Los Angeles.

Thankfully none of his loved ones had been hurt, but as the impacted communities try to rebuild their lives, the 64-year-old was keeping his spirits up in anticipation of the grand opening of what he sees as being in many ways the crowning glory of his illustrious career while being the start of a bright new dawn for Everton.

Meis said, 'I hope that Hill Dickinson Stadium will help shape much of my legacy. There are a lot of projects to come in the UK and for me, it's probably the second-biggest market in the world because there are so many football clubs and it's not just the Premier League, but the Championship and lower divisions.

'What I would love to happen is for me to have the opportunity to tell the story to owners about this and how it wasn't just about architecture. Lots of architects can deliver a stadium, certainly lots of sports architects as there are a lot out there. There's something different about this, it really was about capturing the magic of Goodison and the uniqueness of this club.

'I think all of those things created a really unique building that will ultimately, I believe, create a home pitch advantage, because all those elements are there. It wasn't just another building, just another fanbase and hopefully it wasn't just another architect, that's what I would love my legacy to be.

'What Archibald Leitch did was be brilliant about creating these experiences through the engineering of the stands that changed the game while being able to evolve himself, using those ideas that he developed and that's why he became known for delivering these special places.

'I don't want it to be a one-off. I've done buildings all over the world, but I've been very focused on this, and I just hope there's something there that carries me to that next important English football club.

'It's really important that this is just the start of a new generation of memories and the magic that happens. It's all about the pitch.

'I'm really proud of how the building looks, how it fits on the dock, all of those things, but the most important thing is that it helps us win matches. We don't know that yet. I believe it will, and I believe 100 per cent that it's going to be the start of the club ascending to where it used to be.'

The length of Meis's stadium journey is also illuminating as he points out a sketch he did for an Everton stadium design in Walton Hall Park that dates back to 2014 – before Farhad Moshiri came to the club.

Although the Blues would eventually construct a 2,200-capacity ground, renovating a Liverpool County FA site at Walton Hall Park for their women's team to use between 2020 and 2025 before they moved into Goodison Park, plans to switch the club's home there – it's little over a mile from the Grand Old Lady – were abandoned in May 2016, just a few weeks after Moshiri's takeover, following strong opposition from protesters among the local population.

Meis said, 'The only other site we looked at in the beginning was Walton Hall Park. Initially, that's where we thought the building was going to go. At that time, I was thinking "pavilion in the park". I was imagining a white gazebo-type thing in a park.

'It must have been just a few months later that it became clear that probably wasn't going to be viable. There were some other sites, besides Bramley-Moore Dock, but we never really studied them very much.

'It was a bold decision because we didn't know how much it was going to cost on the dock. We knew it was going to be difficult, but I think there was a commitment on the club's part that if we're going to do this, and Bill Kenwright was a big proponent of this, we need to do this big.

'They wanted to do something that was important to the whole city and the region, not just the club.'

When Everton ditched their Walton Hall Park plans, with the aforementioned two possible alternative sites identified, then chief executive Robert Elstone hoped they would provide the club with a 'more straightforward, deliverable opportunity' to build a new stadium.

However, constructing a major sports venue at a location that was predominantly water at the time, could only be accessed from one side and had a tight footprint was anything but a simple solution.

Meis said, 'I was very much captivated by the high risk/high reward nature of the dock. However, I can't even tell you how many times I would wake up in the middle of the night after we started laying it out, and I thought, "It can't fit there!"

'I would look at the Google Maps images and I'd walked around it. It just didn't feel right and it felt like the only way it could fit is if we went east–west.

'I'm pretty sure Old Trafford is east–west and you can do it, but it's not ideal as there are issues like the sun angles in the goalkeeper's face and things like that.

'We wanted it to be north–south as we knew it was better. We put the drawing down and it looked like it fitted, but I'd still wake up thinking, "Oh God, measure it again."

'I was sure it was going to come back to us at some point and that wasn't even the worry of how do you make it a buildable site as that really took Laing O'Rourke, the engineers and a lot of people to work out how they would dredge and fill and all of that.'

In addition to the logistical obstacles, there was also the furore over the stadium construction resulting in Liverpool being stripped of its UNESCO World Heritage status after a United Nations committee claimed the developments threatened the value of the city's waterfront.

The decision, made following a secret ballot by the UNESCO committee at a meeting in China in 2021 – in the week before

Everton formally took control at Bramley-Moore Dock – was due to what was described as 'serious deterioration' of the site.

However, the city's mayor Joanne Anderson (no relation to namesake predecessor Joe) described the ruling as 'incomprehensible'. She said, 'Our World Heritage site has never been in better condition having benefitted from hundreds of millions of pounds of investment across dozens of listed buildings and the public realm.'

Meanwhile, Liverpool City Region mayor Steve Rotheram, an unabashed Kopite, added that the decision was 'a retrograde step that does not reflect the reality of what is happening on the ground'.

For his part, Meis was just as bemused and said, 'I was sensitive to the UNESCO issue and the historic issues of cutting through the wall and things like that, but I really believed from the very beginning that we could achieve all that and be respectful to the history.

'We weren't going to drop a spaceship here, it was going to be sensitive, one way or another. I wanted it to look like it grew out of the dock with this wave coming over. In the end, it was a pretty big investment, just to get to a buildable site. We're kind of lucky that we made it through all of that.

'I've seen a couple of other articles that have touched on it. I recently met Andy Burnham [the former MP who was re-elected to parliament in June 2026 and soon became prime minister], who I didn't realise was an Evertonian, and he made a pretty passionate statement about it.

'I think it's unfortunate that UNESCO gets in its own way a little bit. Sometimes, under the banner of protecting something, they're actually just letting it fall apart, and that's what was happening with the docks.

'I totally understood why it was historic and why it was valued but if you don't do anything with it, eventually it will just crumble and fall into the Mersey. I was committed to an idea that if we do this right and are protective and respectful of the heritage, ultimately activating that area and creating developments, then people will come and experience it.

'It seems to me that UNESCO needs to think about what ultimately their real mission is. This is so you're not just protecting something by cordoning it off, or putting it in a bubble, but you're actually finding ways for people to invest in it and evolve, because I think that is really important.'

Meis, scarred by seeing another riverside stadium project at a major European club fall by the wayside – his vision for a 21st-century colosseum for Roma by the banks of the Tiber was unveiled publicly in 2014 when he was still imagining Everton's 'pavilion in the park' but never came to fruition – explains how Farhad Moshiri's sometimes capricious nature threatened to derail the process.

He said, 'I don't think I ever had technical doubts other than irrational fears that the direction was wrong and it wasn't going to fit by a couple of feet.

'I knew that technically we could do it, we could figure it out. I had real doubts about it happening though and I remember having a meeting with Bill Kenwright and Farhad Moshiri when Farhad asked the question, "Do we have to build a new building? Could we not renovate Goodison?"

'I don't think he completely understood the limitations of Goodison. I'm very respectful of how in Europe and the UK, they are much more protective of their heritage buildings. In the US, I can't tell you how many times you've had an owner say, "This building we only built 30 years ago, is crumbling, it's going to fall down."

'It wasn't about the fact that it couldn't physically be done, other than there are site limitations. The worries I had were really the financial ones as I knew it was a big investment and there were figures of around £100m just to convert it into a buildable site.

'That was a big decision. For me, being committed to a site, you had to argue whether you're getting a return on that £100m because you could build it somewhere else without that spend. For me, that was a bold, and really heroic decision by the club to stick with it.

'Between the boardroom upheaval, the challenges on the pitch with the turnover of managers, all those kind of things would worry me on a daily basis.

'Most of my career, I haven't had those worries. I don't get up every Saturday morning and watch my client, rooting for them and concerned over the result, but there was a lot of that, and thankfully we got there.'

And therein lies the rub. This was much more than just a business arrangement and Meis now finds himself as a 'True Blue'.

He concluded, 'Not that I'm an expert in the Premier League, but as someone who has been involved in sports for so long, I've also tried to remind people that it's such a hard business. Only one club holds that trophy at the end and then you start over again.

'It's interesting because I was with the Philadelphia Eagles just a few weeks ago, another club I'm very close to as I designed their building, Lincoln Financial Field. I became a big fan of them too and they were my NFL team, and I just dropped in to see them after they won the Super Bowl this year. You get through that and it's so hard.

'In the NFL, so much of it is about attrition with players staying healthy. It's a gruelling schedule and a brutal game so a lot of it is just kind of surviving. To win a Super Bowl is really hard to do, so I asked the question, "How long does the glow last?" Their owner didn't even miss a beat and told me, "Until the next game."

'These projects are complicated at the best of circumstances, it's not easy for anybody. There are other clubs who have had lots of dreams shattered and it's easy to think we're the only ones this has happened to. One of the things I've learned in becoming an Evertonian is that there is a lot of recognition of our self-suffering, we've been through a lot.'

21

# Postscript – summer 2026

WHATEVER JOB you do, there is a good chance that those outside of your profession – regardless of how well-meaning or sympathetic they might be – ultimately have little or no comprehension of the actual demands of your role.

As someone who has worked professionally in the newspaper industry for 26 years now, since just shy of my 21st birthday when I first entered a newsroom straight out of university, I can tell you that certainly applies to journalism in general and covering Everton for the *Liverpool Echo* in particular.

There is a misguided urban legend among some in Merseyside who think the *Echo*'s staff somehow operate out of Manchester, stemming back to when the on-site printing presses closed in the late 2000s, yet our office is very much in the heart of the city centre and you can see Hill Dickinson Stadium from the top of the street!

Also, certain naive individuals are under the misapprehension that once the final whistle blows on the last day of the Premier League season, it is somehow time for my colleagues and I to put our feet up.

We still have the same intense demands as the rest of the year, to publish several articles each day, and the era of sticking cricket and athletics on the back page during the summer is long gone in England's most passionate football city.

Without the natural rhythm of the fixtures, it is a time of year when we often have to be creative and put our thinking caps on in terms of producing content.

However, for better or for worse, there always seems to be something going on at the Blues, and that certainly proved to be the case in 2026.

Barely 48 hours after Liverpool had sacked Arne Slot a year after he had guided them to the Premier League title in his first season in charge, transfer talk – incoming and outgoing – was starting up.

An article by Patrick Boyland in The Athletic on 2 June stated that Everton wanted to hand Iliman Ndiaye a new deal on improved wages as a reward for his form since his £15m move from Marseille in July 2024.

However, despite having been in talks since the start of the year his camp had rejected 'multiple' contract offers for the star, who it was said was 'likely' to have a projected transfer value of around the £70m mark.

David Moyes had already delivered a strong verdict on the prospect of a potential exit for the player.

I was in the room when Moyes addressed the issue head-on while speaking in the embargoed section of his pre-match press conference – to preview the visit to Brentford on 11 April.

Asked whether Everton could move on from having to sell their star players amid speculation over top teams casting admiring glances at Ndiaye, Moyes said, 'He is the last person I would consider selling. There are others as well [who he wouldn't want to sell], but my point is I have no interest in hearing the talk if there is talk out there.

'I don't think there is any club that is not a selling club at the right value for their player. I am not saying that means he is for sale, I am not, I just think it is a genuine thing where there is a price where people would say, "Well, we'd have to do something."

'But it is getting too hard to build teams and also supporters are looking for a quick return which managers are not getting. So why would we be giving up our better players?'

However, during the build-up to Senegal's opening World Cup match against the nation of his birth, France, Ndiaye – who would go on to score a stunner to clinch a 5-0 romp in the final group game against Iraq that secured qualification to the knockout stages – gave a couple of interviews in which he speculated on his future.

One, published by website Sportbible on the morning of the game itself, seemed particularly telling. He said, 'It [the season] has gone OK, personally, I think I could have been better. The start of the season was very good but the second part, not so much. I don't think it's fatigue. For me, the team has not been at its best. You can speak individually, but when the whole team is not working, you can't really say this player is fatigued or not doing well.

'At the same time, I don't think I've played enough games. I went to AFCON but actually, I don't think that's enough. I want to be playing in Europe, in the Champions League, I want to play in all of these games.'

Those words seemed to contrast sharply with the tone delivered by Kiernan Dewsbury-Hall when reflecting on the campaign in an Instagram post a couple of weeks earlier, 'Awful end to the season after a promising campaign, miles off it to be honest. A long summer now to review and come back bigger and better next year. Thanks for all the love in my first season here.'

However, having failed to win promotion to the Premier League with his local club Middlesbrough, it was understood that Championship Player of the Season Hayden Hackney was favouring a move from the banks of the Tees to the banks of the Mersey.

Boro had a second bite of the cherry when it came to trying to go up, despite losing their play-off semi-final to Southampton.

The Saints had turned to sinners as they admitted they had spied on three opponents throughout the season en route to reaching Wembley and were duly thrown out of the fixture dubbed 'the richest game in football'.

When issuing what was a rather unremorseful statement in response to the ruling, the disgraced Hampshire outfit name-checked the Blues.

Southampton chief executive Phil Parsons said, 'We believe the financial consequence of yesterday's ruling makes it, by a very considerable distance, the largest penalty ever imposed on an English football club.

'Luton Town's 30-point deduction in 2008/09 – to date the most severe sporting sanction in the English game – was levied against a club already in League Two, with no comparable revenue at stake.

'Derby County's 21-point deduction in 2021 cost them their Championship status. Everton's eventual six-point deduction in 2023/24 followed losses of £124.5m, a figure dwarfed by what has been taken from Southampton in a single afternoon.

'The largest financial penalty ever levied by the Premier League, against Chelsea in March of this year, was £10.75m, and was accompanied by no sporting sanction whatsoever despite involving £47.5m in undisclosed payments over seven years.'

Hackney, who was about to enter the final 12 months of his contract, was left in tears by the 1-0 Wembley defeat to Hull City.

With his side reinstated, the midfielder, who had been sidelined for the final two months of the campaign with a calf injury, returned to make a 20-minute cameo off the bench against the Tigers but was unable to prevent them from falling to a heartbreaking loss with Ollie McBurnie netting the only goal of the game in the 95th minute.

Speaking on the *Royal Blue* podcast on 5 June, Joe Thomas said of Hackney, 'Everton have a very firm interest and have tracked him for some time. I think they have made considerable efforts to make their interest in him clear, and they want him at the club.'

Yet, later that same evening, Sky Sports News reported, 'Everton have been knocked back by Middlesbrough after an initial approach for Hayden Hackney. The two clubs' valuations are miles apart, so Middlesbrough have told Everton to go away and think again ... talks are not ongoing at this stage.'

After announcing earlier in the day that the club was continuing to liaise with representatives of Idrissa Gueye over his future, with the midfielder's existing deal expiring at the end of the month – they would later confirm on 24 July that he had left – Everton were left reeling on 10 June by a costly punishment that came their way, being told that they had to pay Burnley £35m over the impact of a breach of the Premier League's financial rules.

The case – heard by a Premier League commission – relates to the 2021/22 season, when Everton were found to have broken profit and sustainability regulations (PSR) over a three-year period.

Burnley argued the breach impacted their chances of staying in the Premier League and sought compensation for the losses associated with being relegated; they were awarded £26m in damages and a further £9m in interest.

In response, Everton said they were 'surprised and angered by the decision' and claimed, 'This ruling sets a dangerous and unworkable precedent for English football, given it is constructed on a principle that a club can be in breach of financial rules at any point in a financial year.'

Rules also ensured that those dishing out this punishment were the same panel that handed the Blues their initial ten-point deduction in November 2023, which at the time was the biggest sporting sanction in the 135-year history of English top-flight football.

That trio – David Phillips KC, Alan Greenwood and Nick Igoe – produced a verdict that was subsequently pulled apart by the appeal board who gave Everton four points back, stating that they 'made legal errors' on two grounds, yet here the game's equivalents of hanging judges returned like bad pennies.

Club sources insisted Hill Dickinson Stadium chiefs would robustly and thoroughly contest the ruling while David Moyes told talkSPORT, who he was working for as a World Cup pundit, 'I felt that we had paid our dues,' and revealed that he had been told by the Friedkin Group that the decision would not negatively impact on his summer transfer budget.

Moyes was still feeling the heat from considerable sections of the fanbase after the way the previous season had ended.

When back on talkSPORT following the announcement of the 2026/27 season fixtures on 19 June, name-checking a couple of teams who played in the two smallest grounds in the Premier League and had never won a major honour between them did not go down well with many supporters, regardless of the pair both finishing above the Blues in May.

Asked by Jim White about his aims for the campaign, Moyes said, 'I don't know if a club like Everton now, we can make big, huge strides but we see how well the likes of Bournemouth and Brentford are doing, so there's no reason why we all shouldn't have those ambitions to try and at least match those clubs and how they go about it.'

With the 63-year-old entering the final 12 months of his current deal, we all wait with bated breath to see whether the club's most consistent manager of the Premier League era can revive their fortunes as he did during his lengthy first spell in charge.

Curiously, he was installed as an early bookmakers' favourite to become the next Scotland boss following Steve Clarke's resignation as soon as Scotland's World Cup elimination was confirmed.

Moyes is a proud patriot who carries his reading glasses in a tartan case, but he has never managed in his home country, the Scottish FA would not be able to offer him anything close to his Blues salary and he is well aware of the limitations in talent available for playing personnel in his nation.

It will also be intriguing to see if TFG start to take this passionate and storied football institution to their hearts after what has been a distinctly cool and hands-off approach from Dan Friedkin himself, at the time of writing ranked 249th with an estimated net worth of $13.2bn (£9.9bn) by the Bloomberg Billionaires Index, a daily ranking of the world's richest people, compared to the way he handles affairs at Roma.

After being saved from football oblivion, loyal but long-suffering Evertonians thought this would be a 'Cinderella story'. However, they are still waiting to go to the ball, and like Cinders herself, they feel like the poor relations, while those at the top appear to focus on their sister club.

Hopefully, it is not just a case of Everton merely being too good a deal to miss out on. However, there are already whispers coming from well-placed sources on the Houston grapevine suggesting as such, and claiming that interest in the club's fans, history and culture is modest beyond retaining their Premier League status ahead of offloading to a new buyer in the not-too-distant future.

Time will tell through the owners' actions – or lack of them – as there is great potential in this project if just given some proper TLC.

But let us not end on a potentially sour note, especially given that as I write this, the club are closing in on signing their first new face of the summer having struck a deal with Middlesbrough for Hayden Hackney following that chasm in earlier negotiations.

An initial £16.5m fee has been agreed in a package that could eventually be worth £25m if all clauses and bonuses are met for the best player in English football's second tier in 2025/26, who football data comparison tool Comparisonator revealed completed more successful passes per 90 minutes (55.65) than £220m pair Moises Caicedo of Chelsea (52.8) and Declan Rice of Arsenal (52.14), who led the way in the Premier League throughout the season.

Also, Andy Burnham, a Blues season ticket holder, and someone I interviewed across the road from Goodison Park in 2023 on the subjects of mental health and the new stadium, was poised to become the new prime minister and has since taken up his position in 10 Downing Street.

After decades of decline, their move to the Mersey sees Everton playing in the best stadium in the land with the potential to at least move towards the Premier League's established powers on a financial footing.

If anyone encapsulated such powers of recovery at their new home, then it was Michael Keane. Having briefly lapsed into free agency, the man who nine years on from his arrival remains the club's most expensive defender came back to feature in 35 matches in total in 2025/26. Then, having penned a new deal for a tenth season, he and bride Emmie celebrated their wedding day soon after the campaign finished.

A few months earlier, I asked him what it was like as a Blues player turning out at Hill Dickinson Stadium and as always, he gave me an honest, insightful and articulate answer, 'Everton is a huge football club, but I think playing at Hill Dickinson Stadium makes us feel like an even bigger football club, that's how I feel as a player.

'I feel like going there every couple of weeks to play football is a massive occasion and we're desperate to do well there. We want to make it a fortress for ourselves but just the stadium itself is really special. It's so loud and the pitch is a bit bigger, which I quite like personally.

'I think it's just an incredible place as the atmosphere is really good and hopefully the fans have really enjoyed it because the players are buzzing every chance we get to play there.

'I don't think they could have done it in a better way. Stepping away from Goodison and all the history there, it was always going to be tough.

'You're not going to replicate that, you're going to build a modern version of that, but I think they've done a really good job in making sure the atmosphere is good, making sure the fans are close to the pitch, and making sure it's just an amazing place to be in and to look at as well.

'It's an incredible place and we're lucky to play there. I think with the steep stands and the sheer size of it, it makes it difficult for opponents when you've got 50,000 Evertonians shouting for us.

'I think it's tough for anyone else to play there. I also think that results help with that. We've had a good start there, we've got momentum at the stadium at the minute and the longer we can keep that going, the more confident we'll be as we get used to it.'

22

# New stadium timeline

**11 March 2016**

Having purchased his initial 49.9 per cent controlling stake in Everton, Farhad Moshiri pledges to tackle the stadium issue. He tells the *Liverpool Echo*, 'Goodison Park has served the club extremely well, but we need to make sure the club has a suitable stage to perform on for the future. We will review the best options and how to finance, especially as it is likely to cost a little more than the £3,000 it apparently did back in 1892.'

**14 October 2016**

Club officials, including Farhad Moshiri, Bill Kenwright, Denise Barrett-Baxendale, plus Liverpool mayor Joe Anderson and architect Dan Meis, visit proposed stadium sites at Stonebridge Cross in Croxteth, and the waterfront Bramley-Moore Dock in Vauxhall.

**7 November 2016**

With supporters pushing for the Mersey riverside option, Moshiri declares that the club has 'taken soundings from fans' and says, 'In our mind, we know where we want to go. We are committed.'

**2 February 2017**

Joe Anderson says Everton's proposed new stadium at Bramley-Moore Dock could play a part in the city's bid to host the Commonwealth Games in 2026.

**23 March 2017**

Everton's Land Purchase Agreement for Bramley-Moore Dock is sealed with the club signing an initial 'heads of terms' agreement to acquire the site from Liverpool Waters developer Peel for a fee understood to be £22.5m.

**31 March 2017**

Liverpool City Council agrees a deal to help Everton build their new stadium at Bramley-Moore Dock. The council's cabinet says it will act as an effective guarantor for the club's plans by setting up a Special Purpose Vehicle to attract investment. The announcement comes as the city of Liverpool – having previously planned to host the 2026 Commonwealth Games – attempts to be awarded the 2022 Games with the stadium the centrepiece of the bid.

**7 September 2017**

Liverpool loses out to Birmingham in its bid to host the 2022 Commonwealth Games, ensuring that Everton's new stadium will not need to incorporate a temporary athletics track.

**23 November 2017**

Everton exchange contracts for the Bramley-Moore Dock site, signing an agreement to secure a 200-year lease on the proposed location of their new stadium.

**24 January 2018**

Everton reveal 11 key principles that will shape their new stadium – and the future of Goodison Park. They are – Our Fortress; A new home for Everton; A platform for growth; The People's Club; An iconic landmark for Liverpool; Easy to get to, easy to get home; A legacy for Goodison Park; Respecting heritage; Harnessing the environment; Embracing technology; The right deal for Liverpool.

**2 April 2018**

Speaking in a series of fans' workshops with Evertonians at St Luke's Church next to Goodison Park, Dan Meis reveals the Blues' plan to build a large home end based on Borussia Dortmund's 'Yellow Wall' at their new stadium. Emphasising Everton's commitment to make the new stadium a 'fortress' – retaining and amplifying Goodison Park's intimacy and atmosphere – the American declares his desire to create the 'greatest home ground in English football'.

Joe Anderson suggests for the first time that Liverpool City Council may not lend Everton the money it needs to build a new stadium with the club potentially looking elsewhere for financial assistance.

**13 August 2018**

Everton name Colin Chong as stadium development director to spearhead the move to Bramley-Moore Dock. Chong is a construction industry specialist whose CV lists several major projects including redevelopment work at Old Trafford and the building of Wigan's DW Stadium, as part of 35 years in the trade.

**15 November 2018**

Everton embark on what they describe as 'one of the most important processes' in their 140-year history with the start of the formal public consultation on their proposed new stadium.

**20 December 2018**

Everton reveal they are planning a capacity of 52,000 for the new stadium, but the projected figure could increase to 62,000 in the future.

**12 February 2019**

The new stadium proposal is given 'more than a vote of confidence' with key results revealed from the first public consultation process. Over 20,000 people took part in the club's first stage of public consultation with 94 per cent of respondents agreeing that the waterfront site is an appropriate place to build a new ground. Of the 20,168 people who responded, nearly 2,000 were non-Everton supporters, yet the bulk of those fans were still in agreement over the move.

**25 July 2019**

Everton unveil Dan Meis's stunning designs for their new stadium. Meis Architects propose to use 'traditional' brick, glass and steel with the use of brick on the outside ensuring the ground looks at home in the dockland setting.

**26 July 2019**

Just a day after the renderings were revealed, the club's second stage of public consultation begins. In an exclusive interview with the *Liverpool Echo*, Dan Meis declares, 'There has always been that mentality that we're not building a Bentley, we're building a Ferrari. It's going to be new and have amenities but it's a performance building, it's a proper football ground.'

**13 November 2019**

Plans for a new stadium are given major public backing as part of a groundbreaking second consultation process with results revealed. The Blues received over 43,000 responses to their summer survey about the People's Project (both the move to Bramley-Moore Dock and the legacy for Goodison Park). Ninety-six per cent of people who took part want the project to continue, 98 per cent of all respondents support the design of the 52,000-seater stadium with 99 per cent of Everton fans backing Meis's July renderings. The second stage of consultation reached 2,726 non-Everton fans – 24 per cent of whom have no interest in football – and included a 19-

day touring exhibition that visited 12 locations across all six Liverpool City Region boroughs.

**23 December 2019**

Everton reveal their stunning final designs as they submit their planning application to Liverpool City Council.

**14 January 2020**

Everton announce they have enlisted the help of two major international banks to secure the majority of funding required to build their new stadium. The Blues confirm they have been working with JP Morgan and MUFG (Mitsubishi UFJ Financial Group) over the past 12 months to assist in finding the private institutions that could lend the club the bulk of the expected £500m construction costs. It is also revealed that Everton have struck a £30m deal with Alisher Usmanov's holding company USM over naming rights on the new stadium.

**19 February 2020**

Everton appoint Laing O'Rourke as the contractor for the new stadium.

**24 June 2020**

Dan Meis confirms he is 'not currently engaged' in the Bramley-Moore Dock plans and claims that stepping away was one of the greatest disappointments in his career. He adds, 'Let me be clear. I am fully confident that Bramley-Moore will be built. It is both right for the club and the city.'

**24 July 2020**

Everton are 'expected to be awarded' planning approval for their new stadium in October, a major document reveals, as the

Liverpool City Region Combined Authority releases its post-COVID-19 Economic Recovery Plan.

**16 December 2020**

The *Liverpool Echo* reports that Everton are not expected to hear the outcome of their planning application to build a new stadium until early next year. The Blues had been hoping to receive an official answer from Liverpool City Council in December but the local authority being left stretched by the demands of the pandemic means the detailed proposal submitted by the club has yet to be fully worked through.

**15 February 2021**

Liverpool City Council releases a planning report recommending that Bramley-Moore Dock be approved.

**23 February 2021**

The planning application is approved by Liverpool City Council. The local authority held a special planning committee comprised of 11 councillors to unanimously come to its determination on the proposals. Everton's legacy project for Goodison Park is also unanimously approved.

**26 March 2021**

Everton confirm that work at the new stadium can finally begin as Robert Jenrick, the secretary of state for housing, communities and local government, who has been reviewing the planning permission for the last month, decided not to call the project in further, as happened with their previously doomed plans to move to Kirkby.

**14 June 2021**

Everton start preliminary works at Bramley-Moore Dock. Specialist firm Boskalis Maritime sends a boat out on to the

Mersey to carry out various checks on the dock, including looking for any unexploded devices as well as looking at the state of the dock wall plus a survey of micro-biological organisms that may be attached to the dock or living in the water.

**1 July 2021**

Everton confirm they will begin work on their new stadium on 26 July. Chairman Bill Kenwright says, 'We are thrilled to be able to confirm that construction work will commence on our new stadium later this month.' Meanwhile, it's revealed that the enabling works, to prepare the land before the stadium construction begins, are to be paid for by money from majority shareholder Farhad Moshiri.

**26 July 2021**

On the day the club formally take control of the Bramley-Moore Dock site, stadium development director Colin Chong outlines, 'Our intention is that we'll be formally breaking ground on the eastern quayside in the early part of August,' while revealing that fans will be able to follow progress on the site through a webcam.

**10 August 2021**

Everton announce that they have held a project commencement ceremony at Bramley-Moore Dock to mark the breaking of ground in the construction of their new £500m stadium. Bill Kenwright says, 'This is a momentous day, one that we have all been waiting for. To know that Evertonians and the people of this great city are together with us on this journey is a special feeling. Now that the work has commenced we can all watch our magnificent home as it comes to life.'

**27 September 2021**

Everton confirm the operation to re-house the marine wildlife living in the water at Bramley-Moore Dock will be completed by the end of the week. Two floating cormorant pontoons were also installed in the neighbouring Nelson Dock to provide an alternative habitat for the birds in advance of a start on site.

**1 October 2021**
The infill of Bramley-Moore Dock begins. Some 450,000 cubic metres of fluidised sand from the Irish Sea is used to replace the water on the site.

**19 October 2021**
Dan Meis says that he will soon be 're-engaged' on the project. The US architect, whose stunning rendering was revealed in July 2019, made the shock announcement 11 months later that he was 'not currently engaged' in the scheme. However, in an interview with Liverpool-born former professional footballer Neil Danns on BBC World Service, Meis claimed that he will soon be back on board and that it's a 'happy ending'.

**20 October 2021**
Everton confirm the piling process has begun, which includes drilling on the 2,500 concrete piles that will provide the building blocks for the structure. Work has initially begun on the foundations for the North and South Stands, with piling work expected to continue through until the summer of 2022.

**22 October 2021**
Everton confirm the return of Dan Meis to the stadium project. The Blues announce that the architect will continue his association with the process as he takes up a new guardianship role.

**8 December 2021**
The dock infill, which forms a key part of the enabling works, is completed. The three-month process sees a dredger called the

*Shoalway* painstakingly make more than 130 round trips over 20 miles out into the Irish Sea to collect sand.

**21 December 2021**

The first above-ground structure that will form the new stadium goes up. The giant pre-cast concrete panels and pillars are installed, just prior to the enabling and construction works breaking for Christmas, and are the first structural elements of the north-west core, which will incorporate the entrance turnstiles to the North Stand and create support for the entry and exit stairs up to the concourse areas.

**4 March 2022**

Stadium contractors Laing O'Rourke confirm they 'remain committed' to the project following sanctions imposed on Blues sponsor Alisher Usmanov, who had a naming rights option on the ground, after Russia's invasion of Ukraine. Everton had taken the decision to suspend their agreements with all of USM, Megafon and Yota earlier in the week but a Laing O'Rourke spokesperson said, 'We are deeply saddened by events in Ukraine and are doing all we can to support our Ukrainian colleagues. We note that Everton has suspended its commercial sponsorship arrangements with three Russian companies, and can confirm that we remain committed to the contract we have signed with Everton Football Club to deliver its new stadium at Bramley-Moore Dock.'

**11 March 2022**

An emotional Dan Meis declares Everton are at 'the exciting stage' of building their new stadium after setting foot on the Bramley-Moore Dock site for the first time since construction began. He said, 'It's so incredibly exciting and very emotional. It's like being a kid in a toy store and it never gets old. It seems a little absurd that it all starts with a little sketch and then hundreds and ultimately thousands of people come together. It's a giant team of engineers and architects and contractors and a lot of people have put their heart and soul into this stadium, and that's really touching and just phenomenal.'

**29 March 2022**

The new stadium's project engineer hails the 'huge milestone' of the installation of the fourth corner at Bramley-Moore Dock. The first pre-cast concrete wall is lowered into place in the south-east corner of the site, offering a tantalising glimpse of the sheer size of the iconic waterfront build. Laing O'Rourke's David Jackson said, 'This is a huge milestone for us. There are four main cores in the stadium, and we started in the North Stand and then in the south-west corner and now, finally, the south-east corner of the building, which is the final stage of getting up and out of the ground.'

**13 April 2022**

Everton sign an agreement with Laing O'Rourke which will lock in construction costs and see the contractor deliver the next and final phase of development of the new stadium. The deal follows on from the Pre-Contract Services Agreement (PCSA) signed by both parties in February 2021 and the Enabling Works Contract (EWC), which was focused on delivering the preparatory works at the site, including the in-filling of the dock that was completed in December. Under the new agreement, Laing O'Rourke will deliver a programme of works which includes the completion of any outstanding enabling works, the full construction of the stadium and public realm, and remedial works to the Grade II-listed Hydraulic Tower, which will be brought back into public use.

**2 June 2022**

Everton announce that the foundation piling process has come to an end after seven months of work. The dock has been completely filled with sand and the foundations consist of 2,768 concrete piles, each around 15 metres deep.

**24 June 2022**

Work is ready to begin on the concrete foundations that will support the West Stand at Bramley-Moore Dock, the side of the stadium that will face out towards the Mersey. The first of the concrete ground floor slabs is poured as work commences on the main stands following the initial pre-build of the four cores in each corner.

The erection of the four tower cranes is also timed to tie in with the superstructure being built on the west and east sides of the stadium. This is predominantly comprised of precast concrete components which are manufactured off site, transported to Bramley-Moore Dock and then assembled by Laing O'Rourke's specialist team.

**10 August 2022**

One year after work began on site, Everton announce that the first concrete terracing unit has been installed as Laing O'Rourke confirm work is complete on building the four concrete cores to their full height.

**11 August 2022**

Everton unveil the logo and the official website for their future home which from this point – until the club obtains naming rights – is called Everton Stadium.

**18 August 2022**

On his first visit to Everton Stadium after construction of the stands started, architect Dan Meis proclaims that fans will be 'part of the game' in a way that they're not at so many new grounds.

**25 September 2022**
Assembly is under way on the first of the stadium's roof trusses.

**28 September 2022**
Dipesh Patel, principal of Everton Stadium technical architects BDP Pattern, announces that he believes the Blues' future home will be the city's 'fourth grace' and a catalyst to transform Liverpool's iconic waterfront.

**9 November 2022**
Everton confirm that the first of the giant trusses that will support the roof structure has successfully been installed.

**16 November 2022**
The Football Association confirm Everton Stadium will be part of the UK and Ireland's preliminary bid to host the European Championship in 2028.

**14 December 2022**
Everton reveal that the first full-span roof truss has been completed. Each truss, which initially rests on temporary support trestles built into the stand, consists of three sections assembled at ground level and will be lifted into place individually.

**12 January 2023**
Speaking to talkSPORT, Farhad Moshiri describes the new stadium as a £760m project, a figure that is £255m more than the £505m figure for construction that has long been suggested by club officials. Club sources claim that the figure Moshiri quoted is inclusive of every facet of the stadium, from design and planning to construction and even including the potential for further ancillary developments related to the stadium, insisting the cost of construction has not changed and that the contract

signed last year with construction firm Laing O'Rourke has not altered.

**6 March 2023**

Steelwork goes into place on top of the four-level West Stand. The first steel sections, including raker beams, have been installed at the southern end of the stand to provide a dramatic addition to the structure as work gears up to manufacture the roofing barrels on the western wharf.

**15 March 2023**

Andy Burnham proclaims he's certain that Everton's new stadium will be the most iconic ground in English football. The mayor of Greater Manchester, who is a lifelong Evertonian, tells the *Liverpool Echo,* 'It will be the most iconic ground in English football, I'm absolutely certain about that.'

**24 March 2023**

Everton unveil plans for a major new feature at the site of the new stadium, giving fans the chance to cement their place there for posterity. 'Everton Way' will be a walkway that will be paved with engraved stones celebrating Everton's identity, history and the greatest players to have represented the club, with Evertonians having the chance to join those legends.

**27 March 2023**

The primary concrete structure in all four stands is completed. The final roof slab was poured the previous week on top of the East Stand with work on the East and West Stands now turning towards completing the upper bowl.

**12 April 2023**

Everton's new stadium and the City of Liverpool are confirmed as part of the UK and Ireland's bid to host the European Championship in 2028.

**19 April 2023**

Everton hold a 'topping out' ceremony to mark the completion of the structure. Dignitaries from the Blues and their construction partner Laing O'Rourke jointly celebrate the achievement, just 20 months since work began on the semi-derelict site. All four stands have since been erected to full height, with the final sections of steelwork and terracing units being installed on top of the East Stand, where the 'topping out' ceremony and speeches take place.

**24 May 2023**

The distinctive 'barrel' shape of what will become the iconic roof of the new stadium is visible for the first time on three sides as the West Stand steelwork connects to the previously installed North and South Stand roofs.

**27 May 2023**

The holding company behind the new stadium has secured some external funding, according to public documents made available via Companies House. The charge states that 'the lenders have agreed to make a loan to the borrower (Everton Stadium Development Holding Company) relying on, among other security, the security interest created in this deed' and relates to the securing of external funds by ESDHC, for an unspecified amount of money, potentially as some form of bridging loan to ensure the continued development of the stadium build.

**14 June 2023**

Everton are open to talks over whether they should move into their new stadium mid-season or not after explaining how it might not be ready for the start of the 2024/25 campaign.

The Everton Fans' Forum social media account posts that a presentation given to the Everton Fan Advisory Board has been shared with them, and stated, 'Progress on the build remains good but the club stressed completion is during 2024, not in time for [the start] of the 2024/25 season ... Discussions around a mid-season move versus an end-of-season move will be made if necessary once a completion date is known. Test events will be a requirement but it provides opportunities to engage fans.'

**28 June 2023**
Colin Chong insists that the new stadium remains on schedule and that the club are confident it will be completed 'in the final months' of next year. The chief stadium officer, who was also made interim chief executive earlier in the month, states, 'We are confident the stadium will be completed in the final months of 2024,' and adds, 'It raises the question as to whether the club moves in mid-season.'

**28 July 2023**
Dan Meis reveals his personal thoughts on when the new stadium should open, telling the *Liverpool Echo*, 'I really do think there is value in waiting and finishing a season.'

**14 August 2023**
Michael Jones, 26, a lifelong Evertonian from Kirkby, is killed in an accident when working as a ventilation engineer on the construction site.

**23 August 2023**
Construction staff restart work after consultation with Michael Jones's family and the Health and Safety Executive.

**10 September 2023**

Speaking in an exclusive interview with the *Liverpool Echo*, Dan Meis says he believes that interacting with Evertonians helped improve his design of the club's future home.

**14 September 2023**

Everton receive a £100m loan from MSP Sports Capital to help fund the new stadium build.

**20 September 2023**

Howard Kendall will be honoured by having one of the pubs and bars at the club's new stadium named after him. There will also be Dixie's and The Queen's Head – a reference to the venue of the meeting where the club's name was changed to Everton just a year after their formation as St Domingo's.

**23 October 2023**

The installation of the first of over 50,000 blue seats begins. The fitting is part of a five-month process.

**30 November 2023**

Work begins on what the club describes as 'a unique feature that you won't find in a stadium anywhere else in the world'. Giant steel gates that will greet all spectators on their arrival are being installed.

**15 December 2023**

Everton confirm for the first time that the first team's move to the new stadium will take place at the start of the 2025/26 campaign, ensuring that 2024/25 will be their last season at Goodison Park, allowing the club to carry out various test events beforehand at Bramley-Moore Dock.

**20 January 2024**

Work on almost 900 panels that will help to form the barrel roof begins with the installation of the first piece of barrel cladding, the aluminium panels that will form the curved edges of the roof. A further 871 of the pieces – which are perforated to help deal with the waterfront winds – will follow, each put in place with the help of a specially adapted crane attachment that can manipulate the panels to ensure they fit.

**7 February 2024**

The first image of what the home dressing room will look like is revealed. The large, circular dressing room, in the heart of the West Stand, has been designed to maximise team unity and inclusivity.

**24 February 2024**

Everton's new stadium is 'structurally complete' after the final concrete terracing panel was installed. The historic milestone was reached as the final piece of the huge jigsaw was lowered into place in the East Stand, ending 18 months of complex work since the first concrete terrace was positioned in August 2022.

**12 April 2024**

The preparatory work for the pitch, the seeds for which will be planted in the summer, begins on site. The starting point for the pitch preparation is the removal of a layer of stone, known as a piling mat, which supported the heavy-duty equipment used in the construction.

**7 June 2024**

Everton release images of the club crest that will be the centrepiece of the home dressing room being installed.

**20 August 2024**

Interim chief executive Colin Chong confirms that Everton have finalised the funding of their new stadium.

**4 October 2024**

Everton announce a commemorative 'fan wall' at the new stadium celebrating legends and supporters. Named 'The Originals', the artwork will honour Everton players who have realised unique achievements while representing the Blues and those who have truly embodied the Everton spirit on and off the pitch. Evertonians will be able to submit a photograph for the wall, with the personal images set to be pieced together to create a fan-inspired mosaic.

**7 November 2024**

Green blades of grass on what will be the new pitch are pictured coming through. The synthetic stitching of millions of fibres into the newly laid topsoil is under way, using specialised machinery that will slowly work its way across the pitch.

**29 November 2024**

Everton announce their season ticket prices for 2025/26, the club's first campaign at their new stadium. The most expensive season ticket is £900 but under-11s prices have been capped at £199 around the ground.

**13 December 2024**

Everton Way is to be extended further due to popular demand. As a result, its larger footprint means the walkway, which will feature Everton Giants and personalised stones from Evertonians across the world, will now form a wider section along the entire length of the exterior of the South Stand.

**17 December 2024**
Everton confirm the full season ticket sale dates for the new stadium. Sales will begin on Monday, 13 January.

**20 December 2024**
Everton are given the keys to their new stadium in a ceremonial handover just a day after the takeover by the Friedkin Group is confirmed, with new executive chairman Marc Watts present alongside interim chief executive Colin Chong and contractor Laing O'Rourke project director Gareth Jacques. Everton will now oversee a six-month fit-out of the ground's interior.

**13 January 2025**
The first season tickets for the Blues' move to their new home ready for the 2025/26 campaign go on sale.

**14 January 2025**
Everton appoint OCS, a global leader in facilities management, to provide integrated facilities management services at the new stadium. OCS, who currently have around 8,000 clients across the UK, Europe, the Asia-Pacific and Middle East regions, sign a five-year agreement for facilities management solutions, including waste management, cleaning and security.

**7 February 2025**
Photographs show the final preparations being made for the historic first game at the new stadium with pitch markings being laid and the goalposts erected ahead of the under-18 friendly between Everton and Wigan Athletic ten days later.

**17 February 2025**
The inaugural game at the new stadium is held with 10,000 spectators allowed in for the first test event. The under-18s lose

2-1 to their Wigan counterparts with Harry Rimmer and Cole Simms netting for the visitors before Ray Robert reduced arrears late on from the penalty spot to become the Blues' first scorer at their future home.

**23 March 2025**
A second test event takes place, this time with 25,000 fans in attendance and a planned evacuation held 65 minutes into the game as the Blues' under-21s were leading 2-1 against Bolton Wanderers B.

**26 March 2025**
Everton confirm the first major non-football event at their new stadium – a rugby league Ashes test between England and Australia on 1 November with the fixture returning after a 22-year absence.

**18 April 2025**
After holding back on making his first visit until he felt his team were safe from relegation danger, David Moyes reveals that he is 'hugely impressed' by the new stadium after finally going inside the Blues' future home for the first time.

**13 May 2025**
Everton announce that as they move to their new stadium for 2025/26, Goodison Park will not be demolished and instead will become the base for the club's women's team.

**16 May 2025**
Less than 48 hours before Everton's final fixture at Goodison Park, the club confirm a naming rights deal for their new stadium which from this point onwards will be called Hill Dickinson Stadium. The Blues do not confirm the scale or length of the

contract but describe it as a long-term relationship that represents 'one of the largest stadium naming rights deals in Europe'.

**16 June 2025**

Everton announce that they will play Roma in the inaugural first-team game at Hill Dickinson Stadium on Saturday, 9 August.

**24 June 2025**

Everton confirm the official capacity of Hill Dickinson Stadium for Premier League fixtures and sporting events will be 52,769. The club say the initial designated capacity of 52,888, proposed as part of the final design created five years ago, has been reduced slightly following a thorough post-construction audit and review of the seating configuration across the stadium in readiness for the new season.

**22 July 2025**

David Moyes arranges a behind-closed-doors friendly for his Everton team at Hill Dickinson Stadium, the day before they fly out to the USA to take part in the Premier League Summer Series. The Blues come from behind to beat newly promoted League One side Port Vale 2-1 thanks to goals from Charly Alcaraz and James Garner.

Meanwhile, Everton's new flagship store opens at the stadium. Before the opening of the club's new official store, Everton One at Goodison Park permanently closed its doors earlier in the month.

**9 August 2025**

Everton take on Serie A side Roma, also owned by the Friedkin Group, at Hill Dickinson Stadium. The Italians win the main game 1-0 thanks to Matías Soulé's 70th-minute strike before the Blues triumph 2-0 in a legends match of former players from both teams with Phil Jagielka and Steven Naismith scoring.

**24 August 2025**
Everton defeat Brighton & Hove Albion 2-0 in their first competitive match at Hill Dickinson Stadium with goals from Iliman Ndiaye (23) and James Garner (52).

**1 November 2025**
The first major non-football event takes place at Hill Dickinson Stadium as England's rugby league side lose 14-4 to Australia in their second Ashes test match.

**12 November 2025**
It's announced that Hill Dickinson Stadium will stage five matches at the 2028 European Championship to be hosted jointly by England, Northern Ireland, Republic of Ireland, Scotland and Wales. The venue is one of six English stadia chosen, along with Etihad Stadium, St James' Park, Tottenham Hotspur Stadium, Villa Park and Wembley, and will be awarded four group fixtures plus a last-16 knockout clash.

**20 December 2025**
The 1878s display the largest tifo in Premier League history, measuring 700 square metres and displaying the words 'On the banks of the Royal Blue Mersey' ahead of Everton's fixture against Arsenal.

**31 March 2026**
Everton stage their first full international match since Brazil overcame Japan 3-0 in the 1995 Umbro Cup at Goodison Park as Ivory Coast defeat Scotland 1-0 in a pre-World Cup friendly at Hill Dickinson Stadium. David Moyes is in attendance alongside fellow Scots Sir Alex Ferguson and Sir Kenny Dalglish as part of a 33,034 crowd, but their national team are condemned to defeat by a 12th-minute goal from Nicolas Pépé.

**17 May 2026**

With a crowd of 52,590 watching Everton v Sunderland, the club's first season at Hill Dickinson Stadium ends with an average attendance of 52,121, surpassing the 51,603 figure recorded during the 1962/63 title-winning campaign, the only previous occasion in the club's history that they had topped the 50,000 figure over the course of a season.

**9 June 2026**

The first England game at Hill Dickinson Stadium takes place as the Lionesses defeat Ukraine 3-0 in a Women's World Cup qualifier with goals from Jess Carter (14), Georgia Stanway (37) and Beth Mead (67) in front of 26,065 spectators.

**4–5 July 2026**

The best-attended Super League Magic Weekend in history takes place at Hill Dickinson Stadium with a hat-trick of rugby league derby matches across both days.

**11 July 2026**

The England rugby union team play their first game in this country outside of Twickenham since 2019 as they thrash Fiji 73-8 at Hill Dickinson Stadium in front of a record crowd of 50,209 for what is technically a 'home' fixture for the Pacific Islanders.